PROFILES IN QUALITY

Blueprints for Action from
50 Leading Companies

ALLYN AND BACON
Boston • London • Sydney • Toronto • Tokyo • Singapore

This book is published by Allyn and Bacon
A Division of Simon & Schuster, Inc.
160 Gould Street
Needham Heights, Massachusetts 02194

This book is also published under the title
Quality Assurance: Blueprints for Action from 50 Leading Companies

ISBN 0-205-13673-7

Printed in the United States of America
10 9 8 7 6 5 4 3 2 1   96 95 94 93 92 91

About BBP
BBP is a division of the Professional Information Group of Simon & Schuster, a Paramount Communications Company. Serving your needs is the largest, most skilled staff of our editors, authors, business experts and education specialists ever assembled to bring you the most effective information and training available anywhere. We use the latest technologies to interchange this information so that when you use any of our services, you use all of our services — you have access to the united strength and resources of the entire group. You will never find a more dedicated or more technically skilled organization in which to entrust your critical training needs.

BBP, 24 Rope Ferry Road, Waterford, CT 06386

TABLE OF CONTENTS

EMPLOYEE RECOGNITION

Are employees at your company given a real incentive to do quality work? Sometimes it takes more than lectures about quality to motivate workers to give their all. At these companies it pays to provide a tangible payoff for a job well done.

GETTING—AND USING—CUSTOMER FEEDBACK

Where's the best place to learn what standards you should strive for? Go right to the source— the customer. Savvy QA professionals know this, and they are instituting creative ways to gain quality insight from their customers.

ASSURING VENDOR/SUPPLIER QUALITY

Assuring the quality of incoming materials is a logical—and necessary—way to assure the quality of outgoing products. Get vendors/suppliers on your quality team by working closely with them. Also, determine which ones you should be relying on, and which are less than quality conscious.

STATISTICAL PROCESS CONTROL

Statistical Process Control (SPC) is a potent tool for zeroing in on the root cause of defects. And it can be used easily by everyone from workers on the line to vendors. But you need to see that SPC is implemented properly for maximum benefit, as these top companies have done.

your edge. OPC realized that SPC was just such a tool. Here's how the company launched its SPC effort and gave production and quality a big boost. *135*

ROBERTSHAW CONTROLS COMPANY: Here are seven false assumptions that can jeopardize your SPC efforts. Breaking through these dangerous misconceptions can help you implement this valuable quality control tool successfully. *139*

GENERAL ELECTRIC COMPANY: Can SPC being used outside your company help you to assure quality? Yes, if it's used by your suppliers. GE's Aircraft Engine Group offers its advice for teaching vendors the ins and outs of SPC. *142*

DESIGNED EXPERIMENTS/TAGUCHI METHODS

Companies have found that they can eliminate flaws that impair quality by using these tools to study designs and processes. And the good news is that implementing designed experiments and Taguchi Methods is not as complicated or difficult as it might seem.

UNITED TECHNOLOGIES AUTOMOTIVE: *You* know that designed experiments enable you to test designs and processes to improve quality. But how do you convey this idea to managers and other nonstatisticians? *147*

ITT: ITT uses Taguchi Methods to pinpoint and solve production quality problems. In one case, the company realizes seven-figure savings annually. *151*

FORD MOTOR COMPANY: How can you solve quality problems before they happen instead of after? Ford's Casting Division uses five steps to implement design of experiments, and has excellent results. *153*

EATON CORPORATION: What's the best application for Taguchi Methods? Eaton Corporation demonstrates that the greatest benefits can be realized in parameter design. *157*

SHELLER-GLOBE CORPORATION: How does a major supplier to the automotive industry remain competitive? It manufactures top-quality products by using Taguchi Methods. *159*

ECHIP, INC.: If you're just getting your feet wet in Taguchi Methods or other design-of-experiments techniques, you may not be ready for Robust Product Design. Then again, it never hurts to look to what may be the future of quality assurance. *160*

QUALITY AND OTHER DEPARTMENTS

United, you stand; divided, you fall. That statement accurately sums up the relationship between QA and the other departments at your company. When each department marches to its own drummer, achieving your goals may be difficult—even impossible. Working co-operatively is a must if you want to keep quality on track.

INTERNATIONAL SWITCHBOARD CORPORATION: The quality department is often regarded as the ''bad guys'' by other departments. By promoting teamwork with other areas at your firm and hiring wisely, you can break down the barriers to harmonious—and quality-effective—relations. *165*

FEDERAL EXPRESS: FedEx's plan to involve its maintenance department in QA has kept its planes flying high and its customers satisfied. You can assure both interdepartmental cooperation and quality with a similar strategy. *166*

PROMOTING QUALITY IN THE SERVICE SECTOR

Quality assurance is just as important in the service sector as it is in Manufacturing. And it takes the same type of commitment, training, and tools to make it work. The following service sector companies share their successful strategies for "keeping the customer satisfied."

INTRODUCTION

Quality Assurance: the key component in achieving excellence.

Everywhere you go today, people are talking about quality—and the importance of making it better. Some argue that it should be done one way; others are equally committed to their own approaches. How do you know which approach is best?

Why not listen to the winners—the companies that have already achieved excellence in the field of quality assurance? After all, they're the ones with a proven track record. They're the ones who are reaping the rewards for establishing an outstanding reputation for high standards of quality. Those rewards are superior products or services, satisfied customers, and increased profits.

This book is designed to help you gain those same rewards. Within its pages, you'll find some of the most valuable information about quality you'll ever read. The articles give you blueprints for success that over 50 leaders in the field of quality have followed to reach their positions of prominence.

Now you can share their secrets. You can study their action plans to see exactly how they've done it. And then you can customize the information to suit the needs of your company. This will allow you to develop your own unique action plan to build and maintain a superior quality assurance program.

In this book, you'll read about companies that have made quality their number-one priority. They all take pride in their quality efforts and are constantly striving to raise their quality standards. They know, for instance, how important it is to seek customer feedback—welcoming it even when it's unfavorable and using it as a springboard to improve their products or services. They understand that it's essential for their employees to be well trained—to have the know-how to avoid costly defects. They also know that the commitment to quality can't end with the quality department. To be successful, it must be a companywide effort.

Although it would be fair to say that all of these companies excel in achieving a high level of quality, you'll find that each company is especially effective in achieving outstanding performance in a particular area of quality assurance. That's why this book has been organized around 13 main themes: Quality Measurement; Total Quality Management/Continuous Improvement; Communication: A Crucial Part of QA; Giving Employees Responsibility for Quality; The Team Approach to Quality; Employee Recognition; Getting—And Using—Customer Feedback; Assuring Vendor/Supplier Quality; Statistical Process Control; Designed Experiments/Taguchi Methods; Quality Training/Task Assignment; Quality and Other Departments; and Promoting Quality in the Service Sector.

You'll find each company's story under one of these headings. For example, what do the quality efforts at Pacific Bell and Hewlett-Packard have in common? Both companies understand that to gain a true appreciation for the kind of quality that customers are looking for requires going to the source and eliciting customer feedback. And giants like Ford and Polaroid share the philosophy that everyone—up and down the corporate ladder—must be encouraged to take an active interest in quality. So both companies rely on employee teams to zero in on quality problems and come up with viable solutions.

The companies spotlighted in this book realize the importance of finding ways to provide better products and services for their customers. There's no denying the fact that competition is keen in today's marketplace. No company can afford to rest on its laurels. To stay competitive, you must look for ways to narrow your company's margin of error and deliver a superior product or service.

The companies in this book have developed innovative ways to narrow that margin of error. They may differ somewhat on the specifics, but they share the same ultimate goal: to keep the customer coming back for more.

Customers today expect to receive products and services of high quality. That's what you will be able to provide when you follow the lead of these companies and aim for excellence in your pursuit of quality.

QUALITY MEASUREMENT

You can have the most stringent quality standards around. And you can hammer away at the importance of sticking to these standards. But you can't be sure your efforts are on target without an ongoing effort to see how you are doing. That's why quality measurement should be an intrinsic part of your operation.

ENVIRONMENTAL PROTECTION AGENCY

When you have to make a decision that could cost your organization a lot of money, which would you rather have: a lot of information, or the right information? This federal agency has developed an approach to assuring quality in data-gathering endeavors.

Data gathering must take place before any quality-effective decision can be made. For example, R & D must carry out research to determine for Engineering the best design for a new product. Purchasing must do some "homework" to conclude which suppliers can provide Production with the best materials. QA personnel need to scout for facts and figures to ascertain which overall quality strategies would work best for your company.

If this key information is sought and collected in an ineffective manner, poor decisions—and poor quality—will result.

How can you promote quality in your company's data-gathering endeavors? The U.S. Environmental Protection Agency (Washington, D.C.) developed an effective approach for its Environmental Data Operations Divisions. The Divisions collect information for use in protecting public health and the environment. EPA's internal data-gathering operations cost approximately $500 million a year, and the agency relies on information-gathering quality to keep those costs in control. Flawed decisions based on inadequate and inaccurate data could cost billions of dollars.

In the past, it wasn't always easy to generate adequate and accurate data in a cost-effective manner because there was limited communication between the data collectors and the data users/decision makers at the EPA. "The collectors needed to find out what the users needed, and vice versa," says Stanley M. Blacker, director of Quality Assurance Management for the EPA. "We felt that it was important to create links between the data collectors and the data users, especially during planning."

TQM TO THE RESCUE

Blacker believed that implementing Total Quality Management principles would provide an answer to the problem. Using TQM terminology would enhance the quality of the data-collecting operation because, in effect:

▷ Data collectors would become "suppliers"

▷ Data users would become "customers"

▷ Data itself would become the "product"

The first step was to develop some specific tools that the collectors and users could utilize to ensure the accurate and timely generation of data. Blacker's department developed four specific tools:

1 Data Quality Objectives (DQOs). This key planning tool assures that the customers and suppliers understand what is needed. It requires specificity in requesting data, and eliminates vague requests such as, "Collect the best data that you can," or "I'll know it when you show it to me."

Approaching data operations with lack of specificity, observes Blacker, confuses the data collectors and cannot guarantee adequate, cost-effective data. That's why DQOs require each data user to:

✔ define the problem;

✔ state the decision that needs to be made;

✔ establish the "decision rule" (a quantitative statement of the factors that are the basis for making the decision); and

✔ define the performance measures (the type and quality of data—in quantitative terms—needed to make a defensible decision).

Together, data collectors and data users then sit down and "revisit" the information provided by the data users to ensure mutual understanding. "The DQO process forces data users to become increasingly precise and knowledgeable about what they need," says Blacker. The resulting written statement of the need and the performance measures assures the collection of the right data the first time. "The time that the data collectors and data users spend together results in simpler and better-focused data operations," points out Blacker.

2 Quality Assurance Program Plans. These plans describe how each of EPA's 50 major organizations intends to carry out its quality program. Each organization prepares its own plan on how it will implement the Total Quality concept. To do so, it:

▶ defines the activities to be pursued during planning, implementing, and reviewing its environmental data operations, and

► describes the roles and responsibilities of each key individual during each step

This assures clear understanding of the data operations process in each of the 50 organizations. The largest benefit derived is not in having a plan per se, but in having gone through the process of developing the plan. "Management recognizes the thorough analysis required to develop the plans," says Blacker. "These analyses have improved management's understanding of the programs it runs and how better to accomplish its desired objectives."

In addition, such a "blueprint" provides a benchmark for evaluating progress. "Everyone knows what is expected, and success is easily measured," says Blacker. And since each plan was developed by and tailored to each organization's individual needs, management has more of a tendency to adopt and follow them.

3 Management System Reviews. These reviews determine how well each organization is accomplishing the quality process it has established. Each review starts with the organization's QA Program plan to determine how well the organization is adhering to the Plan's "blueprint." "The review establishes where the quality process is working well and where improvements should be considered," notes Blacker.

4 Audits of Data Quality. These audits define whether the planned objectives have been achieved and what the limitations are of the completed "products" (the data collected). The questions asked are:

⇨ "Did the resulting data meet the Data Quality Objectives stated by the data users?

⇨ "If not, what is the data quality, and what are the limits in using the results?"

GAINING ACCEPTANCE BY STAFFERS

The key tools described above are necessary to the success of a Total Quality effort in a data-gathering function. However, they are not sufficient in and of themselves. "You can't just give people new tools and expect them to use them," explains Blacker. "Most people will feel that the tools will either be too difficult to understand or not applicable to their situations. People are not comfortable taking on new ways of thinking, especially when they perceive that things are all right."

To gain acceptance for the new tools, Blacker's department employed three strategies at EPA, strategies that you can adapt to your own needs:

A. Find Champions. Blacker did not try to sell the tools to top management within EPA. Rather, he sought out some middle- and lower-management people who believed in the concept and were willing to become "champions" for the tools. "We found some managers willing to try our new approach and then taught them how to use the tools," he reports. "They became our trailblazers."

B. Develop Trust. It's important to get people to understand that there are different ways to do things, and then get them comfortable with those new ways. This requires developing mutual trust, observes Blacker. "We explained that we were there to work with them, not to threaten them," he emphasizes. "Without trust, people will feel uncomfortable with—and threatened by—even the most valuable and helpful tools."

In other words, it was important to get people comfortable with Blacker's department first, and then with the tools they were offering. "And the only way to do this is to try to understand their positions, what they need, and what problems they are having," he says. "You need to build rapport at all levels." Following this, it was possible to take the people through the pilot programs, teach them how to use and apply the tools, and emphasize to them that the tools were for *their* benefit; to make *them* look good and be successful.

C. Publicize Success. Once the trailblazers were able to generate some successes with the tools, the champions and Blacker's department publicized these successes so that other managers would see the benefits of using the tools. "Organizations need to see the benefits to the bottom line," he notes.

▻ **Quality Data Yield Quality Decisions** ⇨ As a result of this Total Quality effort at EPA, Environmental Data Operations employees are more receptive to producing quality information for particular applications. In addition, there is more emphasis on up-front planning before they go out and collect their data. Such an approach is significantly boosting the quality of the data that staffers collect, and is having a positive effect on decisions based on those data.

By stressing a similar effort to improve data-gathering at your company, you can help assure that quality decisions are made—the kind that assure excellence in each function throughout your organization.

MOTOROLA, INC.

Is your quality organization getting the job done? This Malcolm Baldrige National Quality Award winner shares the 10 factors that it looks at when auditing the effectiveness of its quality assurance effort.

What does it take to make an effective review of the quality systems in your company? Motorola, Inc. (Schaumburg, IL), is in an excellent position to tell you. Its system is so good that last year Motorola became the first winner of the Malcolm Baldrige National Quality Award.

The award, named after the late Secretary of Commerce during the Reagan administration, recognizes companies that, in the words of former President Reagan, "exemplify the belief that quality counts, first, foremost, and always [and] realize that quality improvement is a never-ending process, a companywide effort in which every worker plays a critical role."

THE ROAD TO AWARD-WINNING QUALITY

"Our quality progress started several years ago when we saw a need for much more intensive training in quality at all levels," says Scott Shumway, vice president and director of Quality for Motorola's Semiconductor Sector (Phoenix, AZ). "This led to formation of the Motorola Corporate Quality Council, or MCQC, which directs quality efforts throughout the company." The impetus came from the top, Shumway adds, specifically from Chairman Robert Galvin.

"When it comes to a meeting, the first thing on his agenda is quality results," says Shumway. "If that part is okay, he may leave, because he feels that when quality is going in the right direction, he doesn't have to worry about how we're doing financially."

Motorola's Quality Systems Review is an internal audit program in which a team of five people from the MCQC visits a division and spends a week talking with people and measuring operations against stated criteria. The team looks at 10 performance factors—factors that Shumway says are remarkably similar to the points looked at by the committee that evaluates candidate companies for the Malcolm Baldrige Award.

▭ **Award/Winning Plan** ⇒ The 10 basic factors (with their assigned weights) are:

1. Quality system management (15 percent). "Here we look at the leadership, style, and effectiveness of the management team in the area of quality," says Shumway.

2. Product development control (10 percent). This factor is based on a manufacturing program Motorola developed two years ago called Six Sigma. "Sigma is a statistical unit of measurement that describes the distribution about the mean of a process or procedure," Shumway explains. "A process or procedure that can achieve plus or minus Six Sigma capability can be expected to have a defect rate of no more than a few parts per million. In statistical terms, this approaches zero defects—and it's our goal to achieve this level of quality in everything we do by 1992."

3. Purchasing material control (10 percent). This looks at the level of quality being supplied by vendors and the systems in place to measure vendor quality.

4. Process development and operational controls (10 percent). "This is aimed at the entire manufacturing flow process," says Shumway. "The question is, 'Is it working?'"

5. Quality data programs (5 percent). Are all necessary data available? Is this real information and not just databases? How is the information used—as a tool to improve quality?

6. Special studies (10 percent). How sophisticated are the methods? Are they state of the art?

7. Quality measurement and control equipment (5 percent). "This governs all our standards and calibrations," says Shumway. "Is the system in place and is it properly maintained?"

8. Human resources involvement (5 percent). "The team tries to determine if the people are capable and properly trained," says Shumway. "We want to know if the work force can do the job assigned."

This area is particularly important to Motorola, Shumway explains, because it's a recognized national leader in the participative management process, with people down the ranks involved in decisions—and sharing in the rewards of correct decisions.

9. Customer satisfaction assessment (20 percent). All organizations must have methods and systems in place to assess the satisfaction of customers with shipments.

10. Software quality assurance (10 percent). "This was a later addition to our list," notes Shumway. "We're getting more and more sophisticated in software related to quality. We spent a couple of years getting people prepared in this area before we tailored it into a score.

"We've developed the system to the point that we can see at a glance trends against goals, cost of nonconformance, quality of delivery, service to customers, and so on, complete with a summary."

Putting it all together, the division being examined knows how it is doing. "If they're below the satisfactory mark, they know they need corrective action," he says.

THE AUDIT PROCESS

Motorola's divisions can expect a Quality Service Review every two years. The corporate council puts together a team for each review, and the five members are selected from various parts of the company. There's no one committee that does all the checking, Shumway says.

"We thought about having one fixed team do all the reviews, but decided against it," he explains. "It's better to have people rotated so that every quality director gets an opportunity to work on a team. We also are careful about selecting leaders of each team. No one can be the leader without having participated in Quality Service Reviews in the past.

"At the end of the week of review, the general manager and his or her staff have a session with the team. They go over the review. The strengths and weaknesses are discussed, and recommendations are given to local management as to what improvements have to be made," he says.

Results of the survey are then reported to the steering committee, the MCQC, at the next meeting. Results aren't negotiable; what the team sees is what is reported. At the MCQC meeting, the division manager of the review division reports on what corrective action his or her organization will be taking.

"The Quality Service Review is championed by the corporation," says Shumway. "That's a key point that we've made to other corporations as we share our experiences under provisions of the Malcolm Baldrige Award.

"Our system has worked well for us. Over the years, it's given us uniformity and consistency. Corporate goals are driven down through the organization, and that's a powerful quality tool," concludes Shumway.

FIRST NATIONAL BANK OF CHICAGO

How do you focus attention—and action—where it will do the most good? This major financial institution created a Product Quality Measurement Program that tracks 700 performance indicators.

Many times, there are very good reasons people don't make attempts to improve quality. Among those reasons is the fact that awareness about the need for improvement isn't very high. How can that be turned around? By measuring quality performance and presenting those measurements to management, employees, customers, and suppliers, you can raise quality awareness all the way around. And the result is a more efficient—more profitable—operation.

A bit of background—Banks have traditionally made their money with credit (loan) products, but have offered noncredit (cash management) products such as corporate checking and shareholder services on a loss basis in order to maintain customer goodwill. "Cash management products were generally considered 'giveaway' products," explains Aleta Holub, manager of Quality Assurance for the First National Bank of Chicago, one of the largest banks in the United States.

However, in recent years, with the advent of deregulation and other forms of competition—such as foreign banks, investment banks, and data processing firms—the need to turn cash management products into profitmakers has become critical. There are two major reasons for this:

1. Banks must cut losses and increase profits so that they can pass these savings on to customers and thus remain competitive with those who are not strapped by federal—and other—regulations.

2. With the array of services being offered, customers have more options to choose from. So being able to offer the best service is of greater competitive significance than ever.

Turning losses into profits requires, most of all, increased efficiency. For example, a standard money transfer costs a bank an average of $10. However, if mistakes occur, such as sending the money to the wrong place or not getting it to the right place on time, costs can skyrocket to $400 or more, depending on the amount of money involved and the complexity of the problem.

With this in mind, First Chicago started its quality initiative by creating separate *strategic business units* (SBUs) for each of the individual cash management product families. Each SBU manager—who has the power to control expenses, pricing, product features, customer service, and quality—is an entrepreneur of sorts, charged with the responsibility for achieving the highest levels of quality in his or her SBU in order to make it profitable.

MEASURED RESPONSE

Integral to the success that the SBUs have experienced is First Chicago's Product Quality Measurement Program. The effort is designed to identify, track, and improve performance indicators that the bank's customers themselves consider important.

Customer input, in fact, was and is crucial to the successful implementation and maintenance of the effort. "Doing the wrong things right makes no sense," reasons Holub. "We wanted to make sure that we would be doing the right things right, so we asked our customers:

- ✔ What do you consider good-quality features of a product?

- ✔ What do you consider good quality on the delivery of those features?"

Customers responded with a number of quality criteria, and some of the most important were:

- timeliness
- operations efficiency
- accuracy
- economics
- customer service responsiveness

These responses led to the formulation of 700 quality indicators that the SBUs are expected to meet and *exceed.* These indicators include things like:

- lockbox processing time
- bill keying accuracy
- customer service inquiry resolution time
- cash concentration maintenance accuracy
- money transfer timeliness

Using both the customers' input and industry standards, SBU managers set performance level criteria for the 700 standards, using two measurements: *Minimum Acceptable Performance* (MAP) and *Goal*. MAP is based on customers' expectations, while Goal is the mark that indicates the exceptional or superior performance that the SBUs are striving to achieve. As improvement occurs in each of the 700 indicators, both the MAP and the Goal are raised accordingly.

Performance measured weekly. Charts for each of the indicators are created weekly, graphically depicting how well the SBUs have done and comparing the results to both the MAP and the Goal. (For samples of these charts, see Figure 1.)

These charts are also useful for SBU managers in the weekly performance meetings when the managers report detailed information to top management. The emphasis is on indicators above Goal, indicators below MAP, and any significant upward or downward trends. The purpose of these meetings isn't to create competition among SBUs, but to provide an early warning system for potential problems, ensure the timeliness and efficiency of the bank's services, provide starting points for improvement, and help management project future equipment and staffing needs.

Holding weekly performance reviews might seem like overkill to some, but Holub counters that this frequency seems to be just right. "I studied a number of similar programs in other organizations. Most of them simply had monthly or quarterly reports that they sent to top management. Our reporting is done weekly, and SBU managers actually meet face-to-face with top management and talk about what the charts mean. By meeting weekly, we are able to keep the program highly focused and attain a high level of detail in monitoring performance."

Feedback: Staying on Target—The meetings themselves are also used to open communication with both customers *and* vendors. First Chicago extends an open invitation to customers to attend the sessions, and regularly encourages them to do so. This not only helps customers better understand how well the bank is doing in meeting their needs but also helps the bank better understand changing customer needs. Using the new information that customers share at these meetings, the bank can then modify indicators and performance standards as required. Customer participation also has another benefit: It sends a loud and clear message to customers that they are central to the bank's concern;

that they are what the effort is all about.

To help all customers keep track of how the bank is progressing, it also sends out comprehensive annual booklets that highlight key charts. This booklet allows customers to view the most important indicators at a glance and compare results with previous years.

Vendors, on the other hand, are invited to the meetings to see how well they are doing in relation to the bank's performance objectives. Competitors in computer products, for example, sit side by side and learn—in graphic form—how their products are doing compared to the others. As a result, says Holub, "the bank receives an unfair share of its vendors' attention and service."

GETTING COMMITMENT FROM THE PEOPLE WHO MATTER

While the system itself is rather straightforward, Holub admits that there was some initial difficulty in getting managers and employees to buy into the concept. To solve the problem where the managers were concerned, top management tied a set percentage of the SBU managers' bonus money to their success with the Product Quality Measurement Program.

Getting employees on board presented a greater challenge, however. "At first, we offered incentives to employees based on what *we* thought they would like," says Holub. "For instance, I would like nothing better than the opportunity to have lunch with the president, so we offered lunch in the executive dining room as one of the incentives to improve performance. The problem was that not all employees considered this an incentive; many found this type of event quite stressful."

To remedy the problem, management went to the employees themselves and asked what kinds of incentives they would like. "We had been good about going to our customers to ask what was important to them, and we realized that it was just as crucial to go to our employees to ask what was important to *them*," Holub says.

A BOOK FULL OF BENEFITS

The benefits of First Chicago's Product Quality Measurement Program could fill a small book, but overall the effort has resulted in documented savings of $7 million to $10 million *per year*. For example:

➡ In 1982, the remittance banking lockbox operation experienced an average of one error for every 4,000 transactions. By 1986, that rate had dropped to one for every 10,000 transactions.

➠ Between 1981 and 1983, the volume of lockbox receipts increased 30 percent, but error correction cost dropped from 16 percent of production costs to 6 percent of production costs.

➠ Between 1981 and 1985, the volume of fund transfers increased by 45 percent, but error correction cost dropped from 21 percent of production costs to 10 percent, a savings of over $1 million—more than the cost of the whole Product Quality Measurement Program itself.

➠ The Money Transfer Group maintains a 99.97 percent accuracy rate.

➠ The Check Collection unit maintains a reject rate in check processing substantially lower than the industry's norm of 1.5 percent.

Besides continuing to improve its performance on a percentage basis, First Chicago is moving ahead to devise a system to study individual situations. "Regardless of how good our percentages are, they can still hide important issues," says Holub.

▭ **More Than Numbers** ⇨ "For example, the amount you pay in compensation when you send money to the wrong place is tied to the actual amount of money sent. Thus, incorrectly sending $5 million would seem to cause more of a problem than incorrectly sending $5,000.

"However, if that $5,000 was college money for the daughter of a chairman of the board of a major corporation, that $5,000 becomes much more of a customer-sensitive issue. Our plans for the future, then, are to continually refine the program with the customer perspective in mind," she concludes.

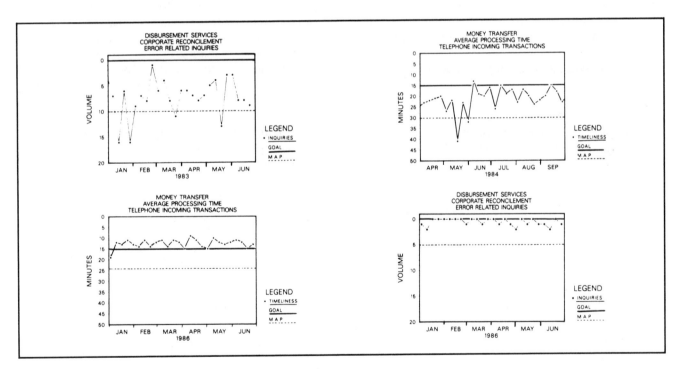

FIGURE 1

INTEL CORPORATION

People working together to audit their own performance keeps quality on track at Intel. Here, the company shares its do-it-yourself quality measurement system.

In many organizations, quality audits are looked upon as a necessary evil—with the emphasis on the evil. But since they must be performed from time to time, it's important that they be done as painlessly as possible, just as they are at this California facility.

Until recently, Intel Corporation had a central corporate audit function, and corporate auditors visited the company's plants worldwide to conduct quality assurance audits. But there were several problems with this central auditor approach:

1. The expense involved in sending auditors all over the world was significant.

2. Negative plant reaction. Auditors were usually viewed as outside "police officers" whose presence was not seen as adding value to the plants. This meant that the two sides were at odds from the start.

When people found out that an auditor was visiting, they quickly got processes and procedures up to snuff. The fixes tended to last long enough to pass the audit, and then things would slide again until the next audit. In some cases, people would steer auditors through the processes and data that were operating properly and try to avoid those that were in need of improvement.

"In this way, they would get the best grades they possibly could and have the fewest number of things to improve," says Gregory K. Pasco, senior quality specialist at Intel's Folsom, CA, facility.

3. Audit team limitations. Since the auditors did not work at the plant full-time, they were neither thoroughly familiar with the processes and procedures they were auditing nor able to work with plant personnel to get the best solutions to any problems they uncovered.

Auditors did not have the formal authority to make necessary improvements. This was left up to local management, and since they were not part of the audit process, they often focused only on fixing noncompliance findings while ignoring improvement recommendations. And since the auditors left immediately after their audits, the audit team could not check firsthand to see whether or not its recommendations were implemented.

What was the bottom line? "Plant managements viewed audits as resource drains without any benefits," answers Pasco.

A SYSTEMATIC SOLUTION

When faced with overhauling the audit function, Pasco realized that what was needed was a way to get people to work together to solve their problems. "I wanted a methodology in which people would get excited about discovering and solving their own problems," he says.

What resulted was a distributed Self-Audit System based on the concepts of individually owned quality and continuous improvement. Under this system, each plant is divided into self-audit areas by process or by station. Local audit groups create "best known methods" to be used as measurement and evaluative tools in conducting quarterly audits of their own processes.

Each plant has a Plant/Auditor/Coordinator reporting to plant management. This person's functions are to:

➡ administer the Self-Audit System in the plant

➡ train the members of the self-audit team

➡ schedule audits throughout the plant and make sure that they occur as scheduled

➡ consolidate corrective action plans

➡ issue quarterly reports on the audits

➡ track corrective action/continuous improvement report line items to completion

➡ coordinate and host all customer audits (under the guidance of the corporate auditor)

Plant Auditors/Coordinators receive their training from the corporate audit department.

TEAMING UP

Each plant also has a Self-Audit Team (composed of functional/content experts from Engineering,

Maintenance, Manufacturing, and Management) for each self-audit area. And these groups are charged with actually conducting the audits in their respective areas of the plant.

"Each Plant Auditor/Coordinator forms the Self-Audit Teams for the plant," reports Pasco. Membership selection is based on finding the best and the most committed people available, rather than enlisting employees who just happen to have some time on their hands.

Some teams continue to keep the same members year after year, while others rotate members. The teams are role models for teaching people to audit themselves as a part of their responsibility for the quality of the work produced.

THE AUDIT PROCESS

Self-audits occur in each self-audit area of a plant on a quarterly basis under the direction of the Plant Auditor/Coordinator. Here is the process, broken down step-by-step:

1 The team goes to a specific area to make sure that personnel are following the proper procedures and specifications.

2 The team's job is to see if anything can be improved.

3 The team leader then assigns ownership for each recommendation (based on a newfound deficiency or opportunity).

4 The leader then writes a report, which is sent to the Plant Auditor/Coordinator.

5 The Plant Auditor/Coordinator pulls together all the reports from the various areas of the plant and sends copies to plant management as well as to the corporate QA audit office.

6 "We review the reports and make additional suggestions at that time," explains Vivian Brown, audit operations manager and senior auditor at Intel's Santa Clara facility.

7 If it turns out that a systems problem exists, plant management forms a Quality Improvement Team to reevaluate the system and make the appropriate recommendations for change.

IMPLEMENTING THE SELF-AUDIT SYSTEM

What does it take to build a Self-Audit System into a company, especially one with a worldwide organization such as Intel? There are a number of keys to success, according to Pasco and Brown:

⊃ **Management acceptance and support** ⇒ According to Pasco, this is the most important key to success. "The plants that are most successful with self-audits are those with management backing," he observes.

"Management must believe that the self-audit concept is valuable to them," adds Brown. "We try to show them that it is added value for them, not something being done to them."

Is management buy-in vital? It is important and makes putting the program in place much easier, Brown believes. But if you can't get buy-in at first, you may be able to get by initially with a management agreement to try it for a while to see if it works. Once they see that it does work, actual buy-in takes place on its own.

⊃ **Flexible methodology and "ownership" of the system** ⇒ Individual plants and operations must feel that they have a stake in the results.

"Once the guideline methodology for the Self-Audit System was developed, we went on a worldwide tour to sell it to management and QA functions at each plant. Presentations were made one-on-one and in groups with management staffs," explains Pasco. "Our goal was to sell them on the concepts and the idea of creating their own program, not selling our specific program to them."

Each plant was encouraged to draft its own self-audit procedure, one that would adapt the new concepts to the needs of its operations. As such, the local, site-specific specifications became the controlling documents. "Our corporate methodology, which provided the guidelines outlining tools, concepts, goals, and end results, was simply an educational document," says Pasco.

"We had some specific requirements from customers that we had to implement in certain cases," adds Brown. "However, we left the rest up to the individual plants. We wanted to set down guidelines, not rigid rules."

⊃ **Training Plant Auditors/Coordinators** ⇒ and getting them to communicate with each other on a regular basis. Ongoing interplant user groups share problems, solutions, tools, and the evolution of "best known method" for each type of factory or organization, observes Brown. "The auditors meet with each other to share successes so that the plants don't all have to 'reinvent the wheel.' ''

Auditors meet annually at worldwide quality auditor conferences; these are week-long sessions and workshops designed around education and communication. "By the end of the week, they all have a common vision," says Pasco.

❑ **A positive—not punitive—attitude** ⇨ Along with the keys already mentioned, it's absolutely critical to educate plant management not to use audit results as punitive information. Management response to self-audit findings will determine its implementation success. The only way employees will report audit findings honestly and openly is if they know that their reports will be accepted without retribution and responded to positively.

"We don't want management to 'shoot the messenger,' '' says Pasco. "This cultural change helps management adopt a continuous improvement and teamwork mind-set."

❑ **More than a quick fix** ⇨ Finally, management must realize that self-auditing is a permanent discipline, not a Band-Aid approach. "It is not designed to be a one-shot thing that will be discontinued after problems are initially resolved," emphasizes Pasco. "If it's abandoned, the same problems will be back six months later."

INTEL'S SELF-AUDITS: THE BENEFITS ARE SELF-EVIDENT

Intel has seen numerous positive results from its self-audit program. One significant result is the change in culture that has occurred in the plants. "People now know that it is okay to have problems and 'turn in' themselves or the system," says Pasco. "They know that if they report things that are wrong, they will not be penalized or simply told to fix it."

Before the Self-Audit System was put in place, the term "audit" was considered a bad word. "Now it's a good word," says Pasco. "People actually look forward to conducting audits." During audits, employees are communicating with one another like never before, discussing problems and trying to come up with solutions and process improvements.

The Self-Audit System has placed Intel's factories in a constant state of readiness for *customer* audits too. "We don't need a week's notice or have to turn the plant upside down to get ready for a customer audit," says Pasco. "The plants are ready all the time."

They must be, because since implementing the Self-Audit System, Intel has not had even one unsuccessful customer audit. "In one year, we had 85 customer audits and numerous other customer visits, receiving high marks on all of them," he reports.

Some customers are so impressed with Intel's internal audit system that they are forgoing their own audits. One customer has commented that it doesn't feel it can add anything at all to Intel's audits. Another plans to audit the company only every second year, instead of annually.

❑ **The Bottom Line** ⇨ "There is no doubt in my mind that we have gained more business as a result of the Self-Audit System, by demonstrating to customers that Intel's processes are in control," Pasco concludes.

TOTAL QUALITY MANAGEMENT/CONTINUOUS IMPROVEMENT

Many leading companies are turning to Total Quality Management (TQM), and for good reason. TQM brings the entire organization into the quality picture, enabling staffers across the board to "do it right the first time."

E.I. DU PONT DE NEMOURS & CO., INC.

Like many organizations, Du Pont launched its quality improvement effort in response to a problem it had discovered. But unlike many, it made a commitment to Total Quality Management and has reaped a number of benefits as a result.

When the Polymer Products Department of E. I. Du Pont de Nemours & Co. (Wilmington, DE) conducted a cost of quality survey a few years ago, it found that internal and external failure costs amounted to approximately $400,000,000, which was about twice the earnings of the $3.5 billion business. To address this problem, the department launched a Total Quality Management (TQM) effort, employing three "bodies of knowledge":

1 Organizational Effectiveness. Learning in this area is allowing the organization to:

- establish a leadership process designed to evoke purposeful, business-directed activities from the entire organization;
- develop a culture based on openness and trust;
- improve the quality of thinking using frameworks and models; and
- provide methods to—

  - ▶ develop shared responsibility teams
  - ▶ build common visions and goals
  - ▶ increase delegation
  - ▶ develop understanding and trust so that needed changes can take place
  - ▶ increase the quality of individual and group thought processes and contributions

2 Marketing Management. Learning in this area is allowing the organization to:

- encourage an outward focus on markets and customers;
- provide a way for everyone in the department to differentiate their offerings in the marketplace; and
- provide methods to—

  - ▶ determine the perceived values held by customers and prospects
  - ▶ segment major markets into manageable pieces

  - ▶ analyze competition and make educated guesses as to their strategies
  - ▶ define offerings that would give the department a competitive edge

3 Quality Management. Learning in this area is allowing the organization to:

- satisfy the needs of internal and external customers;
- stress the importance of prevention versus correction of failure;
- establish the practice of continuous improvement on a project-by-project basis;
- stress the value of performance measurements as a way to hold improvement gains; and
- provide methods to—

  - ▶ identify problems and areas for improvement via cross-functional discussions, cost-of-quality estimates, and work process analysis
  - ▶ eliminate chronic problems through diagnosis to determine root causes and execution of improvement projects
  - ▶ maximize product and process consistency using statistical process control and experimental process design
  - ▶ minimize future internal and external failures by emphasizing quality assurance (prevention and appraisal) in the project and process planning stage.

TQM IN ACTION

"We see TQM as a process for continuous change and improvement in everything that an organization does," says Thomas C. Gibson, currently consultant/Quality Management Services for Du Pont.

TQM, according to Gibson, must start with a focus on the customer. That is, TQM is designed to promote continuous improvements in products, services, and work processes. "Work processes are interactions that begin in the field with the customer," explains Gibson. They involve gaining an understanding of customer values and needs and translating those needs into goals that people within the organization can understand.

"Unless you understand customer values and needs, you don't know what you should be producing or what corrections and improvements need to be made to satisfy those needs," he continues. If customer focus is not at the beginning point, then you may end up making improvements in your organization and operations that are not pertinent at all.

Work processes can also involve relations with suppliers—developing working relationships and partnerships with suppliers so that they understand how you are trying to serve customers as your products and services enter the marketplace.

TQM can help you meet these challenges, but it also requires that you:

1. Provide leadership. This is, by far, the overriding "driver" of making process improvements, says Gibson. TQM is all about change, and if you don't have leadership in place, people will be reluctant to change.

"People only change when confronted with strong leadership, crisis, or both. Therefore, unless you are willing to be at the whim of crises, strong leadership is the only reliable change force you have."

2. Provide training in improvement methods. Once leadership is in place, the next step is to train participants and focus on three important improvement methods:

- Increase customer focus.
- Upgrade operating networks. All interactions that take place must start with the customer, work back through internal operations, and then move back to suppliers. "Isolate and eliminate all the failures and glitches that exist in your operating networks," Gibson suggests.
- Broaden employee involvement and upgrade the quality of their thinking. This helps to ensure constant improvement. "If you think only in terms of today's activities and customer needs, you won't have any assurance of being better six months from now," he notes.

3. Execute projects for continuous improvement. "This is really the payoff step," says Gibson. In other words, this is where you obtain the results of your specific project-by-project activity. A project, according to Gibson, is any organized effort aimed at improvement.

In the area of customer service, for example, you can train the people who deal directly with customers on how to develop in-depth working partnerships with customers—the kinds of relationships and partnerships that allow the current and future needs of the customer to be understood. Examples of projects that might be effective in this area are:

➠ Training sales and marketing representatives in skills needed to get better information from customers. "This is the kind of training that you would normally give to marketing researchers," explains Gibson. By giving this training to sales and marketing reps, they can continually gain information that is vital to understanding customers' real needs and values.

"Most customers are very willing to provide this kind of information," emphasizes Gibson. "It is simply a matter of training reps to conduct these interactions and dialogues."

In one client organization, a department has set up a sales rep hotline. At the end of each day, the sales reps call the hotline to report any new information they have gathered during the day that they think will help improve the department's offerings to customers.

➠ Training customer service representatives (those who actually take the orders) to conduct similar partnership-type dialogues designed to continually gain understanding of customer values and needs.

➠ Conducting periodic, planned, and direct surveys of customers. "Again, customers respond well to direct requests from suppliers that are aimed at better understanding their needs," he points out.

You can create a system to organize the data and get it in front of management people and those responsible for developing strategies, and then make sure that the strategies dictated by the survey results are implemented.

Most companies that have problems with customers, Gibson believes, are those that do not have adequate systems in place to get information from customers on where improvements are needed. They have systems to gather information on sales volume, return on investment, percentage of orders meeting customer ship dates, and so on. However, they don't have data on what customers will need in the future or where failures are occurring in operating networks at present.

"In other words, the kind of information they have helps them react to problems, rather than to be proactive and improve things before they become problems," Gibson explains.

For instance, few companies have information systems that provide data on where the "mini-crises" occur each day in the plants, in the field, with customers, between Marketing and R&D, and so on. "As such, these companies don't find out about the mini-crises until a major crisis occurs," he notes.

Here are some examples of mini-crises that could benefit from being addressed by projects before they contribute to a major crisis:

PROBLEM ► Not getting adequate interaction between functional leaders within the company.

Solution: Find a way to train and lead these people to work better together.

PROBLEM ► First-through yields in a production process are only 85 percent when they should be in the high 90s.

Solution: Create a project to find the reasons that the yields are not higher.

PROBLEM ► Lack of cooperation between operators running a production line and operators in the control lab, evidenced by the lab not getting control data back to the line people quickly enough.

Solution: Create a project to get operators to understand the importance of working together and then train them to do so.

PROBLEM ► A supplier doesn't have an updated understanding of your current needs.

Solution: Create a partnership with the supplier and explain your needs.

RESULTS THAT ARE SIMPLY POSITIVE

As a result of Du Pont's efforts with TQM, a number of positive results have occurred. "We are seeing sales reps taking people from the plants and labs with them on calls and forming teams with similar functions at their customers' locations," reports Gibson. "Using this approach, they are resolving problems that existed for years because no one understood them well enough until people with like-function responsibility began talking about them."

Other improvements Du Pont has seen include the following:

✔ Teams of functional managers from R&D, Marketing, Production, and other departments are working together and cooperating on projects.

✔ In the manufacturing area, teams composed of first-line operators, supervisors, and engineers are finding ways to make mutual contributions to improving processes. "As they see the results of their efforts, they gain enthusiasm for making even more improvements," says Gibson.

✔ First-through yields on production lines have increased from 75 percent to 90 percent.

✔ Many departments are reducing their cost of quality by 5 to 7 percent a year. "Quality-related costs in the typical manufacturing operation are in the range of 20 to 30 percent," says Gibson. "If you can reduce the cost of quality by 10 percent annually, you're talking about 3 percent of sales revenue. That's real money savings."

✔ In one case, a department had been selling a resin to a customer for years. At certain times, the resin would not work well for the customer. The department created a team composed of representatives from the department and from the customer's organization. It turned out that the parameters that the department was measuring during production were not exactly consistent with the properties that the customer needed.

The team more clearly defined exactly what key characteristics needed to be measured, changed the process, and installed new controls. Not only did the improvements meet the customer's needs, but departmental manufacturing yields increased and costs were reduced.

WHAT DOES THE FUTURE HOLD?

In the future, Gibson believes, many Du Pont groups will include the annual cost of quality studies as part of each department's annual business planning process. Each department would then be required to analyze its internal and external failure costs, identify areas for improvement, and measure progress on these improvements over the year.

If past successes are any indication, Du Pont has much to look forward to in the areas of quality improvements and cost reduction.

ALUMINUM COMPANY OF AMERICA, INC.

Consistency in every phase of operation is the key to Alcoa's successful Total Quality effort. Learn the eight essential elements of this company's quality-consistent organization.

Total Quality is a noble goal, and more and more companies are starting to strive for it. But many run into a roadblock when they develop the impression that using a certain program, technique, or concept is all they must do to meet the Total Quality Challenge. It takes much more than that, actually. And among the more crucial elements is consistency in all you do.

Discussing coiled rigid container sheets, one of the products produced by the Packaging Systems Group of the Aluminum Company of America (Alcoa), Group Vice President Ron Hoffman had this to say:

"Our customers want coils that allow their manufacturing lines to operate at their peak. The coils must arrive on time, they must be consistent across the width and throughout the length, and consistently be at the specified customer maximum size. Consistency over time is essential. Each coil must be the same as the last and the next. And along with optimal line performance, our customers expect zero errors in invoicing and other administrative services, as well as on-time delivery and product packaging integrity."

The fact that the terms *consistent, consistency,* and *consistently* appear so often is no accident; the terms are fundamental to the quality improvement effort.

"Inconsistency always costs someone down the line—whether it happens to be the person at the desk next to you or the final customer," points out Doug Ward, statistical quality control (SQC) manager for Alcoa's Rigid Packaging Division (Pittsburgh, PA). "Eliminating inconsistency is really the name of the game."

But how does Alcoa eliminate inconsistency? "We know what each customer requires, we consistently meet our commitments, and we continually improve our products and services through time."

To this end, a total commitment to quality was adopted. The quality effort is an all-encompassing result of years of learning and, frankly, false starts. What has resulted, however, is an excellent quality blueprint for the future.

FALSE STARTS

Ward says that it was through false starts that his division is now able to firmly grasp the essence of quality. "Part of the reason we had those false starts was lack of a deeper knowledge of what a total commitment to quality is all about," he says.

While the Rigid Packaging Division (RPD) used control charts as far back as the early 1950s, it wasn't until 1983 that some of the company's business units became reassociated with statistical process control through customers who were starting to use SPC and encouraging their suppliers to do the same.

After attending some Deming and Juran seminars, as well as other awareness activities, representatives of the RPD realized that SPC held great promise.

"The concept of looking at variation through time on a relatively simple graphic display and using that as an important tool to identify 'special causes' made sense to us," says Ward. However, it took several years to begin to more fully understand the real meanings behind the messages of quality:

➡ **Realization #1—Target versus specification.** There was confusion over the difference between conformance to an optimum target and conformance to a specification. The goal, Ward stresses, is to develop a target-based mentality as opposed to simply meeting specification.

For every critical variable, there is an optimal target. This target is a single value that exists inside of a specification at which the customer's performance is optimized. The actual achievement of 100 percent conformance to this target is an essential part of never-ending improvement.

➡ **Realization #2—Terminology.** Another concern was the lack of consistent definitions for seemingly simple terms such as *quality, control, capability,* and so on.

"We used these terms all the time, but we didn't

realize the importance of having clear, understandable, and uniform definitions of these words within our culture, as well as with our customers and suppliers," notes Ward.

It's essential that everyone involved in the quality equation speak the same language. Today, people at RPD are working hard to use these terms, and others of a more technical nature, uniformly.

➡ Realization #3—Training. The linkage between awareness and training and application was another issue. Employees spent many hours in classes learning about tools and terms with which they hadn't previously been familiar. But it became obvious that unless the training was closely coupled with practice and real-life application, the effectiveness of these hours was greatly diminished.

As Ward says, "The 'half-life' of training effectiveness *without* an improvement opportunity immediately available is incredibly short. And the more complex the training, the shorter that half-life."

➡ Realization #4—Goals. In 1983 the goals were related to commitments to statistical tools such as SPC. "We were approaching the tools as goals in and of themselves," explains Ward. "We didn't necessarily understand at that point that the goal really was to improve the product and the services going to our customers."

As a result of this realization, Ward passes along the following message: "It's important not to latch on to one tool and simply go forth and find a problem to solve. You must begin to learn and understand the overall concept of quality.

"Along the way, there is a tremendously valuable statistical 'tool kit' that will be studied and incorporated when it is necessary and appropriate to do so. The total management of quality goes well beyond simply learning statistical tools and concepts, but an effort that is built on these principles has a strong foundation."

➡ Realization #5—Programs. It is very difficult to avoid managing the improvement effort as simply another "program," even though you say up front that you will not do this. A cultural change is required, and this simply will not happen as a result of slogans, speeches, or a commitment from management that is not knowledgeable. "It is easy to confuse doing things right with doing the right things," Ward says.

➡ Realization #6—Customer-driven effort. In 1986, the RPD started to understand that quality wasn't an issue for Manufacturing alone, and that it wasn't limited to dimensional and physical property improvement.

"We now realize that improvement is for everyone," emphasizes Ward. "When you adopt a mentality that quality has to do with customer satisfaction, and when your measurement is how well your customers rate your performance, you start to realize that the product is not just aluminum, but all of what everyone does that directly or indirectly affects the customer."

➡ Realization #7—Scope and direction. In the mid-1980s, the RPD and some other business units started to develop an appreciation of the breadth and depth that a total commitment to quality brings. "This understanding does not come overnight, but it is essential if you are going to move forward," observes Ward.

"It is difficult to balance the accomplishments of yesterday with the need for never-ending improvement that tomorrow demands," Ward admits. But resting on your laurels is something you can't afford to do. Your quality effort has to be focused on meeting *tomorrow's* standard—not yesterday's.

"For instance, there are a number of problems we measured per 100 units yesterday that today are defined per 1,000 units. However, the understanding of never-ending improvement means that we must require scales per 10,000 tomorrow, and per 100,000 in the future."

➡ Realization #8—Structured approach. Recently, the RPD has come to understand that there is a crucial balance between the technology of statistical methods and the organization's culture. "The pieces involved in the improvement of quality must be managed together, not as separate entities and activities. The management of quality improvement requires a structured approach, and this process is the Plan-Do-Check-Act cycle," says Ward.

When it comes to *culture,* this means that "management needs to provide specific expectations, environment, philosophy, and a consistent set of policies and procedures by which to operate. Also needed are technical systems and people to manage them, but if management does not provide an opportunity to practice the skills and utilize the knowledge, then we have actually accomplished very little."

In terms of *technology,* "the ultimate depth of the statistical and problem-solving methods is unknown.

It's amazing to review articles and texts from the early 1900s which are every bit as valid today as they were then. Likewise, new developments are coming forth all the time. The technical challenge is to understand and implement the concepts, not just learn the mechanics.''

THE INTERNAL CUSTOMER: A CRITICAL ELEMENT OF SUCCESS

Like other successful companies, Alcoa recognizes the importance of instilling the internal customer concept. That is, when quality concepts and tools are used within each function to produce the consistent results required by the next internal customer, the final result is consistent quality that is on target for the external customer. Without this internal consistency, external consistency cannot be assured.

Accurate internal quality targets don't just happen, however. Information on customer requirements must be actively solicited. It is important to determine what optimum targets are required by customers, translate these requirements into measureable product, process, and service characteristics, and then supply these characteristics consistently.

According to Ward, ''It is important to have an effective way to communicate with customers to determine their requirements and how well we are meeting them. The effort is not just about training, it is not just about learning how to do SPC, it is not about being oriented toward a particular tool or activity,'' he stresses.

''It is about meeting our customers' needs. The effort is all about improvement as measured by the customer.''

EARLY PAYOFFS

While the RPD's Total Quality effort is still relatively new, results and benefits are already being seen. Some of the more obvious include:

- Product quality improvements as noted by customers
- Reduced setup time
- Improved yield

- Increased uptime on capital-intensive equipment
- Manufacturing flexibility
- Reduced inventories

''One of the subtle—yet more important—benefits of the effort to date is that larger numbers of people regularly question assumptions about what 'everybody knows' is important,'' says Ward. ''This sometimes painful activity *always* leads to improvement in our overall understanding about what is really happening in the process. We have a number of projects where people have been able to get to the roots of long-standing problems and actually correct them.''

▢ **Improvement in Action** ⇨ For example, the RPD has a new, 500-foot coil coating line with equipment designed to trim, level, wash, and apply a protective coating to coils of rolled aluminum sheet. The line is in place to meet the need in two fast-growing segments of the rigid container sheet market: food-can stock and wide-coated endstock.

''In specifying the equipment, the division established critical performance requirements for equipment acceptance. A highly trained multidiscipline team divided the line into six segments and identified 135 effects (64 main variables and 71 variable interactions) that could affect our ability to consistently produce at the optimum targets.

''Using design of experiments techniques (involving 15,000 measurements in 15 separate experiments), the team determined which variables were the most important in understanding not only how to set the average but also how to reduce the variation. Results are now allowing engineers and operators to set and control the line to yield the specific characteristics required for the final product.''

These, then, are the initial payoffs of the Total Quality approach. What does the future hold?

''There is much more to learn and do than previously imagined, and in many ways we have only begun,'' says Ward. ''The deeper we go, the more we must consider, but the basic underpinning of the effort is extremely simple: Variation from what the customer really requires is costly and must be eliminated.''

ALLEN-BRADLEY COMPANY

The need to modernize sparked this company's move to Total Quality Management. The result? Final test yield percentages in the high 90s and a significant reduction in warranty returns.

One of the marks of a truly quality-minded company is that it strives for constant improvement. Even if things are already going well, there's no reason why an organization can't challenge itself to do even better when it comes to quality.

Many companies implement quality management systems because they need to improve quality. Unlike these companies, however, Allen-Bradley Co. (Milwaukee, WI) found itself in the enviable spot of launching its quality system to position itself for even greater competitiveness in the future.

This manufacturer of industrial automation and quality management components and systems, formed in 1903, has always had a tradition of high quality because of its Old World German and Swiss culture. "The company had the Old World mentality of the value of quality," explains Roger Hartel, vice president of Quality Assurance for the company's Industrial Computer and Communications Group (Highland Heights, OH). "As a result, it always had an enviable market position with all of its products."

CAUSE FOR CHANGE

In the mid-1970s, however, three important things occurred that forced the company to reevaluate the way it managed quality:

1 **Management decided to move the company into the "electronic age."** Until that point, all the company's products were electromechanical. Management realized that the future of the industry would be electronic. As such, the company's quality system would need to be refocused.

At the time, quality was based on a lot of inspection, testing, and rework. This worked well, because the majority of defects in the electromechanical devices were very visual (parts out of shape, out of dimension, cracked, or broken). "Quality problems in electronic components, however, are more subtle, hidden in the software or electronic circuitry," points out Hartel.

Such problems can occur as a result of temperature changes, interactions between and among different products, and so on. "A problem might be there one minute and gone the next," he adds.

Because of this, the company needed a quality system based on prevention, rather than appraisal, simply because appraisal would be difficult; and it would certainly not be cost-effective.

2 **Allen-Bradley was also in the process of acquiring a number of new companies** as part of its strategy to move into electronic manufacturing. But these new companies did not have the strict quality culture of the original Milwaukee facility. And when management attempted to transfer this culture to them, it met with great difficulty.

3 **Part of the company's strategy in moving into electronics involved moving into the world marketplace.** That meant that it had to become world-class in its operations, and, of course, this required quality based on prevention, not appraisal.

EARLY PROBLEMS

To address these challenges, Allen-Bradley implemented a Total Quality Management System (TQMS), one that emphasizes continuous improvement in quality, productivity, and customer satisfaction. It is based on the belief that everything can be improved and that improvement must be continuous.

Early efforts involved implementing many of the standard quality control systems, such as statistical tools and training, problem-solving techniques, manufacturing controls, and supplier management. While the efforts themselves were not difficult to implement, management met with resistance in many locations for two reasons:

➪ Those locations that were part of the "Milwaukee quality culture" didn't see the need for a new system, since their quality was already so impressive.

➪ Those locations that were recently acquired by the company often reported that they were too busy solving quality problems to find the time to adopt a new system.

Pressure from management to adopt the new system was one component of success, but another event spurred adoption even more: "Many of the divisions realized the need to move into a just-in-time (stockless) production system," reports Hartel. "In so doing, they quickly realized that they would never be able to manage such a system without a prevention-based quality system."

In other words, there was no way to be able to predict how many individual units would have to be fed into a process in order to produce the right number of final products in a short-run system. "You simply cannot do JIT when you have low yields or when you handle quality by inspection and rework," emphasizes Hartel.

TEAMWORK: A CRUCIAL ELEMENT

Teamwork plays a vital role in TQM. Prior to the introduction of the system, people at Allen-Bradley performed their work to high standards, but did not necessarily do so in a spirit of information exchange and cooperation. "They lacked the awareness of what their internal customers needed," he says. Each department, in other words, set its own standards and procedures without consulting other departments.

An important part of TQM involves turning this mentality around to one of teamwork and cooperation. "The idea is to define how the organization as a whole wants to do business," says Hartel. The next step is to break down these goals into individual steps and elements as they affect quality and service. This requires the visible and permanent involvement of all functions. Hartel refers to the process, which addresses how each function serves and is served by all other functions, as "defining and managing interfunctional deliverables and receivables."

Today, the concept is often referred to as parallel engineering. Unlike other companies that have just begun to adopt this strategy, however, Allen-Bradley launched its teamwork concept a decade ago.

▷ THE PROCESS IN ACTION ⇒ From the time a marketing person has the glimmer of a product idea or receives a suggestion from a customer for a new product, until the time the product is actually manufactured and shipped, most companies allow the functions involved to operate somewhat independently of one another. Allen-Bradley insists that all the critical functions work together as a team to design, develop, and manufacture the product. Each function becomes both a customer and a supplier of the other functions. In every instance, each function considers the ramifications of its actions on all the other functions.

CERTIFIABLE QUALITY

Another critical element of TQM success is departmental certification. Each department in the company is required to determine what systems must exist in its department in order to satisfy its part in reaching the company's overall goals. Management then audits these systems to verify that they are in place, that they are working, and that they are achieving the quality improvement results that are expected. When a department achieves these three goals, it is formally certified.

Each year, the department must also be recertified. Recertification audits ensure not only that the systems are in place, working, and achieving quality goals, but that they are *improving*.

"Each certifiable department must enhance its system by adding new elements to its quality activities," emphasizes Hartel. "Status quo causes atrophy, and there is no place for atrophy. We must continue to grow and improve in our quality efforts."

Therefore, the department must establish its quality improvement goals and state how it plans to achieve them. An additional component of recertification involves surveys of internal and external customers that assess departmental performance.

THE BENEFITS IT BRINGS

As a result of its TQM system, Allen-Bradley has seen dramatic decreases in its internal and external failure costs. For example:

- Final test yield percentages for most products are in the very high 90s. Also, many *first* test yield percentages are in the very high 90s.
- One division that quadrupled its size over the past 10 years has seen an absolute reduction in warranty returns over the same period (representing over a 75 percent reduction in warranty returns).
- Between 1982 and 1988, the company saved in excess of $100 million as a result of reduced quality costs. "We have a payback in excess of 13 to 1 on everything we have invested in quality improvement," Hartel says.
- Allen-Bradley has experienced a dramatic increase in market share, "and we feel that a major portion of this is attributable to improved quality and reduced cost," concludes Hartel.

ROCKWELL INTERNATIONAL

True quality assurance doesn't come from any one technique or magic "tool"—nor does it apply to only one aspect of your operation, as managers at Rockwell realized firsthand. Instead, it's a continuous, "total" strategy that involves the commitment of every employee.

Today, every company is feeling the pressure of increasing competition and looking for a solution. The day when you could turn to a "quick fix" and feel that you'd solved the problem is long gone, however. One or two well-placed programs or the implementation of one or two "tools" (SPC or quality circles, for example) simply won't do the trick. The times require more than a Band-Aid approach.

Companies in the automotive and automotive parts industries know that this is a luxury that no longer exists. Competition is international, it is stiff, and it is getting hotter and hotter. "Only the strong survive" is the philosophy by which companies in these industries live.

Here, the very best of the very best compete for the top honors: the lion's share of manufacturers' business and the lion's share of consumers' business. As a result, it is here that one can find the very best and most successful quality improvement strategies being implemented.

The Automotive Operations Division of Rockwell International (Troy, MI) represents an excellent example of a company that has taken the bull by the horns and is molding itself into a world-class supplier. In the early 1980s, Automotive Operations had one primary goal: to improve quality in order to remain competitive. In retrospect, that sounds a bit like simple survival. Today, it has added two additional goals—goals designed to place it in the forefront of its industry:

▶ **It decided to become a system supplier.** "We supply axles, brakes, and drive-line components to truck manufacturers," explains Jim Warren, director of Product Assurance. "Recently, we have also moved into the clutch business, and we will soon be going into the transmission business."

What's the strategy? "We are moving from a component supplier to a system supplier of components," he replies. What customers ultimately want is a system of parts that work together. The implications of this for suppliers are staggering. Instead of a dozen suppliers supplying a dozen individual components, it may be in the future that one or two sup-

pliers will supply complete systems.

The challenge is obvious: Improve quality to such a point that Automotive Operations is one of those premier suppliers.

▶ **It decided to improve warranties while at the same time reducing its warranty costs.** As part of its competitive strategy, Automotive Operations implemented a 5-year/500,000-mile warranty program three years ago. In order to prevent warranty costs from increasing as a result of the program, it also launched a "50 and 5" program aimed at reducing warranty costs by 50 percent over a five-year period. "We are approaching our third year of this program, and our cost reductions are already ahead of schedule," reports Warren.

RESTRUCTURING THE QUALITY PHILOSOPHY

Before its efforts to improve quality began, the division had a "traditional" QC program. "We called it 'the checkers checking the checkers,' " says Warren. Inspectors checked the operators' work, auditors checked the inspectors' work, and staff auditors checked the plants' work.

"We found out that, no matter how many levels and types of checkers you have, there is still plenty of room for cat-and-mouse games," he admits. "We realized that we would have to convince people of the importance of doing work right the first time."

One of the first lessons management learned was that quality improvement was not the result of implementing one or two "programs" or "tools." That is, while SPC, quality circles, JIT, Taguchi Methods, and Quality Function Deployment were helpful in improving quality, they were not, in and of themselves, keys to success. In a paper given at the 1989 ASQC Quality Congress, Warren makes an excellent point: "Even though American businesses have gone to Japan for the 'answers,' they are still not successful, because they have not gone through the thought processes to get the answers for themselves."

Warren has found that the real key to quality improvement is top management understanding and commitment to the process. Once that has been established, the proper programs and tools can be selected.

○ **Case in Point** ⇒ One of the company's plant managers, in seeking to find out why quality improvement at his plant had stalled, decided to personally chart peformance on a particular machine. His goal was to show operators his personal commitment to improvement, but he found a few surprises in his experiment:

● He could not get the gauge to repeat during the first hour.

● He took the gauge to the gauge crib to try to replace a part on it, but found that the crib had been out of those and many other spare parts for months because of budget cutbacks.

● Upon returning to the machine, he found it in need of maintenance.

● In addition, the machine was operating in such a way that chips continued to jam it, leading to further delays.

"All in all, he learned very little about control charting, but instead experienced firsthand the environment that he had created by his own management actions," observes Warren.

Through experiences like this, management learned that quality is such a broad subject that it applies to everything the organization does. "There is no magic formula," adds Warren. "Quality is not the result of any specific tool or technique. Rather, it requires three things":

1. Management understanding and effective leadership of the organization.

2. Proper use of the appropriate technical tools.

3. Employee involvement.

This is the framework for Automotive Operations' Total Quality Control (TQC) effort. "TQC is a very broad-based strategy that relates far beyond just product quality to every aspect of the business," he explains. "It requires every employee's participation; it requires dedication, planning, and constant review."

Creating a successful TQC effort, then, is not an overnight task. It requires many months of careful planning and analysis, taking everyone's perspective into account.

CHANGING ROLES

How does the quality department's role change in a TQC environment? "We are catalysts," Warren replies. "We show the various parts of the company how quality applies to them and then provide the expertise in specific technical tools when they are needed."

The current phase of implementing TQC in Automotive Operations involves the "internal customer" concept. "If we can't make the internal customer happy, department to department, section to section, machine to machine, or desk to desk, there is no way we will make the end customer happy," he says.

Training and implementing the internal customer concept involves finding out what each "customer" in the organization needs from his or her "supplier." People will be trained to ask:

✔ "What do you need from me?"

✔ "What do you do with what I give you?"

✔ "Are there any gaps between what I am supplying and what you need?"

At that point, quality plans will be developed for each department so that progress can be measured and tracked. "With quality, if you can't measure it, you can't implement it," Warren concludes.

NCR CORPORATION

The continuous improvement process at NCR uses five critical dimensions to prevent defects *before* they happen—and it works.

Do you rely on traditional, "after-the-fact" inspection to assure the quality of your company's product? If so, you might like to switch to a preventive—and ultimately less expensive—QA strategy. Here's an approach called "process management" that focuses on building quality into the product from the earliest stages of production.

Almost every quality professional is looking for a QA approach that is more efficient than the traditional inspections at the end of the line. Patrick Murphy, director of Quality for the U.S. Marketing Group of NCR Corporation (Dayton, OH), believes that NCR has developed a better way.

"We've been successful in reducing the number of full-time quality inspectors in our plants by putting quality responsibilities into the line organization," he asserts. "We've done it through what we call *process management*, which is accomplished through managing 'internal relationships.' "

What are internal relationships? Murphy explains: "No matter what job is performed, the person performing it has a customer. For NCR personnel, that customer is someone else in the company. People perform tasks for someone else down the line."

FIVE CRITICAL DIMENSIONS

Many companies have adopted a similar "internal customer" philosophy. But few have broken it down into its logical components, as NCR has. The company has defined five critical dimensions of what it calls *preventive quality* (because defect prevention is the objective of process management). Here is a closer look at each of those five dimensions:

1 Ownership NCR builds its product with a process known as the *platform approach*. "The general manager at the plant 'owns' this process," explains Murphy. "That's who defines the design time, testing, and development costs. The process outlines input requirements from suppliers and manages material that comes into the areas, such as operating software, buses, power supplies, and cabinetry."

The manager then passes the production process to someone else, and must conform to the requirements of that internal customer. "Input, work tasks, and output make up a boundary for a process," says Murphy. "That involves all kinds of relationships as it goes down the line. It's the owner's responsibility to understand those relationships with both internal and external people."

2 Definition This area is a little more comprehensive, Murphy says. It includes nine components that can be stated as questions you might ask yourself:

► Who is the customer of this process?

► What are that customer's output requirements?

► What is the output?

► What is the work task?

► What is the input?

► What are the input requirements?

► Who is the supplier?

► What is the work activity of the process?

► What is the boundary, from input through tasks to output?

As you can see, this will result in a definition that works from the customer back to the supplier. Conformance to the requirements is then passed back to the customer.

3 Measurement "This is the part of the process where we measure over time to see that we have the definition right, and have control over the relationship between the supplier and the customer," says Murphy.

"We use standard terms here, such as parts per million, but it's not done the same way for every process, because there's a difference in their products, requirements, and capabilities."

4 Control NCR has a list of 31 assessment questions that fall into five categories called *process ratings*. "In the control part of the process improvement strategy, you ask and validate whether you do have measurements in place, have corrective action programs, and have some benefits that are being realized,'' Murphy explains.

5 Continuous Improvement The goal from this point on is to continually improve the process. In NCR's case, the goal is a number-one rating, which is the best one to strive for. It means the quality review organization has reviewed the process and determined that all customer dissatisfaction has been eliminated.

''We haven't reached level one on many processes yet, though several of our plants have reached level two,'' says Murphy. ''But there could still be further improvements. The owner of the process could find competitive and technological advances that could be made.''

TWO AREAS FOR SPECIAL ATTENTION

In a quality program like this, some training will be needed. NCR has four different courses in process management, each calling for two- or three-day seminars. Most people in manufacturing facilities have taken the courses. Training starts at entry-level jobs and becomes part of job descriptions. (An effective ''memory jogger'' is the company's Process Management Pocket Guide, reproduced here as Figures 2 and 3.)

NCR NCR Corporation

PROCESS MANAGEMENT Pocket Guide

What is Process Management?
A commitment to excellence in which all functions focus on continuous process improvement and defect prevention, resulting in increased customer satisfaction.

What is a Process?
Anything is a process if it has measurable input and output, has added value, and is repeatable.

Process Management Process

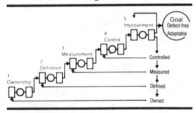

Key Factors for Process Management Success

- Management leadership:
  -top down
  -committed
  -active
- Clearly understood and agreed on Goals
- Breakthrough thinking-not the same old way
- Appropriate Process Measurement methods
- Teamwork
- Training
- Sharing, Promoting and Reinforcing successes

Process Management Model

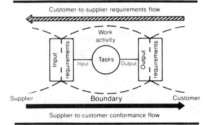

Process Definition Steps

1. Identify process OWNER.
2. Define WORK ACTIVITY.
3. List CUSTOMER(S).
4. List OUTPUT REQUIREMENTS for each customer.
5. List OUTPUT(S) for each customer.
6. List TASKS within the work activity.
7. List INPUT REQUIREMENTS.
8. List SUPPLIER(S).
9. List INPUT(S) from each supplier.
10. Determine starting / ending process BOUNDARIES.

Formalized Definition

- **Thoroughly Defined**
- **Agreed Upon**

Process Management Actions

1. Communicate process management
2. Determine processes you own
3. Define process elements
4. Establish measurement systems
5. Implement process control actions
6. Implement process improvement actions
7. Assess each process and plan for continuous improvement

Root Cause

''That condition (or interrelated set of conditions) having allowed or caused a defect to occur, which once corrected properly, permanently prevents recurrence of the defect in the same, or subsequent, product or service generated by the process.''

Process Management Links to Quality, Productivity and Customer Satisfaction

A quality product or service is one that meets customer expectations. We all have customers, they may be both internal and external to NCR.

True improvements in the quality of products and services have multiple positive effects on NCR:

-lower costs   -increased customer satisfaction
-lower prices   -increased market share
-higher productivity   -increased profits

FIGURE 2

Such a program also involves a couple of particularly important areas that must be managed. ''I wouldn't call them pitfalls,'' says Murphy. ''But there are areas that demand your special attention.'' These are:

● **The relationship between the internal customer and the supplier.** Suppose you have significant organizational changes and the owners who are strong proponents move to new management assignments. ''They'll take the quality program with them,'' he says. ''That's great, but you'll have to renew your education program with those who fill their slots.''

● **The application of your program to marketing and staff areas.** These organizations are not the same as Production and Development. ''The principles of quality process management are conceptually straightforward, but execution is difficult in Marketing,'' says Murphy. ''There are so many subprocesses and so many intertwined activities that formalization, rigor, and measurement are hard to accomplish while conducting the ongoing flow of the business.''

BEGINNING THE PROCESS

Once training has been completed and you're committed to giving special attention to those areas that need it, you need to decide where to begin the program. It might be wise to emulate NCR, which started its program by attacking the areas that had the highest impact on customer satisfaction.

The first was order processing, which begins with releasing a new product to the sales channels and ends with the rendering of an invoice to the customer.

"We got an enthusiastic reception, and it was infectious," notes Murphy. "But we know we can go further once we have done all we can with process management." At present, about 15 to 20 percent of revenues at NCR go into the cost of quality management and improvement. But they're working to reduce that percentage, he notes. Process management should certainly assist them in meeting their aims.

"We think quality process management is one of the most powerful strategies available as we enter the decade of the nineties," says Murphy. "We think it has important implications for our cost structure and for our ability to provide superior customer satisfaction and value." And it just might have the same implications for you.

Process Management Tools

These tools are not a substitute for good judgement or process knowledge. They are aids to help convert data into information which can then be used to make objective decisions.

Process Flow Chart

Shows a visual representation of the sequential steps in a process which also indicates the relationship between the component parts.

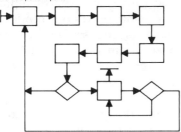

Indicates problem areas, unnecessary loops and complexity, and where simplification of a process is possible.

Cause / Effect Diagrams

Used to organize potential factors that produce an observed result.

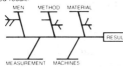

Helps identify and organize process variables or factors that are potentially responsible for the quality of our processes

NCR is the name and mark of NCR Corporation   E&M-W
© 1987 NCR Corporation. Printed in U.S.A.   July 1987

Histograms

Bar charts showing distribution of measured data; if done with averages, should be used carefully.

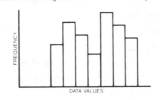

Pareto Charts

Bar charts showing relative importance of specific problems.

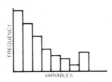

Should be based on data, not opinion.

Scatter Diagrams

Shows relationships of two variables.

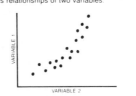

Should be done on single items, not averages.

Trend Charts

Shows the time-order sequence of values.

Control Charts

Shows level of statistical control (predictability).

Natural Pattern (in statistical control): Most points near center-line. A few near control-limits. Rarely any points outside control-limits.

Variables Data $\bar{x}$, R Chart

Attributes Data

Chart	Records	Subgroup Size
p	% or fraction of nonconforming units	varies
np	# of nonconforming units	constant
c	# of nonconformities	constant
u	# of nonconformities per unit	varies

PROCESS MANAGEMENT THE NCR WAY

"We take Customer Satisfaction personally."

"Product Excellence through the Engineering and Manufacturing process."

"Superior quality in everything we do is the objective."

FIGURE 3

UNION CARBIDE

This company's goal-oriented total quality program, called "Excellence Through Quality," covers all the bases. See what makes it work.

If you've ever wondered what an organization could accomplish if it made a complete commitment to improving quality and put all its resources into the effort, then look no further. Here's a nuts-and-bolts description of how one Union Carbide division went about achieving total quality improvement.

When management of the Specialties Department of the Union Carbide Polyolefins Division took a look at the future in the mid-1980s, it realized that, while there were already some important quality efforts taking place, more could still be done.

"The individual programs were successful, but they were not sufficient to carry us into the future in terms of customer needs," says Connie E. Carroll, currently production engineer and formerly quality training coordinator at the company's Seadrift plant (Port Lavaca, TX). "The goal was to pull all of the quality-related activities into a comprehensive and coordinated plan."

The result was what the company calls the "Excellence Through Quality" (EQ) program. The program has two goals:

◻ **Goal # 1** ⇨ **Be recognized as the quality leader by customers, competitors, and the industry.** This goal, in general, involves *external* efforts, such as:

● understanding customers and their needs

● determining how well customers perceive their needs being met

● striving to do things right the first time

● consistently providing the quality that customers need

One of the strategies used to achieve this goal is "Outward Focus," which is based on the recognition that the business needs to be market-driven. That is, Marketing and Production must become sensitized to how their products are used and what is important to the customer—not only in terms of product quality, but in terms of services such as delivery, paperwork, product certification, technical services, and literature. "The more sensitive the business is to what makes customers happy, the more we will be able to develop mutually beneficial, long-term relationships with them," explains Carroll.

Part of achieving these results involves mutual visits. The business invites customers to visit its facilities, see its processes and functions, and talk with people in the facilities to get to know them in person. Conversely, the customers invite Union Carbide people (sales representatives, production operators, QC laboratory analysts, technical staff, maintenance support personnel, distribution attendants, and so on) to visit their facilities to see their products in use.

"Our people come back with a keener understanding of how our products are used and what variables in the product properties are most important to our customers—what makes our products more 'processable' for customers," says Carroll. The result is that employees begin working harder at meeting customer requirements, not just at meeting internal specifications.

"They have a reason for doing this now that they understand firsthand why certain things are important to customers," Carroll adds.

◻ **Goal # 2** ⇨ **Make quality and excellence a way of life for everyone.** In general, this goal involves *internal* efforts, such as:

● taking an integrated approach to meeting customer needs within the business by actively promoting teamwork

● emphasizing open communication

● training employees in quality-related skills like team problem-solving, statistical analysis methods, and technology

● recognizing and rewarding high-quality output and pride in work

● identifying and recognizing the potential as well as the actual contribution of each employee

● placing responsibility for quality on the line organization

● promoting a proactive mind-set for dealing with issues

- reducing quality-related costs in all functions and disciplines

- managing the role that raw material suppliers play in the quality and consistency of the final product

REACHING FOR THE GOALS

To assist in reaching the two goals it had established, the organization set up a multilevel quality-reporting structure:

1 Department level. The Specialties Department (located at administrative headquarters in Danbury, CT) first named a quality director who reports directly to the vice president/general manager; his function is to promote and guide implementation of the improvement effort throughout the Specialties Department.

The next move was to name a training manager to design and coordinate the training effort throughout the department.

Then, the department created a Quality Council consisting of the vice president/general manager and his staff. This council was charged with the following duties:

- identify major improvement projects

- establish annual improvement goals based on the identified projects

- set the priorities for the major resource-intensive projects

- allocate the available resources based on these priorities

- ensure progress on the few critical projects

- monitor the overall effectiveness of the program

Reporting to the Quality Council are six Quality Steering Committees representing:

1. Seadrift plant manufacturing operations

2. Bound Brook (NJ) plant manufacturing operations

3. Sales, marketing, and administration areas

4. Distribution and logistics areas

5. Research and development areas

6. Raw materials area

Each Quality Steering Committee is composed of that operation's or area's functional manager, his or her immediate staff, and the quality manager or

quality director. And just what do the committees do? They:

- identify and prioritize potential improvement projects and "breakthrough" projects

- select the few critical projects

- allocate resources as needed

- define control teams as needed to hold current performance levels

- audit the results of individual improvement projects and the overall program in their operations or areas

2 Plant level. At the Seadrift plant, the quality efforts of the host polyolefins business areas, the tenant chemicals business areas, and the plant support groups are coordinated by a quality manager, who reports directly to plant management.

This plant quality manager also oversees the activities of four diagnostic engineers, who act as resource persons for problem-solving teams in applying statistical methods of analysis and also facilitate those teams.

The plant version of the Specialty Department's Quality Council is the Seadrift Performance Excellence Council (SPEC), which is composed of the plant manager, assistant plant managers, the quality manager, and the employee relations manager. Each business area with production facilities at the plant has a plant quality steering committee, reporting administratively to the SPEC and functionally to the business's quality council.

The Specialties Department and Seadrift plant coordinate their activities through an "Excellence Through Quality Team," which is made up of the department's quality director, the plant's quality manager, the department's training manager, the plant's training coordinator, and the four diagnostic engineers.

OPPORTUNITIES FOR IMPROVEMENT

Once these structures were in place and training in quality improvement techniques was under way, the business began to identify areas and opportunities for improvement. They included:

➪ **Strategic Planning.** Business directors and key managers engage in a strategic planning process to establish and maintain an integrated, long-term plan for all phases of the business. "We see this strategic planning as a dynamic, ongoing process that lies at the very heart of our quality management philosophy," emphasizes Carroll. "Strategic planning must and will occur year after year with the full participation of key managers from all functions of the organization."

◻ **Excellence Models.** The steering committees "crystal ball" what their business performance and management responsibilites will be five years in the future as a result of utilizing quality improvement methods. The committees conduct annual self-audits to compare current performance with the goals of the Excellence Models they develop. They also establish specific projects to address the deficiencies they find during the audits.

◻ **Cost of Quality.** The business uses Juran's "Cost of Quality" concept to prioritize project nominations and to monitor the effectiveness of the overall program. The business defines its cost of quality as:

➡ the sum of all resources that must be committed to preventing the manufacture of product that will not meet the needs of the customer

➡ resources required to determine the status of any project

➡ costs incurred when product of low quality is made, and

➡ the cost of disposing of that product

"These latter two comprise the cost of nonconformance or the cost of poor quality," explains Carroll. Estimating the potential effect of each of the nominated projects on the cost of poor quality enables management to prioritize projects. Improvement teams are then commissioned to address the critical few projects that will yield the greatest improvement for the lowest investment.

◻ **Control Charting.** This is used to define the normal operating range of a process and then signal any real-time deviations from the normal range so that troubleshooting and corrective actions can be taken.

"We found that the operating personnel gained a greater degree of control over the process following implementation of control charting," says Carroll. "It also provided a greater understanding of the capability of the process itself and of the correlations between several variables. This increased understanding ultimately led to greater consistency in the managerial function or product quality under consideration."

◻ **Vendor Improvement.** One of the first proj-

ects that the raw materials steering committee undertook was designing and activating a Vendor Improvement Program (VIP). "At the time, we knew very little about the variability of the materials we received from vendors and had little control over them," says Carroll.

The VIP involves telling vendors that they will have to improve their product and service quality and ultimately be certified by the Department if they wish to remain vendors.

Vendors are rated according to product quality, packaging quality, delivery schedule, paperwork, technical support, literature, and so on. Audit teams from the Department visit vendors on an as-needed basis (but at least every two years) to monitor progress and areas for improvement.

◻ **Breakthrough Teams.** The Seadrift plant and the Specialties Department have a history of getting to the bottom of vexing problems by using problem-solving teams. So, when management opted for the "Excellence Through Quality" program, many employees were not strangers to the problem-solving process that is now such an integral part of the program.

"Our plant has had 20 to 30 'quality circle type' teams operating since the early 1980s," says Carroll.

More recently, the more formalized "breakthrough teams" (as they are now known) have addressed problems with the invoicing system, product consistency, and rail costs.

One of the more notable projects involved working hand in hand with a customer to resolve a product processing problem. The team addressing the problem invited customer representatives to become full-fledged members of the team, and together they experimented with the problem and arrived at a solution.

"Through the efforts of the breakthrough team, we not only solved the technological problem, but—more importantly—we transformed the nature of our relationship with the customer into one of mutual trust and respect."

◻ **Formula for Success** ⇒ So what's the formula for a successful breakthrough team?

Key # 1: Management support. Carroll says it all starts here. "The common denominator differentiating the successful teams from unsuccessful ones is the level of management support," she explains.

Key #2: A team charter. Once management lends support to the team concept, the next key is to properly "charter" the team. In other words, the more specific management is about what it wants the team to accomplish, the more likely it is that the team will, indeed, accomplish it. In the chartering process, management provides the team with a formal written charter that specifically defines the scope of the work, the time constraints, the people who are to address the problem, and the resources that will be available to the team.

Key #3: Affirmation of the project's importance. When management charters a team with a project that is truly critical to the business, it is more likely to support the team when the team reaches a roadblock. "Recently, we have been able to improve the success rate of our teams from about 60 percent to 95 percent by emphasizing the importance of both the chartering process and the role that management plays in supporting the team," says Carroll.

A FUNDAMENTAL CHANGE

The "Excellence Through Quality" program has led to fundamental changes in the way the Specialties Department does business—and in how the department is perceived by its customers.

"When I first began working here, I recall a customer calling the plant to report a problem," says Carroll. "Our response at the time was something a bit like 'Our product met your specifications.' That was the extent of our involvement in resolving the problem."

Today, such an attitude or response is not even considered. Now when a customer calls with a problem, the discussion is more likely to run along the lines of, "Why is this certain product characteristic important to the customer? How does the customer use our product? What process does the customer use? Why is the customer concerned about this? What can we do to improve or change the product so that it meets customer needs?"

"The importance of understanding our customers' needs and making every effort to satisfy them has begun to permeate our attitudes and daily routines," says Carroll. "Most important, our customers have noticed and recognized the vitality of these attitudes."

COMMUNICATION: A CRUCIAL PART OF QUALITY ASSURANCE

Can something as fundamental as communication spark outstanding quality improvements? You bet! In fact, it would be fair to say that communication is the glue that holds your entire QA effort together.

BOEING COMMERCIAL AIRPLANES

It doesn't always take a hot new program or the expertise of an expensive consultant to improve quality. Boeing Commercial Airplanes turned to an age-old method to boost quality: It improved its communication—and quality improvements soared.

▶ **DILEMMA:** *What do you do when your industry is deregulated and you must improve quality and lower production costs at the same time?*

▭ **SOLUTION** ⇒ You make sure the job is done right the first time by increasing communication across the board and getting everyone in the company—management and employees alike—to work together as a team to solve problems.

When Boeing Commercial Airplanes found out about the deregulation of the airlines industry a few years ago, the company knew that it and its customers—the airlines—would have to lower costs while maintaining high standards of quality in order to remain competitive.

"We recognized that if we were going to remain competitive in the marketplace in the years ahead, we were going to have to change the way we did business," says Jack Wires, vice president of Quality Assurance. "We had to make a breakthrough in the way we produce our products in order to get our costs down, and at the same time increase our quality."

So, Boeing implemented a new, sweeping, continuous quality improvement process. Its goals were to:

● increase communication

● encourage teamwork

● solve quality and productivity problems

THE TEAM APPROACH

"In implementing the quality improvement process, we took a big step forward," says Wires. "We said that if we were really going to make a breakthrough in the way that we manage our business, increase our operating efficiency, and take the waste out of our system, we had to have all management committed and involved.

"Fundamentally, 85 percent of improvement opportunity is in the hands of management and 15 percent is in the hands of the workers," he continues. "Workers perform their jobs in a system that's been established by management over the years. You can ask those workers to work harder, better, or faster, but there's only so much they can do. So if you really want to make a breakthrough, you can change the system itself, and that's management's responsibility."

With that in mind, Boeing began to form quality improvement teams. These teams are distinctly different from quality circles, a participative management practice that Boeing has had in place since 1980. In the quality circles, people work together to identify and solve problems that involve their particular work area, with the leadership of a supervisor. The problems they address are, by definition, relatively narrow in scope. The quality improvement teams, on the other hand, look at chronic problems that may span a number of organizations, or they look at an entire system.

"Before, management was involved in collective problem-solving only from the standpoint of being leaders of teams," explains Mark Bodensteiner, Director of Quality Improvement for Boeing's Fabrication Division. "There was no team of managers working on the system. So we underwent a major change in emphasis in 1986. We added to our team structures by involving management to a much greater degree." Specifically, this effort:

➠ **Increased awareness of the program.** "The first part of the plan calls for a lot of education to make people aware of what this is all about," Wires says. "We started with management, because management has to provide the will, the belief, and the wherewithal to get this done, all the way from the top management of the company down to the first-line supervisors."

➠ **Developed special training courses** (in statistical process control and team leadership skills) to provide the skills for implementing this new way of working together.

Exactly what elements make up "this new way of working together"? They include:

▶ **A steering council.** Each division at Boeing has

a quality improvement structure that consists of a steering council made up of the vice president/general manager and the directors. This group charters improvement teams to focus on problem areas that have been brought to their attention or that they have identified.

► **Team member selection.** Each team is specifically chartered to focus its attention on a particular problem. In order to make sure that the right people—those who have the knowledge, work skills, interest, and responsibility—are on a team, the steering committee also selects who will be on a particular team. This means that any combination of employees may be on a team, ranging from line workers to supervisors to engineers to managers. The team works together until it comes up with a solution, and then is dissolved.

► **Problem identification.** "We have a Business Process Analysis method, and as the various departments start to look into their business processes—making flowcharts to determine how they do their jobs—improvement opportunities are identified," says Wires.

"For example, where we have no-value-added work or where we have rework, we ask the following questions:

● Why does it happen?

● How can we eliminate this rework?

● What are the improvement opportunities?

"Quality improvement teams are formed to address these problem areas, these areas of opportunity."

FORGING CHAINS OF COMMUNICATION

When you get right down to it, making quality improvements is about making changes. "In order to make changes—and make the *right* changes—you really have to know what the job is all about and where the problems are," Wires points out.

"That's where the employee comes in," he says. You have to:

⇨ Develop a relationship between management and nonmanagement people that will permit a worker to go into a meeting or talk to management and lay things on the table; to tell things the way they are.

⇨ Eliminate the element of fear. "That's one of

the fundamental thrusts of this program," Wires points out.

⇨ Get all the right people involved to focus on the problems and on the changes that are necessary. "Many of the processes at Boeing are very complex, particularly those that cut across divisional lines," he continues. "They involve many people and many functions—engineering, planning, manufacturing, tooling. That means a lot of communication among a lot of different departments."

To facilitate this communication, Boeing is fostering an environment in which workers will communicate with the right people when they see something wrong, or when they see something that can be done more efficiently. "For example, we had people in a particular shop recognize that a change could be made in the way a part is produced," says Wires. "They believed that their suggestion would make it much easier to produce the part while improving its reliability."

These shop workers took the initiative to go to Engineering and relate what they had found. Engineering recognized the value of the workers' recommendations and made the suggested change.

"The first-line supervisor of this particular shop is probably more motivated by our improvement process than anybody I've ever talked to," says Wires. "And he has instilled that motivation in his people. One of the first things he told me when I walked into his shop was, 'You won't believe how intelligent the people who run these machines are. You talk to them and ask them how we can improve our operation and they've got all kinds of ideas—they're an untapped resource.' "

To further facilitate this type of communication, Boeing has also implemented:

■ **Supervisors as "enablers."** "Workers are encouraged to make suggestions to their supervisors," explains Wires. "And when they come up with something they feel has merit, the supervisor acts as an enabler. For example, he or she asks Engineering to come down to the shop floor to discuss the idea."

If you don't have first-line supervisors encouraging this type of communication, there's a strong likelihood that your workers are not going to feel free to communicate their ideas to others. "Workers can submit ideas through the suggestion system, but one of the best ways to obtain improvements is to create an environment in which problems can be brought to the surface and the right people can work together to solve them," maintains Wires. "You don't necessarily have to have a team forced to do this. It's rather straightforward and simple: Discuss it with the people who have the authority to make the change."

■ **A liaison engineer.** This person works between the manufacturing shop and the design group to resolve problems.

■ **Routine visits by engineers to Manufacturing.** "We routinely bring engineers to the manufacturing facility to see how the parts are made," explains Bodensteiner. "Through these exchanges, the engineers can learn to relate to the manufacturing problems, and the shop workers can begin to understand what Engineering's problems are." Boeing also brings Engineering and Manufacturing together to work on problems that involve both aspects of production.

■ **The "customer concept" applied internally.** Developing good customer relations is very important for almost any type of business. In order to accommodate your customers, you must first understand their needs, and you achieve that understanding through good communication.

Boeing is now applying this customer concept internally. This is especially important in the Fabrication Division, which provides a lot of hardware to the divisions that assemble the airplanes. "Consequently, they have a lot of customers within our company, so there has been a lot of customer/supplier communication," says Wires.

"Workers identify, learn about, and achieve an understanding of their internal customers' needs by visiting them and talking to them," explains Bodensteiner. This dialogue begins with supervisors. "They know what organization their work goes to," he continues. "And they go and make contact with those organizations. Some supervisors have taken their workers over to another department or division to see where the part they make goes when they have finished with it."

Wires offers an illustration of how this emphasis on serving customers' needs is working: "I spoke to several employees in a particular shop who told me that they were talking to their customers for the first time. They knew that the part they worked on went to a different part of the factory in their immediate vicinity, but they didn't really know the particular department or the people in it.

"So when we implemented our new quality improvement process, these workers went down around the corner to find out where their parts went and what the next operation was. They talked to the workers there, who said, 'Oh, yes, we get this part. But before we can do this particular operation on it, we always have to cut off a corner.' Then the workers who were visiting said, 'We can make the part so you won't have to do that.' " This is a clear-cut example of how increased communication can eliminate rework.

COMMUNICATING OUTSIDE THE WALLS

For companies that are trying to improve communication—and in the process, quality—there may be a tendency to overlook the importance of improving communication outside the walls: with suppliers and customers, that is.

"The suppliers have to be on board in this quality improvement activity as much as Boeing does," says Wires. "We buy approximately 60 percent of the parts that we use on airplanes. So there's a lot of activity out in the supplier world that's important to us, and we want to get the highest quality product from our suppliers at the lowest cost."

Fortunately, Boeing's suppliers are very enthusiastic about the increased interaction. Some of them already have quality improvement processes in place, but others are now implementing their own quality improvement plans, which Boeing is helping them to develop. "In the long range, we just can't help but see an improvement, both for ourselves and for our suppliers," says Wires.

As far as customers are concerned, "we have asked them to identify more specifically what their requirements are and to provide us with feedback so that we can satisfy those requirements," explains Bodensteiner.

"What we have done is to communicate with our customers' airlines. For example, we invite them to participate in our educational seminars on what quality is all about," he continues. "That way, they understand what Boeing is doing to improve our method of operation and improve quality."

EARLY RETURNS

What have been the results of this emphasis on quality improvement through increased communication? Boeing, which employs about 49,000 people, is still in the early stages of its new process, which they project will take six years to implement fully. But already they have seen a number of improvements in:

➡ scrap and rework reduction

➡ the bottom line

➡ morale

"The feedback that we have received from workers who now have an opportunity to get involved is just fantastic," reports Wires. "They feel that management has finally recognized that workers can offer some good ideas for improving the company; they have a greater feeling of belonging." Also, increased interaction with people from different departments and levels of management is giving workers a better picture of the overall product, the quality goals of the organization, and their roles in meeting those goals.

Wires cites a sterling example of the prevailing employee attitude regarding the new, more open atmosphere: "I had one worker come up to me and say, 'You know, it's really great to come to work now. I really feel a part of the team. Before, I just put in my time, but now I feel like I'm really contributing and that my efforts have a greater impact on how well the company can perform.' "

If you can motivate your company's employees to start thinking that way, it won't be long before you'll be reaping big quality improvements of your own.

ORTHO PHARMACEUTICAL CORPORATION

A quality assurance manager conducts an independent research study and learns that quality problems aren't always technical. Her results indicate that communication plays a bigger part in quality than may have once been believed.

Troubleshooting quality problems is a common but challenging task for any quality professional. How do you figure out what's going wrong when you're missing deadlines, or a product is recalled, or your suppliers aren't meeting your specs? As tough as quality problems can be, the fact is that the more practice you get solving them, the easier it becomes.

"I have worked in the product development area for three companies, helping to bring products to the point of quality assurance specs," says Mary Lou Zett, manager of Quality Assurance Compliance for the Advanced Care Products Division of Ortho Pharmaceutical Corp. (Raritan, NJ).

In analyzing problems that occurred during technology transfer (the process of bringing in a newly created technology from the supplier with whom the work was contracted) or with product quality in general, Zett found that the cause of the problem could almost always be traced back to some aspect of:

● communication (participants' interpersonal skills and how they interacted with each other), or

● something in the organization that prevented information from flowing properly or that prevented participants from getting all the input they needed to come to the best decisions.

As part of some independent research she was conducting, Zett interviewed upper-level QA managers from approximately 240 companies that purchased new technology from contract research groups or other suppliers. Industries represented included pharmaceutical, medical devices, food, cosmetics, and household/consumer. Drawing on the results of her research, Zett came to a number of conclusions relating to success in transferring technology from suppliers.

The first thing that needs to take place, she says, is the coordination of communication between participants and departments within the purchasing company (the "customer"). Until this occurs, it will be impossible to establish coordinated communication with suppliers. Some of Zett's suggestions for improving internal communication are:

1 Approach top management in your organization and explain the importance of improving communication at various levels. Ask for their support in making such improvements.

2 Try to develop a better understanding of your role in the organization as well as the roles of the people with whom you interact. "We all perceive ourselves as having certain roles," Zett notes. "However, we may not be as aware of how these roles interact with, supercede, or usurp someone else's power or influence."

3 Analyze the communication that occurs between you and other participants in the decision-making body that formulates product quality requirements. Be particularly aware of situations involving:

► conflict generated by power plays

► lack of trust

► insufficient motivation for certain participants to provide their input

These three situations can be particularly destructive to successful communication related to the development of product quality requirements, according to Zett.

4 Take the time to discuss problems in a nonthreatening way. "For example, if you have material coming in that was bought by the purchasing department before you actually approved product specs, then you need to discuss this problem with Purchasing," she says. Take this opportunity to explain how participants fit into the process and how what they do affects the rest of the process.

5 Expose participants to communication training. Topics should cover, at minimum, conflict resolution, understanding each other's jobs, building trust, and eliminating conflicting roles. Some of this, naturally, may have to be handled by your company's training department. However, there are some things you can do on your own.

For example, Zett has offered an "information day," in the division's research library in which she displayed tapes, books, reports, and other materials on communication skills. "A lot of people showed interest in learning more," she reports.

TAKE IT TO SUPPLIERS

Once you have taken steps to improve communication within your own organization, you can begin to make some efforts to improve communication with suppliers. Such communication, especially in the area of technology transfer, is particularly crucial. Why is this so?

"Product specs are not just specs in terms of test criteria, but they also ensure that the supplier developing the technology is in compliance with government regulations and follows good lab practices when they test the product or technology they will be transferring to you," Zett emphasizes.

To improve communication in this area, she suggests that you:

✔ Have documented procedures for the technology transfer process.

✔ Document what the supplier says it will do (promised performance), and create a system to monitor what it actually does, asking questions like:

- How is the process proceeding?
- Is it going according to plan?
- Are there time deadlines and milestones "pulling" the technology through the system before it's ready?
- Is there any element of "crisis management" being used as the technology begins to flow?

✔ Arrange meetings with suppliers to emphasize the importance of good communication. At Ortho, for example, Zett serves on a supplier quality management committee that arranges "supplier days," during which suppliers' top managements visit and learn about the company's philosophy of quality and how to formally engage in productive communication.

THE SHAPE OF THINGS TO COME

Where will this emphasis on communication likely lead? "Once people understand how they fit into their organizations and what roles they play, they can begin to develop cohesiveness," Zett says.

The cohesiveness can be identified by more open, frequent, and cooperative interaction. Once this occurs—and provided there is a strong commitment to quality from the top of the organization—there really is no need for a formal QA department, according to Zett. At that point, quality professionals can begin to use their technical expertise and interpersonal skills to act as liaisons between various key departments, performing an auditing rather than a control function.

AVATAR INTERNATIONAL INCORPORATED

Do you think your workers' commitment to making quality products would measure up to the commitment that Japanese workers have? It would—if you followed the Japanese example and made quality a team effort.

In a recent survey of managers of Japanese-owned companies located in the United States, conducted by the Society of Manufacturing Engineers, 68 percent of the respondents rated Japanese workers' desire to produce quality products as excellent. However, only 37 percent believed that American workers' commitment to quality is that high.

Why do Japanese workers have this edge? Dr. Deanna Berg, Vice President of Avatar International Incorporated (Atlanta) and quality assurance specialist, believes it's because Japanese organizations have done a better job of communicating the importance of quality to their employees, and they have set up structures that encourage and reward quality efforts. In contrast, giving lip service to only the *idea* of quality is a common failing in American organizations.

"Many American organizations send out mixed messages about how important quality is," explains Berg, who recently spoke on the topic of building team commitment to quality at the American Society for Quality Control's annual quality congress. "They may say that quality is important, but when the choice comes between getting something out the door fast and doing a quality job, they emphasize getting it out fast. This tells employees that quality is important if you've got the time, but if you don't, then it's the first thing to go.

"Japanese companies tend to send a more consistent message, taking more of a long-term management approach rather than focusing on short-term profits." Berg maintains that if people can see a connection between doing a quality job and the effect that that has on the company and on themselves, they're more likely to put the effort into it.

Yet many American organizations simply don't draw those connections for their employees. You'll end up with a much more motivated and efficient work force—as well as higher quality in their output if you can:

- encourage and increase communication within your company at every level
- keep employees informed of the impact their jobs have on the organization as a whole
- get them involved in devising and implementing improvements

Before you can implement a plan to build team commitment to quality, however, you must deal with the following essentials:

1. Obtain a clear commitment to quality at the organizational level. If you want your program to succeed, you will need the backing of top management and the cooperation of managers and supervisors throughout the company. The idea is to change the ways managers, supervisors, and employees interact with one another, so that the ideas of team spirit and open communication permeate the culture of your organization. That won't happen unless your supervisors and peers are just as committed as you are.

In order to obtain that support, outline the benefits of your proposed program. "Impress the importance of quality on your superiors," suggests Berg. "Get them to read some of the literature on the important roles quality and customer service will play in determining which companies survive in the future."

2. Budget the resources that people will need in order to work together as a team. To ensure your program's impact and successes, it's crucial to invest the necessary time and money for training and materials. "In order to have quality products or service, you need to have quality people," notes Berg. Areas in which employees will require training include statistical process control and team development skills such as team dynamics and interpersonal communication.

PUTTING YOUR PLAN INTO ACTION

With those two steps taken care of, you can address these other areas involved in building team commitment to quality:

■ **Define what you mean by quality.** What is your goal in terms of quality? What's the ideal? Take into account not only your own perception but also the perception of your customers, both internal and external, advises Berg.

■ **Measure how far you are from your definition of quality.** Determine what the difference is between the real and the ideal: where you are now and where you want to be. Berg illustrates one way of doing this in the following example: "Let's say you're in a service industry and you conduct a customer satisfaction survey to measure quality of service.

"Ideally, you want 100 percent of your customers to rate you a 10 on a 10-point scale: That's your definition of quality. The results of the survey show that your customers rated you a 5 on a 10-point scale. In this example, the difference between 5 and 10 is the difference between where you are now and where you want to be."

It's important to take this measurement before you implement your quality program. Why? It will enable you to:

► track the concrete results of any changes you implement,

► act as a motivating force for employees in providing them with a goal to work toward,

► provide the basis for a reward system for everyone as you track your progress and quality improves.

■ **Make sure employees understand what you mean by quality.** "Get employees to buy into the emphasis on quality by asking them for input and ideas on what improvements might be made," says Berg. Essential ingredients for open communication include:

✔ **Trust.** "Team members will be willing to contribute their ideas, energy, and time to team efforts only if they are confident that their peers will not only listen to and value their ideas but will also take an active role in the team effort themselves," maintains Berg. That's why it's vital to a team's success to develop a supportive group dynamic.

✔ **Listening skills.** If a team member feels that no one listens to his or her ideas, it won't be long before that person decides not be an active group participant, Berg points out. Stress the importance of hearing each other out, without interrupting.

✔ **Conflict management.** "In most organizations, people are not only discouraged from sharing mistakes and bad news, they're encouraged to

suppress it," says Berg. "People don't go out of their way to tell their managers what they're doing wrong. But you have to be willing to encourage people to disagree with the ways things have been done before if you want to hear suggestions for improvement.

"So, as a manager, you have to develop an atmosphere where people feel free to disagree and aren't afraid that they're going to get punished for it. Develop a trusting atmosphere that encourages risk-taking and the expression of disagreement."

✔ **Periodic assessments.** It's important to the health and success of the team to take time out from focusing on tasks and evaluate group dynamics, notes Berg. Ask team members to be candid about how they interact with one another. Are there any problems in the way they relate that interfere with the quality of their teamwork? "It's unusual for any team to proceed without experiencing some difficulties," says Berg. "If you confront these problems openly and welcome them as opportunities to improve team dynamics, you will greatly enhance the team's effectiveness and longevity."

■ **Demonstrate to employees the benefits of participating in the quality effort.** "They need this information," stresses Berg. "Let them know how making changes is going to help both them and the organization."

■ **Reinforce the commitment to quality.** Unless employees hear and see multiple, consistent messages that affirm the importance of quality, they may get the impression that the whole program has blown over. You need to reemphasize the focus on quality in meetings, in classes, and in informal, day-to-day contact—and again, not just in words but also in actions.

"You have to make a clear, consistent statement, in actions as well as words, that quality is important," stresses Berg. "Continue to measure and pay attention to the level of quality being produced. And be sure to keep people informed of how well they're meeting quality standards and goals."

GETTING PAST THE OBSTACLES

Berg identifies a couple of obstacles that can stand in the way of a successful quality effort:

✘ **Putting a plan into action too quickly, before building a broad base of support.** This problem is all too common, cautions Berg. "Companies find a process they like, so they implement it immediately, but they fail to do a good job of building commitment to that process,'' she says. ''They don't overcome the resistance to it.

"So, at best, people get mixed messages about how important the program is, and don't put as much energy into it as they do when you take the time to determine exactly how you're going to integrate it into the ongoing way of life of the organization.''

✘ **Failing to put enough money into developing the necessary skills.** If you simply form employees into teams without giving them the tools they need to measure and evaluate the quality of their work or to function effectively as a team, then you can't expect to reap impressive results from team efforts. This is an important point to bring home to your supervisors if you decide to implement a team-based quality improvement plan.

WORTH THE EFFORT

It may take a lot of time and energy to build team commitment to quality throughout your organization, but, as Berg notes, it's a lot more effective and takes fewer resources than going around and policing people.

If workers are concerned with quality and committed to providing quality service or producing quality products, they'll be happier and more involved with their jobs. As a result, you'll see consistent and ongoing improvement in quality levels overall.

GIVING EMPLOYEES RESPONSIBILITY FOR QUALITY

Management might have impressive quality goals indeed. But it's the front-line employees who must put those goals into action. How can you encourage your front-liners to take personal responsibility for quality? It helps to create an environment that invites employee feedback and participation.

VENTURE INDUSTRIES

Employees can be strong allies in the war against defects—but only if management provides a conducive environment. Here's how one company moved to break through the barriers of fear and misunderstanding that get in the way of effective employee involvement.

Sure, many companies *claim* that they are seeking employee involvement to help the organization overcome quality problems. But do the management teams at those companies really provide the environment necessary to get employees to make valuable contributions? They will if they follow the example of this Michigan automotive supplier.

Like most automotive industry suppliers, Venture Industries (Fraser, MI) found itself in a highly challenging marketplace during the 1980s. "The automotive industry was going through an unprecedented transformation, and we realized that there would be tremendous opportunities for companies that were responsive to the needed changes," says Theodore A. Lowe, vice president of Quality Improvement and Corporate Planning.

Since the injection molding firm's inception in 1974, Venture's unwritten quality policy has been "to give the customers what they want, when they want it." As Venture grew in size from three employees to more than 1,200, senior management realized that to continue its success, a quality improvement process was needed that would allow every employee to contribute ideas and improvements.

While a number of other auto industry suppliers attempted to implement the popular quality improvement tools of the time—quality circles, SPC, Taguchi methods, QFD, and JIT—Venture's management believed that something else was needed. Those tools helped improve quality to a degree, but they were, in and of themselves, insufficient to guarantee continuous improvement.

◻ **FOCUS ON PEOPLE** ⇒ "Many companies sent their people through the appropriate training, but weren't getting the results that they needed," says Lowe. "They had been concentrating their efforts on products and processes; they hadn't been paying enough attention to the third part of the equation—*people*."

A company, according to Lowe, can only achieve its full potential when its people achieve their full potential. And one of the most important steps in helping people do this is to drive out fear.

FEAR CRIPPLES INVOLVEMENT EFFORTS

"In many businesses, fear has destroyed teamwork and prevented a positive bond from being built between managers and workers," says Lowe.

"Fear robs an organization of its potential; it is the major reason for the difference between the full potential of the people and the current achievement of the organization," he says. That is, fear limits the collective potential capability of people, which means that it restricts the capability of the processes and products of an organization.

What, specifically, are the fears that people in organizations have? Lowe outlines these six:

✍ **Employee fears**

- Fear of reprisal by management
- Fear of providing information ("kill the messenger" syndrome)

✍ **Employee and management fears**

- Fear of change
- Fear of failure

✍ **Management fears**

- Fear of giving up control
- Fear of not having enough information

FOUR PHASES THAT GET YOU BEYOND FEAR

To overcome these fears and to begin developing full employee involvement, Lowe believes that there are four important phases that must be introduced:

■ **PHASE 1. Management belief in the involvement of employees.** Management beliefs tend to establish a company's environment. According to Lowe, the beliefs that are necessary for employee involvement are:

► People want to contribute

► People can be trusted

- ► Change is good
- ► Problems are opportunities for improvement
- ► Continuous learning and improvement are essential for survival

"Management should promote teamwork, help, teach, listen, and lead," says Lowe. This is contrary to traditional management practices of planning, organizing, staffing, directing, and controlling.

▷ **The management challenge**—As a sign of its commitment to belief in employee involvement, the Venture executive staff assigned itself the following responsibilities:

✔ To provide direction to the organization by establishing and achieving a shared understanding of the corporate mission, quality policy, broad goals, and business plan.

✔ To create a work environment (the "Venture Way") that is supportive of the mission statement and quality policy.

✔ To establish the quality improvement structure and strategy and allocate the necessary supportive resources.

✔ To provide visible and active leadership by meeting regularly to plan, monitor, evaluate, and recognize progress, and to identify and address issues and concerns.

✔ To demonstrate the managerial behavior that can be modeled by the organization, showing commitment to learn and improve, and assuring the dignity and development of every individual at Venture.

■ **PHASE 2. Management practices related to the involvement of employees.** "Management practices reinforce management belief," notes Lowe. "Contemporary responsibilities must be reinforced by supportive actions if fear is to be driven out of an organization."

Examples of good management practices include finding and providing rewards for things that are right, looking for what is good about ideas, seeking further improvement of ideas, and praising action "above and beyond the call of duty."

Good management practices at Venture that are designed to further employee involvement are the business planning process and the "President's Audit." All employees are involved in the business planning process and quality improvement process, establishing goals in quality, productivity, responsive-

ness, people development, and plans to achieve the goals. Top management visits the company's locations on a rotating basis, where they discuss progress and obstacles to progress.

"It's important to note that these meetings take place on the shop floor, not in conference rooms," emphasizes Lowe. In short, management asks employees, "How can we help you?" They then listen to employees and share their visions for the future.

■ **PHASE 3. Management systems and processes related to the involvement of employees.** Management beliefs are supported by management practices, which—in turn—need to be reinforced by management systems and processes, says Lowe. Such systems include:

- ► appraisal systems
- ► corrective action systems
- ► development systems
- ► reward systems

You can't expect every new system to be 100 percent successful, cautions Lowe. One system that Venture management implemented to encourage employee involvement was called the "Problem Solver" system. Forms and boxes were placed in each plant for employees to suggest ideas for improvement. The ideas were picked up every day by a "referee," who reviewed the ideas and assigned them to the appropriate managers or staff people for resolution.

"The system didn't turn out to be particularly effective," he admits. In plants where management believed in and practiced employee involvement, the Problem Solver system proved to be unnecessary; employees already felt comfortable talking to management about ideas and problems. On the other hand, in plants where employee involvement was not as far along, employees were still skeptical that anything would come of their contributions.

A more successful system is called Employee Communication Meetings. The president and CEO of Venture, Larry J. Winget, meets with various levels of employees from different functions, where they have the opportunity to share what's going on in the business, as well as to discuss employee concerns and opportunities for improvement.

Employee performance and appraisal is another critical area, notes Lowe. Traditional systems destroy teamwork, foster mediocrity, increase variability, confuse people with other resources, and focus on the short term. The real purpose of performance and appraisal systems should be to:

✔ nurture and sustain individual employee contributions to continuous improvement and teamwork

✔ provide an assessment or evaluation of performance for both management and the employee

"We are working on a new appraisal system for employees that is designed to reward teamwork as well as individual performance," adds Lowe.

■ **PHASE 4. Changing employee beliefs and attitudes.** "Once the first three phases are in place, the fourth phase may fall into place on its own," suggests Lowe. However, to ensure that it does, Venture has created the "Venture Quest Process." The object is to give employees a continuous method and guide for continuous improvement.

Training for this process is based on the theory that learning comes from doing, not just from sitting in the classroom. The first 16 hours involve training employees to understand key quality principles, including a step-by-step approach (called the Venture Quest Cycle and based on the Deming Circle of Plan-Do-Check Act) that they can use to practice continuous improvement.

The training starts with an exercise entitled "Imagine," where employees imagine the type of company they want in terms of how employees and managers behave. "We ask them to help create that vision of what we will be and how we will operate in the future," Lowe explains.

At the end of the 16 hours, each employee or team is then asked to take on a Quest project—either a problem needing a solution or a process needing improvement. That is, instead of receiving a certificate after the 16 hours of training, participants are given "learner's permits" to go out and practice quality improvement.

"We then ask them to return within three months and report on their projects," he says. After completion, employees receive gifts and recognition at celebrations. They are then given a "license" to practice continuous quality improvement forever.

MAKING THE THREE-STEP TRANSITION

While the organization is passing through the four phases outlined above, a more subtle—but equally important—three-step transition also needs to take place:

Step 1. Awareness. There must be an awareness and perceived need for change, and a general understanding of what the change requires. "A sense of urgency should be developed without creating a feeling of panic," adds Lowe.

Step 2. Shared Vision. There must be a shared vision of the future so that everyone is working together toward the same goals in the same direction. "In addition to knowing what changes you need, you also need to know what your end results should be," says Lowe.

Step 3. Action. There must be good "action steps" available to employees. This involves training people in effective personal skills and practices, as well as new group problem-solving skills.

At Venture, employees attend specially designed workshops where they are exposed to the need for their ideas and improvements, and also help to identify the elements of waste that exist in the organization.

This is a crucial element of success, says Lowe. He cites an example that is used to demonstrate the importance of securing the collective brainpower of all employees:

Twenty years ago, a Japanese automaker was taking 65 hours to build a car. The company solicited 200 ideas per employee per year on how to improve productivity. Within 14 years, the automaker was down to 13 hours spent building each car.

Within the same time frame, an American automaker was taking 28 hours to build a car. After implementing the thinking of executives and engineers only, they cut the time to 27 hours per car in the same 14-year period.

"So we ask employees to brainstorm in a structured session, where they discuss everything that prevents them from doing their jobs right or any waste that they experience," describes Lowe.

The next step is to develop a priority list of items to tackle. In one injection molding plant, participants came up with a list of 89 items to tackle. These included:

✎ Create new purging boxes for all machines,

which would reduce scrap and changeover time.

✎ Repair broken skids instead of disposing of them.

✎ Develop a system to prevent oil leaks on injection molding presses.

✎ Plan for auxiliary equipment improvement.

✎ Devise a way to get better scheduling information.

✎ Improve plant cleanliness.

✎ Create a procedure for tool repairs.

✎ Suggest improvements to reduce packaging problems.

✎ Improve lighting.

✎ Arrange for some building repairs.

✎ Create standard methods for procedures that did not have standard methods.

The group placed 54 of these ideas in Category A (those ideas that they felt were in their own control and could be addressed immediately). They placed another 25 in Category B (those that would require additional resources, such as appropriations for new equipment). They placed the final 10 in Category C (those that would require the cooperation of others outside the group). From there, the group addressed each category individually:

➡ **Category A.** The team assigned ownership for these 54 tasks immediately and set target dates for completion.

➡ **Category B.** They prepared financial justifications for each of the 25 projects in this category, and Lowe arranged to get the necessary appropriations for them. "Within a month, we had these plans put together," he says.

➡ **Category C.** "By the time they were finished with the A and B projects, they had gained enough confidence and expertise to believe that the C projects were, to some extent, within their control," says Lowe. "They simply influenced the people who did have control and got what they wanted."

EMPLOYEE PRIDE AND CONTROL RESULTS IN QUALITY IMPROVEMENT

Prior to launching its quality improvement effort, scrap had been 3 to 4 percent in the plant and there was an average of two customer complaints per month. "Currently, scrap has been decreasing consistently for 14 consecutive months, and we have gone eight months without even one customer complaint," reports Lowe. "The cost of quality has decreased from 13 percent to 7 percent, and we are still improving on that."

In closing, Lowe points out, "The employees now have pride in their work and feel that they can control what they do. We have given them the opportunity to be honest without fear."

MARTIN MARIETTA MICHOUD AEROSPACE

Personnel involvement leads to big quality gains, and Martin Marietta shows you how. By asking employees for their input, this company achieved significant improvements. You can, too.

A space age quality/productivity improvement process at Martin Marietta Michoud Aerospace (New Orleans, LA) rests on the philosophical underpinnings of an old Chinese proverb:

If you tell *me how to do something, I will forget it. If you* show *me how to do something, I will understand it. If you* involve *me in doing it, I will remember it forever.*

Saul R. Locke, productivity director for the aerospace firm, has used this proverb to show employees "how they become their own quality and productivity champions. I act only as an integrator. No one works for me, or does what I want because I tell them to."

Since 1980, Locke has brought dramatic gains in quality and productivity to the division's diverse space programs, including the space shuttle's external tank, the aft cargo carrier, and design of logistic and common modules for the future space station. And although some of those gains took place because of newly automated processes, Locke notes that people make the difference, *especially* when it comes to automation.

▷ **People Are the Key** ⇒ "Someone has to think of the idea, someone has to build the machine, someone has to install the machine and implement the idea, and someone has to run the machine," he says.

In fact, Locke believes the most dramatic gains occur when people begin to take the initiative to make improvements. "We never implemented any idea the departments did not want to do. I worked to make them believe the ideas for quality and productivity improvements belonged to them. Then, as soon as an idea was approved and implemented, department budgets were adjusted accordingly. This step made the idea real and part of the normal process, not a special program."

CARROTS AND STICKS

Fortunately for Locke, concern for quality begins at the top of his organization. Martin Marietta's chairman has stated, "We simply have to be—and I believe there is signficant evidence that we are—committed to working productively every day. We have an ethical obligation and a social responsibility to produce products of the highest quality at prices our customers can afford, and our commitment is an integral part of discharging that responsibility."

Locke convinced top management to use the carrot-and-stick approach to prove that they were serious in their support for the improvement plan. "I talked with the president and suggested that he must hold the department directors accountable for improving quality and productivity," he recalls.

"Now, directors are evaluated on their performance in the quality and productivity improvement process. When the president told the directors that quality, and subsequently productivity, was their individual responsibility, the effect flowed through the organization. The directors called in their managers and told them the same thing; managers told supervisors and foremen; and supervisors and foremen made it clear to production workers. In this way, we made sure that quality and productivity were inseparable and not just another slogan."

THE IDEA DEVELOPMENT PROCESS

Backed by this top-level support, Locke began to work with all of the directors of Martin Marietta Michoud's departments. He discussed his concept with the directors and asked each to assign a senior person to work on a productivity and quality improvement council. Then this group met twice a week, and Locke solicited ideas from everyone.

"I never rejected an idea. Instead, I developed a matrix for all of the ideas and defined each in terms of its inputs (money, energy, time, people, all of our resources) as well as its outputs—how efficient and effective the ideas would be. This enabled the group members to measure the usefulness of their ideas and helped them decide which to implement first. But more important, we made sure that no initiative that results in a benefit in one department came at the expense of another.

"Next, I had them set goals, whatever short-term

goals they decided to set. All in all, we had 434 ideas classified in the matrix. The group put them in priority order. Then, to their surprise, I told them to go and do them.'' In short, Locke says, department members thought of the improvement ideas, set their own goals, prioritized them, and were then set free to execute them.

Another key point, says Locke, is that of giving credit to those who deserved it. ''If a production employee developed an idea that resulted in fewer defects and/or a cost savings, we made sure he or she received credit for it and shared in any cost savings from it. Cost savings, we found, came from our original aim—no defects. Of course, with fewer defects, we saved costs. But it was only later that we asked the financial office to estimate our dollar savings,'' he says.

THE CONCEPT IN ACTION

Quality improvements occurred in hundreds of small ways as well as in big ways, such as significant changes in manufacturing processes and factory automation. Locke offers two examples that show how employee concern for quality leads to savings and improved product quality:

Case in Point # 1. ''In the past, we had always used tungsten inert gas welding to join the aluminum alloy 2219 we use in the fuel tanks. But it does not weld very cleanly and requires a lot of rework and finishing. There is another way to weld aluminum, known as variable pulse plasma arc (VPPA) welding. Yet no one had ever used VPPA to work with alloy 2219 in production.

''One of our people found out that technicians at NASA's Marshall Space Flight Center were experimenting with VPPA for production use, so we worked with them to transfer the technology to Michoud. Since we made sure that NASA became a partner early in our improvement process, they were more willing to transfer the welding process to us. As a result, we made better quality welds, eliminated rework, and saved lots of time and money,'' Locke explains.

Case in Point #2. To make the second improvement, also based on an in-house idea, Michoud people used the expertise of two universities to very quickly design two new ways to make and install value-added material.

''The brown stuff you see around the (shuttle's) external tanks on television is called the Thermal Protection System (TPS), which is made up of two parts. One is the sprayed-on foam insulation, and the other is a super lightweight ablation pulling a vacuum. The TPS is made of lightweight silicon resin filled with material, and had always been made by expensive, laborious, and time-consuming handpacking methods. We did a study, which showed that the handpacking wasted lots of this value-added material. Yet the only reason the methods had not been changed was that we were stuck in an 'if it's not invented here, it's no good' syndrome.

''So we went to graduate students at the Polymer Processing Lab at the Massachusetts Institute of Technology and the physics department at the University of Toronto. We told the latter to develop an improved conventional process, while we asked MIT to develop a new technology.

''At Toronto, they developed an inexpensive tooling and compression molding method, which would have saved us lots of money. But MIT developed a new process in which the resin and filler material is mixed with a gas and sprayed over an ordinary garden screen.

''We saved $65,000 per external tank and eliminated defects on future external tanks. We transferred a new technology from a university laboratory right through the system—from the technology resource to our production people—all in one year. None of this would have been possible if we had not asked our people for their ideas and gotten them involved.''

IMPROVEMENT DOESN'T STOP THERE

The positive results in these two cases aren't the only ones Michoud has experienced. The company has also seen:

- 28 percent improvement in manufacturing performance

- 82 percent reduction in planning errors

- 38 percent reduction in engineering errors (the number of requests for correction)

- 27 percent decrease in quality assurance costs

All in all, the ongoing quality and productivity process at Martin Marietta Michoud has created cost savings of more than one *billion* dollars, while the division delivered every tank on or ahead of schedule and reduced nonconformances by 76 percent in a three-year period.

GENERAL MOTORS CORPORATION

People make the difference when automation and quality collide; that's what GM discovered when it automated one of its facilities with improved quality in mind.

If you're like many people in business or industry, you see automation as the stuff that dreams are made of. But all the new technology in the world won't help if employees can't or won't interact with it properly. And when things aren't meshing properly within a company, quality is usually one of the very first victims.

One of the most highly automated and technologically advanced automobile assembly plants in the world is General Motors Corporation's Linden, NJ, facility—one of two plants that build Chevrolet's Beretta and Corsica models. When the plant reopened in 1986 after a one-year shutdown to upgrade the facility, management realized that while the automation and advanced technology that had been added would do a lot to improve quality, productivity, and cost, the advancements alone could not do it all.

"We realized that we couldn't improve quality, cost, or anything else without the total involvement of the work force," emphasizes Plant Manager Dale Snyder. "We couldn't just put in automation and expect it to solve all of our problems. Even though we are one of the most highly automated assembly plants in the United States, we're still about 70 percent nonautomated, so it's very much a 'people' business. In other words, we can only be as good as our people."

With that in mind, GM management set three major goals for the newly revitalized assembly facility:

➡ Improve product quality.

➡ Obtain more reliable productivity.

➡ Reduce production costs.

To achieve those goals, the company focused on the following five areas:

❶ Getting employees involved in the design and engineering of the automobiles that they would be assembling.

In the past at GM, most designing and engineering of automobiles had been done "in a vacuum," according to Snyder. That is, designers would design the cars, engineers would engineer them, process-

ing people would process them, and then the technology would be sent to the production plants for assembly. With the advent of GM's new philosophy, there is a more cooperative approach to the process.

It all began when approximately 30 Linden employees traveled to Detroit to participate in the design and engineering of the automobiles that they would be building at the plant. This was during the one-year layoff, and those who took part gave up unemployment compensation almost equal to their former salaries in order to volunteer for the assignment.

"The idea was to take some of our knowledgeable engineers and line workers and allow them to interact with the designers and engineers in Detroit, providing input so that we could come up with designed processes that would satisfy both the assembly plant requirements and customer requirements," says Snyder. The plant members shared ideas with corporate engineers on production tooling, ergonomics, reasonable loads for humans, and the like.

This approach was such a success that the block of prototype cars that would ordinarily have been built in Detroit were actually built in Linden. "We also ran the entire pilot program of 343 complete vehicles at the plant with our regular line workers," adds Snyder.

❷ Providing employees with extensive initial training and regular programs of additional training as needed.

When the rest of the employees came back to work, they all received two weeks (80 hours) of intensive training. This instruction was not so much on how to perform their jobs as it was on:

► quality control concepts

► basic economics

► interpersonal communication and human relation skills

► productivity and cost-cutting methods

► health and safety

► other topics not usually discussed with line workers

63

"We wanted them to better understand their role and how to do a better job once they were assigned to the line," says Snyder.

As unusual as this training was, it was matched by the novelty of *who* the trainers were. While one might expect management or corporate trainers to handle the responsibility, GM and the union selected a dozen line workers to conduct the training. Employees selected were those who had a background in education and in teaching or training, many of whom had college degrees in education.

Employees were trained in small groups of approximately 20. Snyder spent two hours addressing each group, discussing the company's and his commitment to the changes and emphasizing that GM was serious about what it was promising in terms of employee involvement.

But even after the training, a number of employees were skeptical about how committed management was to following through. "It's now a year and a half later, and we're launching our second phase of training," notes Snyder. "This involves getting every operator off the line for another eight hours of training specifically related to quality."

This alone has begun to convince even the most skeptical of employees. "They believe us because we are doing what we said we were going to do *and* because we are giving them even more training," Snyder points out.

3 Implementing the "stop the line" concept to encourage employees to be responsible for their own quality.

The plant is outfitted with line-stop buttons for every operator's station. This means that if an employee is unable to complete the job or detects a problem from the previous station, he or she can stop the line until the problem is resolved. "This eliminates the need for continuous inspection, repair, and reinspection," says Snyder. "Every operator is now his or her own inspector."

With problems being corrected on the spot, the plant does not need or have a repair line of any kind, which is unusual for an auto assembly plant. Instead, it has a three-bay repair-and-adjustment section.

4 Providing employees with a continual flow of information related to the work they were doing and how their products were performing in the field.

While job-related training is vital, management also realized that employees need *external* information—a continual flow of it, in fact. This information, they believed, should cover things like:

- final product quality
- how well the employees were doing their jobs
- how customers perceive the quality of the cars
- where the plant is improving
- how the plant is doing compared to other plants

To provide this feedback, the plant instituted what is called the Organizational Competitiveness Program (OCP), which involves a group of six management and hourly employees who are assigned full-time to locate, sort out, and communicate the overall "competitiveness picture" to the rest of the employees. In fact, the plant has an "OCP Room" on the shop floor with a conference room where OCP representatives can meet with employees to communicate their information. On the walls of this room are pie charts, graphs, and reports related to plant competitiveness.

In addition, the plant brings in competitors' vehicles and other GM vehicles so that employees can compare the quality of their work with the quality of other plants' work. "This kind of information has never been available to employees before," notes Snyder. However, the company feels that sharing these issues with the workers will help them realize the importance of what they do.

5 Getting employees involved in groups to discuss problems and come up with workable solutions.

It's one thing to share problems and perceptions with employees. It's quite another to invest in those same employees the resources to solve the problems and make continuous improvements—but GM has done this, too. The Employee Involvement Process, an outgrowth of the initial two weeks of training, involves employee volunteers who form into groups of 15 to 20 each, select spokespeople to facilitate the meetings, and discuss specific issues that need addressing.

Teams also select "primary communicators" who act as quality representatives, plant host representatives, cost representatives, OCP representatives, and so on. "Each group is, in essence, a small community where everyone has a specified task," explains Snyder.

Each week, the functional representatives from each group meet with each other to discuss information about their functions and then communicate that information to their individual groups. For example, the quality data (including information from the company's warranty feedback system), and then report on the results of their meeting to their respective Employee Involvement groups.

SOMETHING IN RETURN

As a result of the plant's efforts, employees understand the production processes much better than before, allowing them to produce higher quality automobiles. In addition, since they have had the opportunity to provide input into the processes, they feel a sense of ownership in what they do.

Also, the increase in training, communication, and employee input into problem-solving has brought the employees closer together while building a stronger relationship with management.

What does Snyder see as the bottom line? "The quality on the Corsica and Beretta has been outstanding compared to our competitors'," he points out. The results are particularly significant when one considers that the efforts are only a little over a year old.

"Through virtually every internal and external measure of product quality, all the numbers say we are doing things right," Snyder adds. "Cost-wise, we're continuing to improve and are on target for our goals."

DOW CHEMICAL USA

Can giving employees responsibility for the quality of their work really make a difference? Absolutely, says Dow, which has successfully taken steps to create a quality-committed staff.

There are a lot of programs, gimmicks, and fads that the quality manager can use to improve quality. Some are expensive, some don't deliver what they promise, and almost all fall into disuse eventually. But here's one approach—employee involvement—that isn't likely to go out of style.

For a number of years, Dow Chemical USA has been engaged in efforts to improve safety on the job. "We found that involving everyone in the organization was the most important key to success," reports Joseph Bowman, quality and productivity manager for the company's Industrial Chemicals Division—Texas Operations (Freeport, TX).

"When we saw the success obtained by involving employees in safety improvements, we realized that this would probably be the key to quality improvements, too."

Bowman explains that the company had been successful with quality circles and project teams in the past, but that these efforts were, in and of themselves, insufficient to achieve the kind of day-to-day quality improvement attitudes necessary to reach the company's long-term goals. "Quality improvement needs to be a part of everyone's work every day," emphasizes Bowman.

With that in mind, the facility created a formal procedure for quality improvement, and one of the first groups to volunteer for involvement was the telecommunications department. Employees in this department, which provides services in the area of telephone, radio, broadband, and microwave communication, were often unsure of their roles and the roles of their co-workers. Morale was low, and there was an absence of teamwork.

As a result, "customers" (other Dow employees in the facility using the telecommunications equipment and services) were often shuffled from one person to another within the department when they had a question, a need, or a problem.

"Our goal was to motivate and involve the employees in the department to do their jobs better, to take ownership of what they did, and to take individual responsibility for taking care of their customers," says Linn Brady, P.E., telecommunications manager. "We wanted to improve communication at the various levels in the department: between employees and their customers, and among the various functions in the department."

GETTING TO KNOW THE "CUSTOMER"

The first step in implementing quality improvement in the department was to conduct a survey of the employees. This took place in mid-1986 and involved questions related to perceived levels of service quality, professional image, supervisory communication, opportunities for improvement, and so on. Results indicated a major need for improved communications between employees and their managers.

Following the results of the survey, management took a number of steps designed to solve that communication problem.

■ **STEP #1: "Special Emphasis Day."** This event was designed to help the employees in the department to:

● Get to know one another better

● Understand what their co-workers did

● Realize the need to improve service quality

Employees were assigned seating next to people they did not know, or at least did not work with. Each employee was then asked to "interview" the employee sitting beside him or her and then introduce that person to the group.

Next, the employees broke up into groups of five to brainstorm hypothetical customer problems which were provided by the meeting facilitators. During these discussions, employees began to become better aware of what their fellow employees were responsible for and what problems they encountered in their work.

Finally, the employees participated in skits designed to replicate conversations with angry customers.

■ **STEP # 2: A Teamwork and Morale Task Force,** which was given responsibility for identifying specific actions needed to improve morale and foster team spirit within the department.

Membership included volunteers (one from each work group in the department) and a member of management, with leadership rotating among the team members. The task force discussed the survey results and suggested solutions, including:

★ Revision of policy to promote uniformity throughout all work groups in the department

★ Tours of each work group's area

★ Work group presentations on their job functions

★ A slogan/logo contest and bulletin board

■ **STEP #3: Weekly Meetings.** These aren't the only meetings aimed at improving quality through employee involvement, however. Another part of the ongoing effort involves weekly meetings between the employees in each group and their supervisors, sessions aimed at presenting problems and developing solutions.

The problem-solving process: Each work group in the department follows a six-step procedure in discussing those problems and their solutions:

1 Identify members of the group and review the department's mission.

2 Establish the purpose of the work group and write its mission statements (one for the group as a whole, and individual mission statements for the supervisor and each employee in the group).

3 Define customers and list their expectations, whether they want fast and efficient service, courtesy, or something else.

4 Select processes the group can use to meet these customer expectations. In some cases, the groups are able to select and implement their own processes. In other cases, they must get management approval because of the more universal nature of their recommendations.

5 Prioritize and select these opportunities for improvement. "We recommend that the teams begin with the small projects that they can accomplish on their own and then—when they see some successes—move on to the larger projects that require

management approval," says Bowman.

6 Measure results. One method some groups use to accomplish this is customer satisfaction surveys, which help determine whether the improvements they have made actually have a positive impact on customer service.

INVOLVEMENT CREATES OWNERSHIP

What have been the results of the division's quality improvement effort? Brady points to several. "The employees have bought into the whole effort because they see the opportunity to gain more control over how they do their jobs."

One team, for example, evaluated the phone bills, which indicated that calls overflowing into the company cost more per minute than other calls. As a result, they did some rerouting and saved several thousand dollars.

That employees were willing to make an even greater commitment to improvement became clear when the company conducted another survey in the telecommunications department in early 1987. Results were substantially more positive, with employees reporting better communication while noting more opportunities for improvement in work-related problems. A third survey early last year found employees taking even more responsibility for problems *and* suggesting that the teamwork concept be implemented in other departments.

The work group meetings themselves have become more valuable, since employees now tend to focus almost exclusively on how to solve problems, rather than on trying to place blame. Group members now also share questions and problems with employees and supervisors in other groups when appropriate so that they can work together in solving problems.

"These kinds of conversations are very casual and more and more frequent," reports Brady. "In fact, my staff is now a strong, functioning, autonomous group. I rely on them to make their own decisions and let me know the results."

But the most important result of the whole effort, Bowman says, is that it *worked*. As such, it can be held up as a model for other departments within the company. "Efforts are now under way to do the same thing in other departments," he concludes.

THE TEAM APPROACH TO QUALITY

You can't afford to go it alone when it comes to solving quality problems. Fortunately, you don't have to. See how the following companies have used teamwork to develop innovative solutions to quality problems.

FORD MOTOR COMPANY

Any worthwhile endeavor starts with a plan. Developing a plan—and sticking to it— is especially important when putting quality problem-solving teams into action. See how an eight-step plan has steered Ford's task forces down the road to success.

Ford Motor Company's foray into quality improvement in the early 1980s is now nearly legendary. However, while the company has advanced light-years in terms of improvements, it is relentless in its quest for even higher levels of quality.

One such effort is the team-oriented problem-solving process. The process consists of these eight steps:

1. Set up the team. "Because this business is so complex, you can't make an impact on it without using a team approach," says John Durstine, assistant general manager for Ford's Body and Assembly Operations (Dearborn, MI).

According to Durstine, a quality problem-solving team should meet the following criteria:

☐ Be small enough to be efficient and effective.

☐ Be properly trained in the skills its members will need.

☐ Be allocated enough time to work on the problems they plan to address.

☐ Be given the authority to resolve the problems and implement corrective action.

☐ Have a designated "champion" (who may or may not be the chairperson). This champion should be able to help the team get around roadblocks that arise.

2. Describe the problem to be addressed. At Ford, this involves the "5W2H" process: *who, what, when, where, why, how,* and *how many.* The answers to these seven questions should be *quantified* whenever possible.

"If you can't quantify the problem, then, in many cases, you really don't know what the problem is," cautions Durstine.

3. Implement and verify interim containment action. While the team will need an appropriate length of time to study a problem and develop a solution, it is necessary to implement some early action to contain the problem. There are two reasons for this:

★ It allows production to continue uninterrupted without making the same errors over and over again.

★ The interim containment action also allows the team the opportunity to observe the process in action and work toward discovering the root cause of the problem.

The team should then *quantitatively* verify the effectiveness of the interim containment action.

4. Define and verify the root causes. "Many people like to take a symptom and say that it is a root cause," points out Durstine. "It's important, however, not to fall into this trap."

Durstine admits that he has been on problem resolution teams that have had to solve the same problem several times because they failed to define and identify the root causes.

The Challenge ⇒ How can you be sure that you have properly defined and verified the root causes of quality problems?

The Solution ⇒ If you can answer the question "Why is this happening?" then you are still addressing symptoms. "It is when you are unable to follow the 'why' question with another 'why' question that you are really knocking on the door of the root causes," he explains.

5. Develop corrective actions and verify them. Verify your solutions—again, *quantitatively*—before you implement them. "If you don't, you can lose a lot of time assuming that you have solved your problem, when in fact you really haven't," he notes.

6. Implement the permanent corrective action and reverify it. Again, verify *quantitatively* that the solution works.

7. Prevent a recurrence of the problem. This involves modifying the appropriate management system, operative system, practices and procedures, and so on. In other words, if you solve a problem in one area or on one line, the same problem can occur in other areas or on other lines unless you modify the overall system that governs all areas or lines.

8. Congratulate the team. This is a step that managers in many companies forget. "Teams put a lot of time and effort into what they do, and you should be truly grateful for this," notes Durstine.

ENCOURAGE TEAMS TO STICK TO THE FACTS

By now, you've probably recognized a common thread running through many of these steps. In short, why is the term "quantitative" used so often and with such emphasis in this process? The heart of the process is what Ford calls "management by facts." This involves using any of a number of appropriate tools to discover, address, and solve problems: Ishikawa "fishbone" diagrams, Pareto analysis, Taguchi methods, "x-bar and r" charts, quality function deployment, and others.

"If two members on a team disagree on a cause or a solution, instead of getting into the 'I say, you say' game, ask, 'What are the facts?'" suggests Durstine. "When the facts become available, both people will have to agree on the right action, and it will *be* the right action."

NORTHROP CORPORATION

There's more than one way to get your employees to work together on coming up with quality improvements. See how Northrop's employee involvement program evolved as it adapted different team approaches to meet its quality needs.

One of the nation's first organizations to participate in formal employee involvement programs (starting with quality circles) was Northrop Corporation's Aircraft Division (Hawthorne, CA), which launched its first circle teams in the late 1970s.

The division created a cross-sectional steering committee to set up the initial ground rules. Committee members came from Quality Assurance, Human Resources, Manufacturing, Manufacturing Engineering, and Public Affairs.

At first, participation in the circles was voluntary. If managers were interested in having these problem-solving teams in their departments, they were set up. However, employees were not required to join (except, of course, in departments that were so small that all employees had to become members in order for the team to function).

Members of the circles always came from the same work areas and met weekly to focus on problem-solving and improvements. To motivate employees to participate, the division combined its already existing suggestion-award program, allowing members to share in awards to the extent of 10 percent of the savings realized (with a cap on award amounts).

CIRCLES ARE SUCCESSFUL BUT HAVE THEIR LIMITATIONS

While many circles programs have fallen by the wayside, quality circle teams are alive and well at Northrop's Aircraft Division. There are more than 50 teams in diverse areas such as Facilities, Finance, Quality Assurance, and Material.

However, while circles help solve departmental problems, Northrop found that they didn't address all of its division's needs in terms of tapping employee brainpower.

"One of the roadblocks was that leaders began to realize that many of the problems they were wrestling with crossed over into other work areas," explains Peggy Jo Fulton, manager of Employee Involvement Programs. "Quality circles could not address these, since they are essentially limited to working on their own department problems."

TAKING IT TO TASK FORCES

To reach into areas that circles could not address, the division widened the scope of employee involvement in the early 1980s to include inter-area employee teams called Task Forces. A Task Force is described as "a group of employees and managers from different disciplines that solves specific problems."

Task Force successes at Northrop include streamlining a new Facilities Request system and working out problems of the many departments involved in Tool Control and various interorganizational tooling issues.

MOVING ONWARD TO EPR GROUPS

Another significant shift in the direction of employee involvement came about in the mid-1980s, beginning in the company F-5 fighter aircraft manufacturing area," recalls Elaine Eldridge, manager of Quality Circles in the employee involvement programs department. "The manager there said that circles were successful, but what was needed was a total departmental team approach, a 'can-do' spirit."

The process that was developed to meet that need is called an Employee Performance and Recognition (EPR) program. Since the first EPR was developed, 12 more—involving more than 3,000 employees—have been implemented throughout the division.

Each EPR program is individually designed by a steering committee usually made up of 70 percent nonmanagement and 30 percent management personnel. While the process for designing the program is standard, the programs themselves (including establishing performance goals and appropriate recognition) are conceived by the steering committee. Basically, EPR groups focus on the following three activities:

★ Enhancing departmental performance through the awareness of problems.

★ Setting goals for improvement.

★ Recognizing improved performance.

EPR groups compete against their own team's previous performance and/or against other teams in their own department for awards such as hats, T-shirts, and designated parking spaces.

🗩 **Example** ⇒ The largest EPR program at Northrop is "Team Hornet" in the F/A-18 assembly area. The team boasts major accomplishments, including an improvement in operating costs and a reduction in employee relations complaints.

ENCOURAGING ACCEPTANCE OF THE TEAM PROCESS

Though the awards came eventually, it wasn't all smooth sailing right from the beginning. "At first, with the idea of entering into an 'everyone is equal' team meeting, many of the employees—as well as some managers—felt that it would just be a waste of time," notes Fulton.

"Many of them had been here for 30 years," adds Eldridge, "and felt that since the division had been successful during that time period, there was no need to change anything. It was difficult to explain to them that we needed to improve, even though we were already good."

To address the reluctance on the part of these few, the division:

✘ Asked employees to "hang in there" until they at least completed the training. "We emphasized that we wanted to use their brains, not just their bodies," explains Eldridge.

✘ Encouraged the employees to help improve and design the overall employee involvement effort.

✘ Tried to ensure that managers were part of the groups, either as leaders or as members. "When you have a group without management participation and involvement, you can't achieve very much," observes Fulton.

✘ Allowed managers to reject team recommendations, but only when they had very good reasons for doing so and explained those reasons to the groups.

As a result of these efforts, Fulton and Eldridge report most of the people who came to meetings "kicking and screaming" are now the program's strongest supporters. "They told us at first that the system couldn't be changed," states Eldridge. "Now they are part of making these changes."

HANGING IN THERE PAYS OFF

The division has found benefits of employee involvement programs beyond the individual project paybacks. "When employees who have participated in teams are promoted to supervisors or managers, they tend to be more analytical and better problem solvers and, even more important, have a better relationship with and understanding of their employees," says Fulton.

What element contributes most to benefits like these? Both Fulton and Eldridge point to top divisional management commitment, support, and flexibility as being the real keys to success. "Many companies have started employee involvement programs of one kind or another and abandoned them along the way because of problems," says Eldridge. "Management here, though, has been very patient and allowed us to experiment with the processes until we got them right."

"In the years that we have been doing this, management hasn't once said that we could not address certain issues," adds Fulton. "It has been very cooperative and open; it supports employee involvement at all levels."

That support will enable Fulton and Eldridge to continue to work toward their goal of more self-facilitation and organizational ownership of circles, EPR groups, and other employee activities.

REYNOLDS METALS COMPANY

Using employee and supervisory teams to come up with quality improvements doesn't have to be a complicated undertaking. In fact, Reynolds Metals contends that the simpler your approach is, the better.

Since 1981, Reynolds Metals Company has dramatically improved quality and productivity at its McCook Sheet & Plate Plant (McCook, IL). The vertically integrated and leading aluminum manufacturer has not only modernized and automated its 44-year-old plant with $125 million in state-of-the-art equipment, but it has also modernized and modified the quality circle concept.

Its circle program—Cooperative Hourly and Management Problem-Solving (CHAMPS)—has made employee participation a way of life at Reynolds, says William H. Bateman, Jr., quality control manager at McCook.

"The philosophy behind the CHAMPS program is very basic and very simple," he says. It is based on the premise that the people doing the job know best how to do it better. CHAMPS differs from many quality programs in that it is entirely voluntary. It is made up of teams from all areas of the plants, and most teams are made up of small groups of employees from the same work area.

"Each team meets for an hour each week to discuss work-related problems, investigate causes, recommend solutions, and take corrective action when they are authorized to do so," Bateman explains.

DETERMINING WHETHER CHANGES ARE *REALLY* NEEDED

Bateman notes that the CHAMPS teams do not have the authority to make changes. Instead, when a team comes up with an idea, it must investigate the problem, develop facts and figures to support its proposal, and make a formal presentation to plant management and staff with a recommendation.

"Often, getting from the idea stage to approval may take six to eight months, especially if the recommendation includes the purchase of new equipment. But since the teams meet only one hour per week, there is a lot of time to answer the crucial question, 'Is this really needed?' " says Bateman.

The answer to that question has been yes far more often than not, he reports. During CHAMPS' first four years, for example, teams proposed almost 475

solutions to problems, and management approved almost 400 of them, an approval rate of more than 80 percent. Bateman emphasizes that the total savings of these ideas has been eight times their cost, significant in a major manufacturing facility where cost control is very important.

A CASE IN POINT

For an example of the CHAMPS program in action, consider what occurred in the plate mill. "In this mill, when a plate has completed the hot rolling process, it must be stacked on a wagon and moved to a storage area," explains Bateman.

"We have to put spacers between the plates so they can cool, and the spacers must be heat-resistant and not burn. We had used rectangular strips of aluminum on the hot corners, but the strips marred the surface of the plates. When the plates were cold, we would use wooden boards, but they would release moisture and leave white, chalky water stains.

"A CHAMPS team tackled this problem. It was more of an appearance problem, but the old spacers did make the finished product look bad. So the team went to another Reynolds Metals plant that makes aluminum extrusions, and asked them to design an extruded product up to 130 feet long and with rounded corners. This solution generally worked, replacing the old hot spacers and boards, and not damaging the surface at all.

"However, since the spacers were hollow, heavy plates mashed some of them. So the team designed a plug that fits in the end of each spacer. The plug extends the life of each spacer two or three times. The result has made a tremendous change in surface quality."

UNDISPUTED CHAMPS

CHAMPS success stories like this one demonstrate why McCook was able to double the pounds of aluminum per employee that were shipped over a three-year period. At the same time, CHAMPS enabled the plant to deliver more than 2,000 items to a particular customer without a single rejection.

AMANA REFRIGERATION, INC.

Using teams of employees and supervisors to develop quality improvements is a tried-and-true method. But some problems must be addressed at a higher level. That's why Amana set up task forces that are made up of people at different levels within the company.

Usually when something goes wrong in an organization, any number of people may contribute ideas for correcting the situation. But that doesn't necessarily mean that the *most qualified* person addresses the problem.

Amana Refrigeration, Inc. (Amana, IA), realized that one way to make sure the right person or group tackles quality problems is to set up task forces. At Amana, the need for task forces grew out of a realization that there were some issues that occur at the first-line supervisor level that actually need to be resolved at higher levels.

For instance, this question was posed to one of Amana's production line foremen:

"If you asked your employees how they could make their jobs easier and reduce the number of units that do not comply with Amana's standards, how would they respond?"

What management found was that, yes, there were certain things employees and foremen could do themselves to improve quality. And because of the response and interest of other employees and foremen, the improvement program was expanded to the entire work force. However, the company also found that there were some problems that people at these levels could *not* address on their own.

"There are some items that need to be addressed at a higher level of responsibility," explains Robert Cech, director of Amana's Quality Assurance.

DIFFERENT FOLKS FOR DIFFERENT PROBLEMS

Amana developed and launched a number of task forces, each of which has a unique area of problem-solving responsibility. They include the:

■ **Goals and Objectives Task Force.**

Each of the product lines Amana produces has a Goals and Objectives Task Force. For example, there is one for Amana's cooking products (ranges and microwave ovens), another for refrigeration, another for air conditioning, and yet another for furnaces.

Each of these task force groups has representatives from Engineering, Manufacturing Engineering, Production, Production Control, and Purchasing. Each group is chaired by a QA representative. Group members are responsible for following up on all problems related to their discipline, even if the problems aren't within their specific specialty areas.

For example, if a group has an electrical engineer representing Engineering, and there is an engineering problem with a cabinet, that electrical engineer—even though cabinets are not his or her specialty—is still responsible for posing the problem to the engineers who *are* responsible, and getting back to the group with the appropriate response.

■ **Field Service Task Force.**

Paralleling the Goals and Objectives Task Force—which handles in-plant products—is the Field Service Task Force, which handles items that arise outside the production facility. Representing this task force is Engineering, Quality Assurance, Purchasing, and Service. This group is alerted to field problems via service department contacts and calls or letters from customers and takes appropriate action to resolve them.

■ **Weekly "Q" Meeting.**

Problems that may be beyond the scope of the previous task force groups are presented to the weekly Q meeting, comprised of the company's president, appropriate vice presidents, and managers. "However, we encourage people to solve the problems at the lowest levels possible," stresses Cech, who is a member of this third-level task force.

■ **ABC Task Force.**

This group focuses its attention specifically on supplier problems. Members are representatives from QA and Purchasing only. The task force places suppliers in one of three categories:

1 **The "C" List.** This includes suppliers who are not meeting Amana's quality requirements. In such a situation, the company requires that the supplier's management visit Amana, listen to a presentation of the problem, and provide a written response regarding the corrective action the supplier plans to take, as well as a timetable for completion.

2 **The "B" List.** Following the meeting and the supplier's promise to follow through, Amana moves the supplier to the "B" list and monitors its progress.

3 **The "A" List.** If the supplier does improve as promised, it is moved to the "A" list for a period of time. If it continues to show improvement, it is eventually dropped from the "A" list and is on *no* list. "In other words, our best suppliers are those that are not listed," explains Cech.

If the supplier does *not* improve after being placed on the "B" list, it is moved back to the "C" list and the process begins again.

TASK FORCES ARE TOUGH

What have the task forces accomplished for Amana? Cech says the most important benefit has been a substantial reduction in the number of units that do not meet Amana's specifications. There has also been a substantial reduction in the number of service problems in the field.

In addition, "communication among the various disciplines has improved," he reports. "When someone has a problem, it is immediately discussed and resolved."

Although the concept is reaping valuable benefits, Cech still sees opportunity for improvement. "We're constantly modifying the system in small ways to keep people alert. We will not become complacent by following the same routines; we strive for constant improvement," he concludes.

POLAROID CORPORATION

Quality circles have "life cycles" that must be monitored in order for the teams to stay healthy. Two of Polaroid's top quality pros share their advice for keeping quality teams alive and well.

When companies first introduce the concept of quality circles, employees usually respond to the challenge with enthusiasm and success. Eventually, however, even the most driven employees can run out of steam and lose interest.

Why do such groups die? What are the signs that they are foundering? And what can you do to keep yours on track? According to a pair of top managers at Polaroid Corporation (Cambridge, MA), if you understand the "life cycle" of quality circles, you can prevent their premature end.

"When we first organized our small groups to solve production problems, we assumed that they'd continue to function indefinitely," says Jack Moran, corporate manager of quality systems. Moran and Dick Talbot, corporate manager, creative learning systems, have been monitoring small groups at the company since 1979.

In the beginning, the theory was that once a group was up and running, it would keep going by a sort of perpetual motion. "We found that that wasn't the case at all," Moran admits. "You have to work hard to keep a group together."

Often, the individual who must work the hardest is the person who leads these groups. The person you choose to act as facilitator is pivotal to your groups' success. "Small groups seem to progress in stages, and at each phase, the role of the leader is a little different," Moran points out. When facilitators know what to look for as groups mature, they can keep them motivated.

PHASE ONE: PROBLEM SELECTION

In its infancy, a quality circle identifies a problem and seeks out an effective solution. The result of this early problem-solving process is presenting a well-thought-out solution to management. At Polaroid, for example, groups meet for about one hour a week and have a presentation ready for management after eight or ten meetings.

During the formative phase, the leader helps select the most pressing problems and then guides the group toward finding the causes. "The early meetings are brainstorming sessions," Moran explains.

He offers these suggestions for ways facilitators can energize circle participants during this start-up period:

➡ **Establish what types of problems the groups may deal with.** Issues like pay scales or the volume of the music in the cafeteria aren't usually considered appropriate topics. Instead, the facilitator should focus the group's attention on topics that relate directly to quality of work.

➡ **Ask team members for their suggestions.** The group leader should go around the room and ask what everyone thinks the three biggest quality problems are. As the suggestions come in, he or she should write them down on a blackboard or a big pad of paper so everyone is able to see them. *The facilitator should be sure to write the ideas in the words of the crew members who suggest them*—the wording shouldn't be changed. "The whole idea at this stage is to give the team members a sense that their ideas are important," Talbot points out. "Using their words shows them that you really believe they are."

➡ **Elicit some participation from everyone.** If someone doesn't want to contribute an idea as the leader goes around the room, the facilitator should make the person at least say "pass." This can serve as an icebreaker—a way of loosening a tongue that's frozen with the fear of speaking aloud. "You want to encourage even minimal participation from everyone," Moran says. "We've found that just saying one word can ease someone into the group."

➡ **Agree on a problem to be tackled.** Once all of the suggested problems have been recorded, it's time to establish some agreement within the group about which two or three are the most appropriate to tackle. According to Moran, the consensus aspect is critical to the eventual effectiveness of the group. And this is why the group leader must resist the urge to run the show.

"The facilitator has to be willing to *listen* and not

just impose his or her ideas," Moran says. "If the group feels it 'owns' the problem, it will be much more willing to work on solutions."

PHASE TWO: ANALYSIS AND SOLUTION

As soon as a problem has been decided upon, the facilitator should use a similar brainstorming approach to the one described above to identify its causes and propose solutions. That is, he or she should go around and ask each employee in the group for feedback, writing their responses down on a blackboard or pad.

While there are many ways to approach this process, Moran notes that following a few guidelines will increase the group's chances of success:

● **Cover all the bases.** The leader must be sure to include *all* the possible causes for a particular problem, even the most unlikely ones. For example, let's say the problem being examined is a high defect rate. In studying the potential culprits, the facilitator might be tempted to overlook machinery because your company recently installed brand-new equipment that should be working perfectly. But you never know—so the group leader should consider investigating those machines just to make certain.

● **Gather data.** Once the circle has decided which areas to focus on first, the group should go out onto the production floor to collect pertinent information. If the problem is that you can't meet quotas and one group member suspects that it's because a machine isn't running up to speed, the worker should be encouraged to check the specs for that piece of equipment and bring the information back to the group.

"Collecting data brings workers into the process of problem-solving," says Talbot. "It encourages them to prove their points and makes them a part of the team."

● **Assess the information.** As employee data comes in, the circle leader should examine it carefully. If the data can be plotted on some sort of graph, it will carry added impact and can show causal relationships that might otherwise be missed.

● **Arrive at possible solutions.** In many cases, the solution to a problem will be rather straightforward and inexpensive. For example, if a machine just needs to have its timing set so that it will run at a faster pace and produce more quickly, then it can be

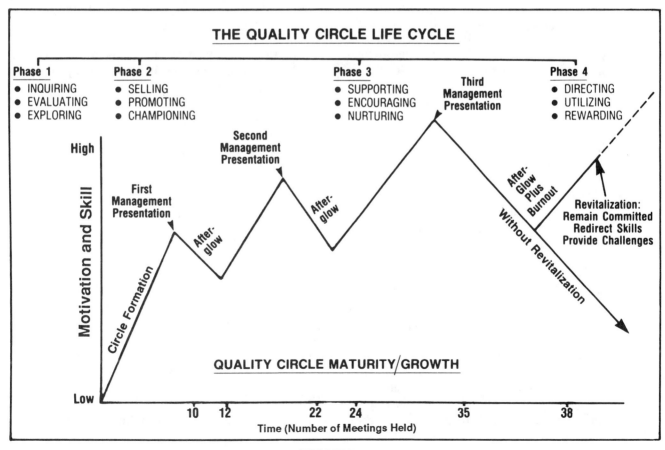

FIGURE 4

simply adjusted, or Maintenance or a vendor service rep can be asked to take care of it, depending on how such matters are dealt with at your company.

On the other hand, if the group is investigating a quality problem and has discovered that faulty materials are regularly making their way into the department from an outside supplier, the solution might be more involved. You might have to implement an intensive preinspection effort, request greater care on the part of the supplier, or switch suppliers altogether. Whatever the case, before any action can be taken, the solution would certainly require management's okay, the involvement of other departments (such as Purchasing), and a great deal of thought and discussion.

● **Post the group's proposed solution for other departments to see.** This will allow personnel from other departments to provide the team with feedback. It will give members of the circle a good idea as to the solution's practicality and viability. The comments the group receives may be helpful in fine-tuning the solution before the circle presents it to management.

PHASE THREE:
THE BIG PRESENTATION

When the quality team has decided a solution is ripe for presenting, the facilitator should contact members of management to schedule a convenient time for a meeting. Then, during the days before the big presentation, the leader should work with circle members to help them overcome whatever "butterflies" they may feel about getting up in front of company "bigwigs."

In fact, the facilitator might wish to devote an entire circle meeting hour to rehearsing the presentation. He or she should try to get as many circle members involved in the actual presentation as possible. Participants should draw up charts and tables to be used as visual aids during the presentation to give it more of a punch. (The workers who are really too shy at this point to speak during the presentation might be glad to take on this task.)

In addition to helping workers hone their presentation skills, the facilitator will need to prepare them for the possibility that their solution might not be accepted with open arms right off the bat. Group members and top managers might have very different ways of looking at the situation, and what seems feasible to the group may seem very *in*feasible to company higher-ups. Or, upper managers may ask the

group to make certain revisions to the solution and present it again (this might happen more than once) before they will grant the solution their blessing.

Whatever happens, the team members should be assured that their efforts *are* appreciated and that they must adopt a "back to the drawing board" mentality if a solution is initially rejected.

Of course, if management wholeheartedly approves the circle's suggestion, there will be great cause for celebration. The facilitator might wish to take the group out for pizza, pass out plaques or awards, or in some other appropriate way, acknowledge its success.

PHASES FOUR AND FIVE:
BASKING IN THE "AFTERGLOW,"
BUILDING ON SKILLS

What is the "afterglow"? According to Moran, this is a period of relative inactivity that often follows a successful presentation. At this point, the facilitator's role must change.

"The leader doesn't have to sell the group on the idea of problem-solving anymore," he says. "So the emphasis shifts to supporting the group as it takes on the next problem. The group can take a week off to pat each other on the back, but then you have to move on."

Once the group members understand the basics of problem-solving, the leader should encourage them to build on their skills. "You have to meet group members at their level," Moran asserts. "Groups require people with both process and technical skills. Sometimes, a group will have workers who really know their jobs but have a hard time speaking up in a meeting. Or a group will have others who are very good at identifying problems but lack the technical skills to verify their theories on the floor. Both types need some guidance [to round out their talents]."

PHASE SIX:
THE BIG FIZZLE

So now the group is working like a well-oiled machine. It has worked its way through several problems and is learning new processes and technical skills, and it has made a couple of successful presentations to management. The team should be reaching new heights of enthusiasm, right?

Not necessarily, according to Talbot. "What we found was that the most critical time in the life of a group is about a year after it starts, just as it reaches the peak of its skills.''

He adds that while the reasons for this decline vary, groups heading for failure usually give some warning. What are these warning signs? Typically, they include:

✔ **Incomplete projects.** Individuals on the team don't follow through on their parts in the problem-solving process.

✔ **Grumbling and grousing.** Circle participants begin to complain that the process is too simplistic or too rigid. They start to question the reasons for brainstorming or list totally farfetched or blatantly incorrect causes for very simple and straightforward problems.

✔ **Projects that are inappropriate.** When a group spends an entire meeting arguing about what color to paint a new piece of equipment, it's time to worry.

✔ **Loss of employee interest and enthusiasm.** This invariably leads to:

✔ **Diminished management interest.** ''As the problems the group chooses to tackle become more trivial, management begins to wonder why it should give up an hour a week of work time to solve issues that are usually settled at the watercooler,'' Talbot points out.

What's the result of these vital signs? Highly trained problem solvers are allowed to ''go out of business,'' wasting precious human resources and considerable investment of time and energy. In short, a quality circle tragically and unnecessarily dies.

PHASE SEVEN: REVITALIZATION

''Once we understood that groups had a life cycle, we began to look for ways we could keep the interest up—to revitalize burned-out groups,'' Moran says. ''Eventually, we began to see that there were two key elements to keeping groups alive beyond a certain point.'' These include:

★ **Making sure the facilitator remains committed and enthusiastic.** When the group starts losing interest, it's all too easy for its leader to fall into the same trap. And the facilitator's increasingly apathetic attitude may in turn feed back to the group. To avoid this situation, the circle leader must convince the group that he or she is serious about keeping it going and presenting its conclusions to management.

One way you can do this is to take minutes of the circle meetings—or assign participants to do it on a rotating basis. A copy can be posted for other shifts, thus promoting an ongoing exchange of information. Plus, a second copy can be sent along to management to apprise them of the group's progress and keep *them* enthusiastic.

★ **Challenging the group's ever-maturing problem-solving skills.** ''After the first year, most groups have resolved the top two or three problems that they came up with during the early brainstorming sessions,'' Talbot notes. ''So they need something more challenging to keep them interested.''

When a group arrives at this point, says Moran, it's a signal for its leader to switch its focus from ''group-driven tasks'' to ''management-driven tasks.''

''In our experience with mature small groups, we've found that the members want to solve problems with a high level of difficulty that the group perceives to be of real importance,'' Talbot says. ''Most companies have long-term goals concerning lower product costs and improved quality. A group could be invited to offer some role in fulfilling those goals.''

The possibilities for mature groups are nearly endless. ''We've had good luck with interdisciplinary groups made up of members from different departments,'' Moran notes. Teams from different departments can get together to work on one problem, approaching it from different directions. Group members can also be challenged by asking them to take over as group leaders.

QUALITY CIRCLES *CAN* LIVE LONG AND PROSPER

By understanding the stages in a problem-solving group's life cycle, a facilitator can be ready to meet the needs of its members at each phase along the way. It takes a lot of work to monitor a circle's ''vital signs,'' but the rewards for the group and the company more than justify the effort.

''At their best, small groups empower their members,'' Moran points out. ''They nurture skills and encourage growth beyond the confines of a particular job. They create self-motivated employees with sophisticated problem-solving abilities and with the desire to have a positive impact on the workplace.''

EMPLOYEE RECOGNITION

Are employees at your company given a real incentive to do quality work? Sometimes it takes more than lectures about quality to motivate workers to give their all. At these companies it pays to provide a tangible payoff for a job well done.

PERPETUAL FINANCIAL CORP.

Incentives are a means to achieve a desired result. This firm shows how it used them to promote superior customer service and to elicit cost-saving quality improvement ideas.

When employees make outstanding contributions to their organizations, they're often recognized in big ways. Unfortunately, many of those who make smaller contributions fail to receive any credit at all.

However, management at Perpetual Financial Corp. (Vienna, VA) knows that small contributions are the backbone of long-term quality improvement and superior customer service. That's why in early 1988, the company developed a plan to acknowledge small but meaningful quality efforts of its employees. It decided to do this by awarding certificates of recognition.

To award the certificates, management formed a service quality committee composed of 16 executives from the company's several subsidiaries. The committee's job was to review nominations for service quality awards.

Employees and customers then were given the opportunity to nominate workers based on their contributions to quality and customer service. Employees could be nominated more than once and even win more than once.

First-time winners received certificates embossed with a silver seal. Subsequent winners received certificates embossed with a gold seal. Each award read:

Certificate of Recognition

For your high standards of service quality which contribute to Perpetual's goal of making quality a way of life.
Award of Excellence

A SALUTE TO ASSOCIATES DAY

To reinforce the company's appreciation of employees and to build on its earlier efforts, management came up with another reward: the Salute to Associates Day.

The Salute was a day long recognition gala. Although the event was kept secret until the day it was scheduled, employees knew something was afoot when each received a letter from Chairman Thomas J. Owen suggesting that they look for something special in the local newspapers during the coming days.

On July 20, 1989, full-page ads in local newspapers and magazines read: "In accordance with federal regulations, Perpetual is publishing a list of its assets." The ad then listed the names of all 1,800-plus employees. It concluded with: "Thanks to the 1,821 associates who helped make Perpetual a $6.5 billion institution. There is a name for people like you: the best."

That day, company managers, who had been preparing in secret for several weeks, rolled out their own celebrations for employees in their departments, offices, and subsidiaries. At each location, employees received poster-sized reprints of the ad and buttons saying "I'm Perpetual's most valuable asset." They also received fortune cookies announcing prizes such as coffee mugs, a day off with pay, sweatshirts, and other such items.

At the end of the day, there was a reception honoring the winners of the service quality awards and a drawing for an all-expense-paid trip to Italy. The winner, a member of the night-cleaning crew, described his prize at "incredible."

BRIGHT IDEAS AND BONUS POINTS

With employee recognition for quality customer service on a roll, early in 1990 Perpetual announced its next quality program: "Bright Ideas."

During this 12-week effort, employees formed teams to develop quality ideas that would either reduce costs or increase revenues. Since the teams were cross-functional, it gave employees the opportunity to get to understand different aspects of the organization, to see how it functioned as a whole, and to get to know employees from other departments.

"It helped them to feel more a part of the organization and see how their jobs fit into the overall effort," explains Ann Kelly, manager of Public Relations. Consequently, this knowledge gave them the opportunity to make more valuable contributions.

But before workers even contributed their quality improvement ideas, Perpetual used incentives to generate participation.

➪ For attending the briefing meeting where the program was announced, employees received a "Bright Ideas" flashlight.

➪ For becoming part of a team and submitting its first idea, each team member received a "Bright Ideas" umbrella.

Once the teams were organized, they funneled their ideas through 20 team coordinators, who passed their suggestions on to one of the 19 evaluation teams.

➪ **One Quality Improvement** ⇒ Kelly herself was on a team, and one of the first projects it addressed was the company's job-posting procedure. At the time, each and every job was described in detail, even when several positions for the same job were open.

"When people received the 40-page list twice a week, few bothered to look at it," she notes. But the team was able to summarize the listings to about one page, and now they are read eagerly by people looking to advance in the organization. "This one project alone saved us $12,000 to $14,000 a year," she notes.

And what about the teams? Teams whose projects were approved by management received bonus points in accordance with the estimated value of the project. They could then redeem these points immediately for merchandise in a catalog.

During that 12-week period, approximately 85 percent of the company's employees formed more than 200 teams. And, 88 percent of those teams submitted quality improvement and cost-cutting ideas.

Was the program a success? You be the judge: Of the 966 ideas that were submitted, 312 were approved. Together, these "bright ideas" reaped combined annual savings and revenue increases of $4 million.

WEYERHAEUSER COMPANY

Want to motivate employees to upgrade quality? Consider this company's incentive plan. It gives employees the power to cite *one another* for providing quality customer service.

When your company makes a commitment to quality, your employees must make that commitment, too. It's not enough to upgrade management's skills, better define customers' needs, and make plans to improve the quality of products and services. To actually achieve your quality goals, you must also persuade workers to dedicate themselves to meeting customers' quality needs.

The Weyerhaeuser Company (Tacoma, WA) has incorporated all of these elements into its Total Quality effort. Yet management has always placed special emphasis on the need to involve employees and link them to their customers.

In fact, to make that link, the company's Financial Services Department created an employee incentive plan three years ago to promote quality customer service.

❏ **The Strategy** ⇨ The STAR Award Program's aim is to encourage continuous improvements in customer service by rewarding workers for their service efforts. And to motivate as many employees as possible, management designed the program to acknowledge the small accomplishments, not just the large ones.

"It's important to recognize *all* improvements and *all* extra efforts put forth by employees," insists Dennis Loewe, Financial Services Controller. It is the sum total of all of these small successes that leads to significant gains, he explains.

"For instance, when you examine all of the little things that occur in a process and improve each of them, the process itself ultimately becomes more effective," Loewe points out. And a more effective process is more likely to meet the customers' quality needs.

EMPHASIZING THE CUSTOMER

To make the all-important customer connection, Financial Services began by introducing the concept of *the internal customer* to its employees.

According to this concept, everyone within an organization has a customer, and that customer is the next person or process down the line that will respond to the previous employee's output. So, in addition to the traditional external customers, employees have internal customers whose workmanship is dependent on the quality of service that has been provided up to that point.

Therefore, employees are encouraged to ensure that their internal "customers" are satisfied by:

✔ Passing on only defect-free services

✔ Doing the job right the first time

✔ Assisting the people they depend on to provide them with defect-free inputs

By focusing on the internal customer as well as the external one, management believes employees will be motivated to do a better job of meeting their customers' service needs.

THE CO-WORKER CONNECTION

It's only logical, then, that if each employee is working to meet the needs of an internal customer (a co-worker), someone else is working to meet *that* employee's quality needs.

In essence, every employee is not only responsible for providing quality service; every employee is also a customer who depends on good service from others. Therefore, each worker is in an ideal position to recognize when he or she receives quality service from a fellow employee.

So, when the Financial Services Department developed its quality incentive plan, it decided to give *all* employees the power to commend *one another* for quality customer service.

In addition to the fact that employees are in a good position to spot quality service, management reasoned that by recognizing one another for all of the small service efforts that occurred on a daily basis, employees would encourage positive behavior in one another. And, in the process, the bestowers of each award would become more aware of their own customers.

❏ **How It Works** ⇨ Management has provided all

employees with blank STAR Award certificates that they can use to recognize the quality customer service activities that they've observed. Workers fill out the certificates, documenting in detail exactly what another employee did to provide quality service.

In addition, workers select from a range of STAR points listed on the certificate and award them based on the degree of effort expended and service provided. Points are awarded on the following basis:

■ **"Quality Customer Service" merits 1 to 3 STAR points.** For example, an employee might earn between one and three STAR points for taking a complete phone message, rather than passing the caller along to the wrong individual. The employee's effort represents "quality customer service," because a complete message enables the appropriate person to respond to the caller's question or problem.

■ **"Extra Effort" merits 4 to 6 STAR points.** To continue with the same scenario, another employee who takes a message may earn four to six points for making an "extra effort." This would include not only taking a thorough message, but also obtaining the information that the caller wanted—without depending on the "proper contact" to take over and respond.

■ **"Above and Beyond" merits 7 to 10 STAR points.** In the same situation, another employee might earn between seven and ten points for performing the first two steps, plus going "above and beyond" the call of duty. This might involve ensuring that the customer is asking the right question and is getting the information he or she really wants.

An employee can also earn seven to ten STAR points by preserving the company's cash, reducing costs, or offering a highly creative or innovative idea that results in improved customer service. In addition, a complimentary letter from an outside customer automatically qualifies a worker for a ten-point award. In such instances, the employee's supervisor usually fills out the award certificate.

Once the bestower of the award has determined the number of points and filled out the certificate, he or she presents the completed, original certificate to the deserving recipient. The bestower also gives a copy to the recipient's supervisor for the supervisor's files, and sends another copy to Dian Nichols, executive assistant, Financial Services, to place in the department's files.

THE REWARDS FOR QUALITY SERVICE

Eventually, employees turn in their certificates, which are then converted into different colored poker chips that represent accumulated points. At the end of each year, workers tally their points and participate in a department-wide celebration. One year, the department held a party in a hotel ballroom and hired a Dixieland jazz band as entertainment. Another year, it hired a country-western band.

During these galas, employees use their poker chips to shop for merchandise awards. The merchandise includes letter openers, brass coasters, sweatshirts, T-shirts, tote bags, clocks, coolers, and pen and pencil sets. All of the items have the department's logo, an upside-down triangle, imprinted on them. The upside-down triangle is symbolic of the department's philosophy, with management at the bottom and customers at the top.

"Employees are so excited about receiving the merchandise that many of them meet in advance, select their gifts together, and then disperse to the appropriate table to be first in line," Loewe reports.

RESPONSIBILITY AND TRUST

An obvious question that comes to mind is, "What is to stop the employees from indiscriminately awarding certificates to their friends?" This is an issue that Loewe and his colleagues considered while developing the program.

"We finally came to the conclusion that we would just have to try the program and see what happened," Loewe says. As it turned out, the employees have proven that they are responsible and can be trusted to award certificates only to those who truly earn them. "They take the program very seriously and are extremely fair," he reports. "In fact, we have found *no* instances of point padding."

A VISIBLE SUCCESS

Loewe says he knows the program is a success by the feedback he gets from people in other departments and business units. They regularly stop him and say either:

★ "I don't know what you're doing, but there sure is a change in attitude in your department!"

or

★ "We want to know more about STAR so we can implement it in our department, too!"

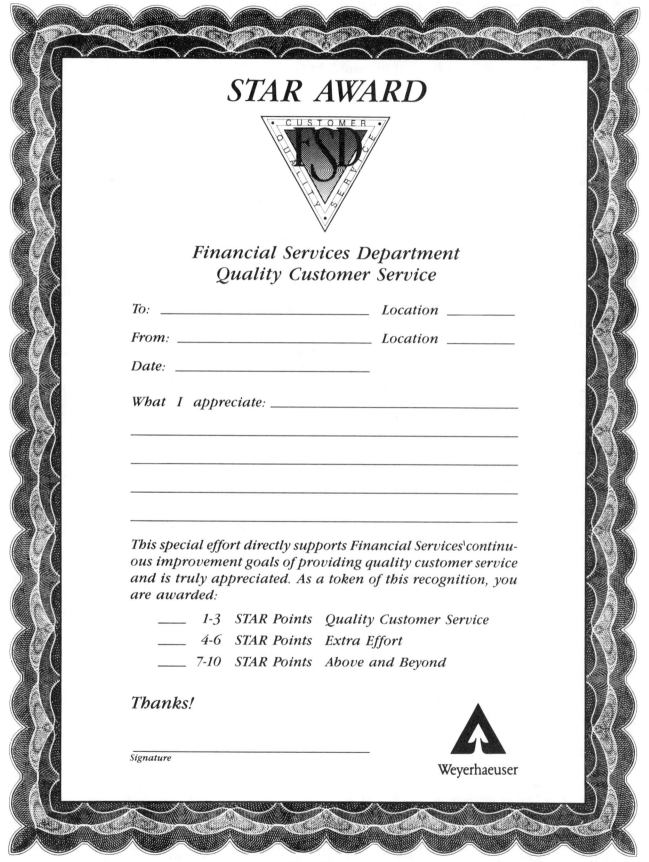

STAR AWARD

Financial Services Department
Quality Customer Service

To: _____ Location _____

From: _____ Location _____

Date: _____

What I appreciate: _____

_____

_____

_____

_____

This special effort directly supports Financial Services' continuous improvement goals of providing quality customer service and is truly appreciated. As a token of this recognition, you are awarded:

_____ 1-3   STAR Points   Quality Customer Service

_____ 4-6   STAR Points   Extra Effort

_____ 7-10 STAR Points   Above and Beyond

Thanks!

_____
Signature

Weyerhaeuser

FIGURE 5

DOMINO'S PIZZA, INC.

As part of its innovative effort to instill quality awareness in its personnel, this company sets up "Olympic" competitions. As a result, employees can have fun and learn about the seriousness of quality all at the same time.

There's no question that the issue of quality assurance is a serious one. But what if you could find a less-than-serious way to improve quality? You'd have to agree that it would at least be worth a try. This national pizza chain decided the fun approach *was* worth a try, and they've seen improvement in service and product quality as a result.

You might think that Domino's Pizza stores are required to purchase all of their food and supplies from the parent company, but that's not the case. The firm is not interested in building layers of management fat into the organization by creating corporate services with captive customers.

To this end, the company has a subsidiary company—Domino's Pizza Distribution Corp. (DPD) (Ann Arbor, MI)—that offers food and supplies to customers but leaves them free to choose any suppliers they wish. And for that very reason, DPD *knows* that it must provide the very best quality and service to its customers if it's going to remain competitive.

In 1984, DPD President Don Vlcek was struggling with the fact that the company's regional offices tended to make more decisions at the regional level than were necessary. "I wanted to get the idea across to the regional managers that decisions should be made at as low a level as possible—by the 'team members' (the company's term for employees) who do the work on a daily basis," says Vlcek. Having decisions made at this level, he believed, would strengthen DPD's competitive position.

Around that time, one of Vlcek's staff people mentioned that a regional manager, while on a visit to one of his region's commissaries (there are between 8 and 10 commissaries in each region), entered into a fun-spirited contest with one of the commissary's doughmakers to see how many batches of dough each could make in one hour. Another staff member then recommended that since the company's 1984 annual awards banquet was coming up in Los Angeles (site of that year's Summer Olympics), it might be a nice idea to arrange a "fun" Olympics between the executives and team managers at the banquet. Vlcek liked the idea, but he took it two steps further:

1. Instead of having the executives compete against the team members in fun competition, it was decided to have team members from each of the company's regions and headquarters compete against one another in *serious* competition.

2. In addition, it was decided that the Oympics would be the main event at the banquet, instead of merely a sideshow.

Now, admittedly, your company may not have the resources—or even the desire—to institute an all-encompassing competition like the DPD effort. But you can still apply some of the principles to foster quality workmanship among the work force. The level of competition and the choice of who will take part are something you and other members of management can decide for yourselves according to the needs of your company.

THE COMPETITION TAKES SHAPE

To prepare for the DPD Olympics, the idea was to review all of the jobs that are performed in the company and set up competitions to determine which of the team members were the best at carrying them out. The competition currently has 15 events based on 15 job categories. (See the box on the next page for a description of eight of those events.)

Each of the company's three regions is free to choose the way it selects the contestants that it sends to the national finals. For the first couple of years, the regions had quarterfinals at each of the commissaries in their regions and then flew the winners to regional headquarters for semifinal events. However, they ultimately decided that it made more sense to select team members who were able to demonstrate more consistent expertise over the course of a year than to send the one-time winners of one-time events.

"They wanted to take the 'one-day luck' factor out of the competition," explains Vlcek. Now, the regions keep track of team member productivity and quality on a daily basis and/or schedule monthly competitions to choose their regional representatives.

The three regional winners in each event then fly to Ann Arbor for the finals, where they compete against each other as well as against the winners from the company's Equipment and Supply Division. During this national competition, contestants must pass written tests that cover questions on company philosophy, attitudes, values, customer service requirements, and so on. DPD passes out a list of approximately 200 questions covering these topics and then chooses about 50 of them to ask contestants.

"The idea isn't the element of surprise," Vlcek explains. "The idea is education. We want our people to learn as much as they can about our company and then to be able to demonstrate and apply that knowledge."

The contestants then engage in competition with their peers from the other regions. "The challenge is to make sure that the competitions really reflect the essentials of the jobs and the daily duties of the team members," emphasizes Vlcek. "We don't want anyone saying that someone won because the competition didn't really reflect the job."

Besides job knowledge and proficiency, there is a time factor involved in most events. So, while one group of judges follows contestants every step of the way, another group times the events with stopwatches. Scoring covers a balance between the excellence of the work performed and speed—quality and productivity, if you will.

Incidentally, many of the judges for the events are DPD customers (the Domino's Pizza store managers). "We have one photograph of a judge studying the roundness of one of the doughballs so intently that his nose is two inches from the ball," relates Vlcek. This photograph hangs in DPD's commissaries around the country with the caption, "If you think our customers aren't very critical of our dough, think again."

The winners selected by those demanding judges stand on platforms and listen to the Olympic theme being played as they receive their medals. "It's a wonderful feeling to see first-line team members who might only earn minimum wage raising their arms and receiving standing ovations from the crowd," says Vlcek.

Adding to the significance of the event is the fact that DPD broadcasts the competition and the awards ceremonies live to its commissaries around the country so that contestants' fellow team members can watch as their friends engage in the contests and receive their awards.

It's more than just medals, music, and ovations, however. Winners receive checks for $4,000, distinguished red "winner" jackets, gold rings, patches, and lapel pins. They also receive write-ups and photos in the company newsletter and have their photographs displayed prominently on the walls of the company's corridors. In addition, DPD forwards the stories and photos to the team members' hometown newspapers.

THERE'S MORE TO IT THAN JUST A GOOD TIME

If this was all there was to it, DPD would still have an excellent program designed to instill pride in its team members and encourage them to do quality work. However, an equally important event takes place a month later when DPD flies all of the winners back to Ann Arbor, where they attend a Detroit Tigers baseball game. (Domino's President Tom Monaghan owns the team.) Before the game, they have their photos taken on the field and then watch the game from the owner's private box.

After the game, they are flown to the company's secluded lodge in northern Michigan for three days of management discussions. The team members meet face-to-face with DPD management to discuss:

- what's good about the company
- what needs improvement
- how those improvements can be made

"The first year that we did this, most of the team members acted as though they didn't have the right to share their opinions," says Vlcek. "We had to pull opinions out of them." The second year, they warmed up more and made some astute observations.

"We not only used many of their ideas; we praised them publicly for bringing them to our attention. Now they tell us all kinds of things." In fact, according to Vlcek, many team members report that the management meetings mean more to them than the money and the jackets they win.

Why? It may be because, in many cases, team members who make suggestions that involve special projects are given the opportunity to manage the projects themselves. For example, a truck driver who won his Olympics competition recommended that a Department of Transportation compliance program be created in the company. He not only was given the opportunity to set up the program himself, but is developing a series of safety seminars for drivers throughout the company and is involved in some of the actual, hands-on driver training.

Other team members have been promoted to management positions as a result of their demonstration of capability and/or their insightful ideas. "Some team members have been promoted to commissary management positions, where they are responsible for 50 team members and as much as $12 million to $15 million worth of business a year," reports Vlcek.

IT'S IN THEIR HANDS

As a result of the Olympics program and its subsequent opportunities, DPD team members now realize that they have their fate in their own hands. "We have been able to send them the clear message that they are in charge of their own destinies," says Vlcek. "This has led to a new excitement throughout the organization." It has also led to a number of direct benefits, including the following:

● In 1986, DPD was able to make 300,000 deliveries with only 13 missed deadlines, a success rate of 99.999 percent.

● Prior to the program, DPD's expenses compared to sales were approximately 18 percent. Currently, they stand at 16.5 percent. On sales of $600 million, that translates into a savings of $9 million.

"I can't say the Olympics has been totally responsible for this improvement, but we haven't implemented any major cost-reduction programs, so the

---

OLYMPIAN TASKS: GOING FOR THE GOLD

Here are eight of the events that take place during Domino's Olympics competition:

★ **Doughmaking.** Contestants measure out batches of dough, double-check the temperatures, make sure that sanitation and sterilization procedures are correct, and conduct tests to determine that the yeast they are adding is active. They must mix the dough the proper length of time to ensure proper consistency and texture. They then recheck temperatures, run the 400-pound doughball through a machine that creates the proper portion sizes, and round them into the shape of a ball. Finally, they place the balls into containers in such a way that they don't touch each other and ruin the roundness.

★ **Driving.** Contestants must demonstrate knowledge of Department of Transportation regulations, maintain accurate driver logs, exhibit positive attitudes, handle equipment properly, and engage in safe practices. Part of the competition involves a 30-minute road test and unloading of a $1,200 order complete with paperwork. Judges use skits and role-playing to evaluate attitudes and other nondriving requirements.

★ **Telephone Receptionist.** Vlcek has found that the way the phone is answered gives people their first impression of a company. Therefore, receptionists need to be cheery, helpful, and knowledgeable. Judges take contestants through a mock telephone quiz with "irate customers" calling to see how they are treated. They also test them on how well they catch certain signs and signals that callers and visitors give, as well as how they react to those signs. "For instance, if a person comes in to apply for a job and has what appears to be a marijuana cigarette hanging out of his pocket, we expect the receptionist to notice this," says Vlcek.

★ **Delivery.** Contestants must deliver a quality product, handle the product properly, inspect equipment, and demonstrate customer relations skills.

★ **Loading.** Contestants must engage in accurate, safe, and efficient loading procedures that avoid the potential for injury and damaged goods.

★ **Delivery Systems.** Contestants analyze current delivery systems, propose improvements to reduce costs, and work with a team to build trust and respect.

★ **Purchasing/Inventory Control.** Contestants identify and solve inventory problems, find ways to reduce costs, demonstrate understanding of the effect of product mix on pricing and gross profit, and react to inventory shortages/overages.

★ **Team Leaders (Supervisors).** Judges take contestants through role-playing situations where "team members" come in asking for pay raises that they don't deserve or where they complain about working conditions.

Olympics must certainly be responsible for a great deal of the results,'' Vlcek says.

● Currently, 96.5 percent of Domino's stores choose DPD as their supplier, even though they are free to do business elsewhere. This is the best evidence that the Olympics is helping to inspire team members to provide the quality of service and products that the customers are looking for.

▭ **What You Can Do** ⇒ If you'd like to inspire your own employees in the same fashion, keep in mind that you don't have to have a competition on the same scale that Domino's does. In fact, you'll get better results if you tailor a plan specifically for your organization. To accomplish this:

➡ **Talk to other managers** to see if there is enough interest in promoting quality workmanship through competition.

➡ **Survey the people ''in the trenches''** to determine which aspects of their jobs would best lend themselves to a contest.

➡ **Study those tasks to generate the criteria under which employees will be judged.** Is speed just as crucial as quality, or does quality stand head and shoulders above all other requirements?

➡ **Decide where the competition will be held.** Certain contests may, by their very nature, have to be held at your facility. But you may also want to hold some events at an outside location to add an air of ''specialness'' to the proceedings.

➡ **Choose appropriate rewards.** The prizes that people receive for winning competitions will be dictated by your budget and your impressions of what employees will find appealing. You may be pleasantly surprised to find, however, that a simple ceremony at which the company's appreciation is expressed may have as much impact as a material reward.

➡ **Don't lose sight of the real message.** No matter how much fun your competition turns out to be, don't let the frivolity get in the way of the true message you are trying to spread: Quality workmanship is wanted, recognized, and rewarded by your company.

GETTING—AND USING—CUSTOMER FEEDBACK

Where's the best place to learn what standards you should strive for? Go right to the source—
the customer. Savvy QA professionals know this, and they are instituting creative ways to
gain quality insight from their customers.

BANC ONE CORPORATION

Finding out what customers want is a prerequisite to effective quality assurance in both manufacturing and service sectors. Here is how one company learns what is important to its customers—and how it uses that information.

Customer satisfaction is the cornerstone of any business. It's really quite simple: If customers don't like your product, they won't be back for more. And if you have a great product but are not providing top-level quality customer service, you'll drive off customers just the same.

In late 1985, Banc One Corporation (Columbus, OH) launched a formal quality improvement effort in its customer service and processing areas. The rationale behind the move was simple: The quality of service that customers receive, the bank found, provides a differentiation significant enough in the minds of customers to determine where they do their banking.

"Quality service keeps current customers satisfied, ensures a better reputation, gains new business, and increases market share," says Vice President and Chief Quality Officer, Charles A. Aubrey.

An Eight-Step Approach ⇒ Aubrey's bank uses the following approach to assure quality service for its customers:

1 Survey customers. It's important to communicate with customers to determine two things:

▷ What service attributes do they consider to be the most important, in priority order?

▷ How is the organization performing in each of these areas?

Some tools that can be used to survey customers include customer contact during service, mail and telephone surveys, suggestion boxes, complaint cards, customer-initiated complaints, and focus groups. Surveys should include questions that will address at least four areas:

► accuracy of service

► completeness of service

► timeliness of service

► behavior /attitude of service providers

Surveys should be conducted on an ongoing basis. "This helps to keep the emphasis and flow of cus-tomer needs—as well as the satisfaction of those needs—at a high-priority level," explains Aubrey.

2 Translate customer requirements into quality measures, objectives, standards, policies, and procedures. "It is important to develop these specifications, particularly for the attributes that customers consider to be the most important," emphasizes Aubrey.

3 Implement these measures, goals, objectives, standards, policies, and procedures that reflect customer requirements. Everyone in the organization must thoroughly understand these specifications and have the ability to carry them out. Management should not only communicate them, but should also explain the reasons for their existence and importance.

"It is important to tell people what you expect of them if they are to know what to do, and do it right consistently," he explains. Once people know what is expected, they invariably conform and meet those expectations. "In fact, performance improvements on the order of 5 to 20 percent can be achieved simply by making it clear to people what is important."

4 Motivate and train managers. Banc One believes that every manager must be a customer champion and lead by example, accepting no less than absolute adherence to the quality standards and procedures developed from ongoing communications with customers.

Why is management's involvement so important? Because management must:

▷ Manage and lead the service quality effort.

▷ Set an example for their employees.

▷ Review the results of quality reports.

▷ Recognize and reward employees for their efforts.

Managers should receive sufficient training in the elements of service quality so that they can begin to utilize the concepts themselves and train their own employees.

5 Motivate and train employees. Employees must also understand the role that service quality plays in their organization and be motivated to meet the standards. "Everyone must know what the quality standards are for their jobs," stresses Aubrey.

6 Create teams of employees to develop improvement projects. While many improvements in service quality can occur simply as a result of being aware of customer requirements, others require specific projects. That is, there are often things that get in the way of employees' meeting customer needs, roadblocks that they themselves are unable to remove on their own. "Significant strides in quality only take place project by project," points out Aubrey.

Employee teams can analyze and investigate problems, and develop, select, pretest, and implement appropriate quality solutions (with management approval).

7 Measure results. The only way you can be sure that you are conforming to your specifications is to measure them regularly, according to Aubrey. "Compare what is actually happening with what is supposed to be happening," he says. "If you find that you don't conform, it is necessary to take steps to assure future performance."

8 Reward performance. One of the most important ways to guarantee consistently improving performance is to recognize and reward individuals and groups who work diligently toward the standards that have been set. "This provides motivation for continued conformance, or for getting into conformance if standards are not being met," he explains. Examples of reinforcement programs at Banc One include:

↪ **For individuals:** "We Care" awards are given to employees who go above and beyond the call of duty.

↪ **For teams:** The "Best of the Best" award is given to the teams with the best projects.

↪ **For branches:** The "Best of the Best" award is given to the branch with the best service (as measured by overt and covert shopping programs).

↪ **For banks:** The "Chairman's Quality Award for Customer Service" is given to the best bank in the Banc One system.

NUMBERS TELL THE IMPROVEMENT STORY

Banc One's emphasis on improving customer service had led to a $6 million-plus savings and revenue enhancement per year by the time the program was in it fourth year. "These figures only take into account the measurable gains," points out Aubrey. "They don't take into account things like goodwill and additional market share."

Further signs of quality improvement come from customer ratings of level of satisfaction with bank service. Four years ago, between 75 and 80 percent said they were "satisfied" or "very satisfied." Today, that figure is between 95 and 96 percent.

In terms of the impact of improved quality of customer service on overall performance, Banc One compares its service levels with national data on other banks and is definitely "ahead of the pack," according to Aubrey. "In addition, the gap is widening. While most of the other banks are also improving service, we are improving it faster and better," he concludes.

PACIFIC BELL

When you're after customer input, why not go to the source? This company trained its customer-contact personnel to gather the information it needs to define quality.

Your company may offer the best service in the world. However, it will not be successful unless it effectively responds to customer needs and desires. After all, your customers ultimately decide what defines quality service. So it's best to get their input on what they really want, instead of trying to determine that on your own.

How do you define quality for a service company? At Pacific Bell (San Ramon, CA), quality is defined this way: "It is understanding who the customer is, what the customer requirements are, and meeting those requirements without error, on time, every time."

Certainly, a better definition for service quality would be hard to come by. Because, regardless of what your company may believe quality to be, it's the *customer's* opinion that counts in the long run. If your customers view your product or services as unsatisfactory, they will go elsewhere, and you'll lose business. It's as simple as that.

Clearly, the best way to find out what customers demand is to get the information "from the horse's mouth." How can you tap into that essential customer feedback? Pacific Bell has developed a way—and you can adapt it to assure quality in your own company's service or product.

FROM WITHOUT TO WITHIN

Until recently, Pacific Bell depended solely on formal market research and external customer surveys to tell it what customers wanted. These outside sources of information were helpful to a point; however, the company was missing out on a valuable *internal* source of customer information—namely, its own front-line employees.

To tap this source, the firm instituted a new program that requires customer-contact employees to seek out information on customer satisfaction and dissatisfaction. The resulting information is used by Service Quality Teams to implement new procedures that will provide improved products and enhanced services for customers.

"Recent research on customer needs and desires has changed our thinking about quality," says Michael Hager of the company's Planning Quality Staff. "In the service sector, the focus is on service performance and the critical role played by the people who are in contact with customers on a day-to-day basis. In many instances, these employees are in the best position to gather information about customer requirements. They make a large number of customer contacts and they have an intimate knowledge of the service processes."

THE PROGRAM, STEP-BY-STEP

To implement a plan like Pacific Bell's Quality Improvement Program, Hager explains that you must:

STEP #1: Listen to customers to discover their expectations and needs. Then determine how your processes affect the services provided.

STEP #2: Systematically document and organize what customers say about the service you provide.

STEP #3: Analyze customer comments to identify which problems occur most often and what services mean added value to the customer.

STEP #4: Involve Service Quality Teams in analyzing results as a starting point for evaluating company processes and procedures.

STEP #5: Change company procedures and processes to meet customer requirements and desires more effectively.

STEP #6: Utilize statistical process control tools to monitor changes in processes.

LISTENING TO THE CUSTOMER

At Pacific Bell, the telephone service representatives are in an ideal position for collecting customer comments. They work at desks where phones and data-entry terminals are readily available. This arrangement makes it easy for them to record information about customer perceptions of service. In addition, they are usually working with calls initiated by the customer; those customers who are involved in a transaction with the company often have definite feelings about the quality of service they are receiving or have received in the past.

Another advantage of using people from the business office environment is that they are close to others doing similar jobs; it is easier for them to maintain a team spirit, enthusiasm, and clarity of purpose.

"With office personnel, our data-gathering operation is completely transparent to the customers," asserts Hager. "The service representatives work within the bounds of normal phone transactions. This means that the employees are not asking extra questions as they would in a survey, but are more *actively listening* for added-value comments. They must not only focus on customer needs that are not being met but also on outstanding work that deserves recognition. This process, in itself, stops us from being on 'automatic' when we talk to customers.

"Outside service technicians also participated in data collection, but there was a lesser degree of success because they usually worked alone. As a consequence, they did not have the same group support structure. In addition, they were not as effective in recording customer comments during a transaction because of the face-to-face nature of their contacts. Notes taken after the completion of the service call often lacked the detail and accuracy required for quality data."

DOCUMENTING CUSTOMER FEEDBACK

Information received from customers doesn't have much value until it's been documented. At Pacific Bell, the documentation is selective. Comments that receive the most attention are those considered "significant." The company is primarily interested in expressions of either dissatisfaction or above-normal satisfaction. Routine comments are generally not recorded. Hager looks at customer feedback in terms of a normal curve like the one shown in Figure 6. The left tail of the curve represents customers who are dissatisfied. The right tail of the curve represents customers whose expectations were exceeded. The middle portion of the curve represents customers who completed a transaction without any significant issues or comments.

At Pacific Bell, the information collected by employees is organized in the following groups:

1 **Customer comments,** which are brief written summaries that describe what is creating "significant " satisfaction or dissatisfaction for the customer.

2 **Identifiers about the transaction,** such as the date of contact, the market segment, and the geographical location of the caller.

3 **Descriptive codes that classify the customer comments** by transactions, attributes, and products.

The coding is done by the person who originally records the comment, but the codes can create some problems, concedes Hager. "Coding can consume more time and effort than just writing down the comments. Having a coding scheme is essential, however, since our objectives include determining the relative frequency of various problems identified by customers.

"Having the coding completed by the person who

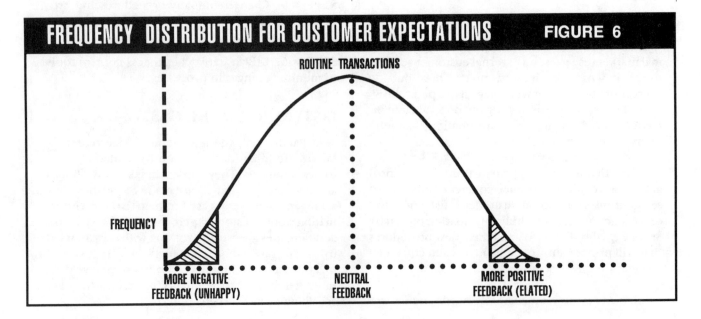

FREQUENCY DISTRIBUTION FOR CUSTOMER EXPECTATIONS **FIGURE 6**

ROUTINE TRANSACTIONS

FREQUENCY

MORE NEGATIVE
FEEDBACK (UNHAPPY)

NEUTRAL
FEEDBACK

MORE POSITIVE
FEEDBACK (ELATED)

speaks with the customer is important; only that employee can detect different nuances in the customer's voice. The observation of voice inflections can be an aid to accurate coding. As an example, some callers have a very accusing tone in their voices, even though the words they use are not that negative. These different tones, in addition to the words of the caller, will be used to identify whether the input is a suggestion, a negative comment, or a positive comment.''

☐ **Pacific Bell's Coding System** ⇒ The coding system itself covers four categories: attitude, transaction, product, and attributes:

➡ **Attitude Codes** are simple; the attitude of the customer is either positive or negative. Suggestions, however, have a classification of their own.

➡ **Transaction Codes** are more complex. They involve a set of codes that identify the type of transaction the customer is having with Pacific Bell, such as taking orders for service, sales activities, installing service, maintaining and repairing service, billing, providing information, or developing products and services.

➡ **Product Codes** are used to identify specific products/services associated with a transaction. Typical product codes for Pacific Bell include access and usage, features, network products, vendors, information services, and billing products.

➡ **Attribute Codes** are the most important in that they pinpoint specific characteristics of a transaction that caused the dissatisfaction or satisfaction. At Pacific Bell, they include:

✔ price/value or the reasonableness of prices

✔ accuracy of records, bills, and information

✔ reliability and a determination of whether everything was right the first time

✔ accessibility to the person who ultimately handled the call

✔ advocacy, or taking a personal responsibility for the customer's problem

✔ capability and competence of an employee

✔ communication, or providing the necessary information in a clear and understandable way

✔ courtesy and respect for the consumer

✔ credibility, including perceived honesty and truthfulness

✔ timeliness, which includes providing service at a time convenient to the customer

✔ product performance, in respect to the customer's needs and applications

''Successful application of the data collection system requires both initial training of participants and ongoing assistance,'' explains Hager. ''This includes both technical and motivational support.

''The initial data collection training is completed in three hours. After the employees have had an opportunity to experiment with the process, they begin to collect data. In addition, one-hour follow-up sessions are usually required. This procedure enables the workers to ask questions about the problem cases they have handled. It also enables management to demonstrate support after they have been collecting for a while.'' (A typical data collection form is shown in Figure 7.)

CUSTOMER SATISFACTION DATA COLLECTION   FIGURE 7

DATE: _____

Input Group _____ Customer Segment P G M R Telephone Number [   ] _____

Customer Comments _____
_____

Attitude POS NEG SUG _____ Type of Contact(Telephone is Default) I ___ (in person)

Product Code _____ Transaction OP ID MA BL IN DV XX

Coding Exception (No is Default) ___ Y ___ 1st Attribute _____ 2nd Attribute _____

Employee Comments _____
_____

ANALYZING THE DATA

Information on the data collection forms is entered into a mainframe computer (called the Customer Satisfaction Information System) that is accessible to virtually all employees involved in the project. They can use either Local Area Networks or dial-up links. The system uses the ORACLE™ relational database software that helps integrate the data with other sources of customer input. Employees can access the system using IBM personal computers or compatibles.

Data summaries and reports can be generated by the Customer Satisfaction Information System, based on the coding. "This allows us to digest large quantities of data," points out Hager. "We can also do an analysis of internal processes to determine underlying causes.

"Once a Service Quality Team gets the 'big picture,' they can get the details if they want to look at any issue that stands out. For their area of responsibility, they can even retrieve the complete customer comments related to specific issues that seem to warrant further analysis."

USING THE CUSTOMER-BASED DATA

"One successful application of the feedback system dealt with our appointment scheduling," recalls Hager. "One of our Service Quality Improvement Teams initiated a special study project. The initial analysis indicated that many customers felt we were missing commitment times. A review of the customer comments showed a problem with the way we explained our commitment times for installing telephone services.

"Changes in the wording of the service representative's script were developed by a group of service reps and managers. Then the team collected information to test for a change in customer reactions. The new data indicated that the revised script was effective in solving the time-commitment problem. So our customer feedback system helped us identify and resolve a 'real' problem."

CHANGES FOR THE BETTER

As problems are identified with either the products or the customer service, Service Quality Improvement Teams work on determining what should be done. Then they help implement the necessary changes across their geographic area.

When customers reveal that service is *worse* than their expectations, Cross-Functional Teams work to provide corrective action. Additional training, improved company procedures, new equipment, or other system improvements are considered and provided where necessary.

On the other hand, when customers consider service *better* than their expectations, the Servce Quality Team is responsible for reinforcing these areas of success to all employees. In addition, the team analyzes the areas in which service is considered outstanding to determine just what makes it so—and how similar techniques might be incorporated into procedures across the board.

LOOKING BEFORE YOU LEAP

Some crucial factors need to be considered before you can successfully implement a plan like Pacific Bell's Customer Satisfaction Program. Items to be considered include *planning, management support,* and a *conducive environment*.

Good planning, before the project is initiated, will reduce the overall cost of most programs. The cost of correcting problems found during planning is less than the cost of correcting problems found during implementation. For example, this system works best if you have a stable management team. If frequent changes are anticipated at a facility, don't implement this system until the organization has stabilized.

Also, management support is critical; few quality assurance programs will work without it. If management had not made computer facilities available and funded the extra cost of collecting data, the customer service project would not have worked, says Hager. Not all management support, however, needs to be financial.

The success of a feedback system requires simply that management provide a clear sense that the data are being used. Personnel involved in each phase of the operation have to feel that they are valued, integral members of a respected Service Quality Improvement Team.

HEWLETT-PACKARD COMPANY

You may have come up with what you think customers want from your company's product or service. But how do you compare your processes with customer needs to ensure a quality fit? This company has an approach that works.

Have you ever sat down with other people at your company to look for a better way to meet customers' quality needs, only to have been disappointed with the results? The reason for your disappointment may be that one important element was missing from the equation: your customers themselves. Listening to them is what provides real insight into meeting their quality requirements.

While Hewlett-Packard Company's Northwest Integrated Circuit Division (Corvallis, OR) is in business to sell chips to other divisions inside Hewlett-Packard (HP), it also serves customers outside of HP. The problem that it faced about five years ago, however, was that many employees either didn't know who their customers were or actually believed that the customers were interfering with them as they performed their work.

Fortunately, management saw the obvious need to address these problems. "We wanted our people to become very familiar with our customers and realize that they were here to serve those customers," says Casey Collett, Ph.D., Total Quality Control manager. "Our goal was to become so responsive to our customers that we would be the only supplier with which they would want to do business."

◗ **A Four-Step Process** ⇒ To meet that goal, the Division launched its Total Quality Control effort in 1983. Collett says it involves four steps:

STEP # 1. On your own, identify what you feel your major business processes are.

STEP # 2. On your own, determine how you are being measured by your customers.

STEP #3. Go out and verify these two perceptions with your major customers.

STEP # 4. Develop a program to improve these processes.

To execute these four steps, division management created a small group of TQC experts, who currently report directly to the division manager and work closely with a steering committee of top managers.

TQC members have expertise in manufacturing, teaching, statistics, and group facilitation. Together, the division quality and TQC departments attack customer satisfaction and internal process improvement issues, respectively.

The Division has also created a three-point TQC model, which has expanded to a seven-point model over the years. (See Figure 8.)

HP'S 10-STEP PLANNING PROCESS

The key to achieving TQC from the customer's point of view at HP is a 10-step business planning process pioneered by planning expert Scott Feamster. This process requires the division to understand and analyze each of the following:

1. Purpose
2. Objectives
3. Customers and distribution channels
4. Competition
5. Necessary products and services
6. Plans for necessary products and services (research, manufacturing, financial, and marketing plans)
7. Financial analysis
8. Potential problem analysis
9. Recommendations
10. Next year's tactical plan

The 10-step business planning process, then, is a systematic way of:

✔ understanding the business you're proposing to be in;

✔ understanding your customers' needs;

✔ understanding the market and competitive environment you're entering, and as a result of these understandings

✔ making solid, well-thought-out plans to meet your objectives.

"When you have developed your strategy, you should have an objective, methodical business plan that looks at what customers need and what you are going to do about those needs," says Collett. "Then you can take this document back to the customer and verify its accuracy."

A crucial element of making the 10-step business planning process work is what John Doyle, HP executive vice president for Systems Technology, calls "imaginative understanding of users' needs" (IUUN). "IUUN is becoming an integral part of how HP does business," Collett reports, adding that the philosophy of IUUN is to hear what customers say their needs are, and apply the creativity and knowledge you have to create solutions for customers.

QUALITY FUNCTION DEPLOYMENT

While IUUN is critical to the success of the business planning process, Quality Function Deployment (QFD) is critical to the success of IUUN. QFD is the philosophy of designing your processes in response to customer needs.

"Before QFD, we didn't always realize the importance of understanding customer needs," says Collett. "As a result, we often invented products that we thought people such as ourselves would want, instead of asking our customers what *they* wanted."

Currently, the Division uses QFD in its R&D and marketing areas. "It helps us find out what our customers need so that we can build these needs into the next generation of our products."

QFD's PLANNING MATRIX

One of the most important tools in QFD is the Planning Matrix. Once you know what your customers' requirements are, the next step is to translate these data into product development plans. The Planning Matrix plots customer requirements on one axis and business processes and their measures or product features on the other axis. The idea is to be able to determine the fit between customer needs and product features. "The Planning Matrix puts a lot more objectivity into the product development process," notes Collett.

◻ **Here's How It Works** ⇒ Down the left side of the matrix are rows of user needs. Across the top of the matrix are columns of product features. With the matrix, you can see where a row intersects with a column and, in that cell, ask yourself if there is a strong relationship, a weak relationship, or no rela-

tionship between what the customer requires and what your company is doing.

If you find no relationship on a highly rated need as ranked by the customer, then you need to look at your product design plan and address the problem, since the customer considers it important. Conversely, if you are building in steps in the design process that have no bearing on customer needs, you may be able to eliminate them. For example, you may be doing test procedures on something that the customer doesn't care about.

R&D then creates another matrix of customer needs by process control characteristics (or internal manufacturing control characteristics) that will have to be met in order to give customers the features that they want. In short, the system translates raw customer data into focused activities for helping Marketing, R&D, Manufacturing, and Quality to make the desired product a reality.

TWO MORE TOOLS FOR SUCCESS

HP uses two other tools to ensure that it is responding to the quality requirements of customers:

■ **Customer Quality Engineers** are electrical engineers who work with Marketing to gather customer data, and with R&D and Manufacturing to make sure customer issues are addressed. The task is not always easy. "Clients ask questions in their own terms," says Collett. Customer quality engineers thus need to translate these terms so that answers to their real, often unarticulated problems can be found. Then they need to translate the solutions developed by the Division back into language that the customers will be able to understand and utilize.

■ **Process Improvement Teams** attack customer issues throughout the Division's team concept. "A few of these teams interface so closely with customer divisions that they ask the customers to be on one of our teams," says Collett. "This certainly gives teams direct feedback from customers."

The teams solve customer problems and then return to customer locations to show them what they have accomplished. "The concept works well, because customers essentially drive the improvement process," she adds.

FOCUS ON THE FUTURE

Things *have* been improving. "Our quality is better, our planning processes are improving, and teams are busy with improvement projects,'' says Collett. ''Sales are up, but we never take customer satisfaction for granted. On an annual basis, we verify with our customers that our processes and the way we are measuring ourselves reflect customer satisfaction. We refine the measures more and more over time to make sure that they accurately reflect what the customer wants.''

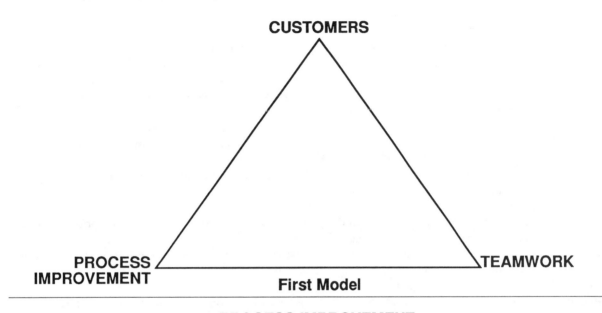

First Model

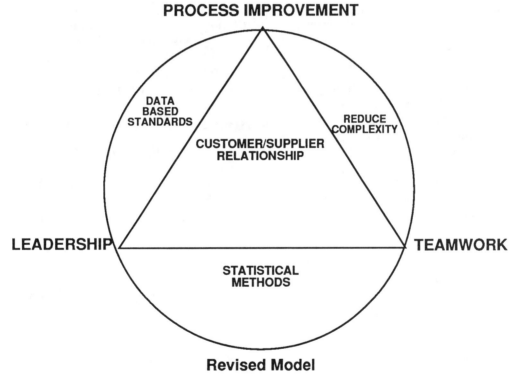

Revised Model

The <u>customer/supplier relationship</u> is central to the model. <u>Process improvements</u> occur through quality <u>leadership</u> and <u>teamwork.</u> Reducing complexity, setting <u>data-based (meaningful) standards</u>, and using appropriate <u>statistical methods</u> are the tools used to achieve the process improvements.

FIGURE 8

BANK OF AMERICA

Do your customers have a forum for speaking out? Bank of America's customers do. This institution shares its unique method for hearing what customers really want.

What better way to learn what your customers want than to hear them candidly discussing what they like—*and dislike*—the most about your company's product or service? The concept is simple, but the design and execution of customer panels require careful thought and planning.

HOW IT WORKS

At Bank of America, five or six customers are selected to represent a particular market segment (such as upscale customers or corporate clients) and brought together to form a panel. A senior manager moderates the discussion and accepts questions from the audience consisting of managers involved in some way in serving the market segment. The proceedings may be videotaped so that employees at lower levels can also benefit from the panel's comments. Action groups meet immediately after the discussion to plan changes along lines suggested by the panelists.

▷ **The Panel's Goal** ⇨ is to give your people the opportunity to hear directly what customers think about your organization, what they expect or need from it, and the extent to which you are meeting their needs.

"Customer panels enable people serving a customer group to step back from day-to-day transactions and take a look at how, as a company, you are serving the group," says Duane Heaps, a vice president at Bank of America (San Francisco) and manager in charge of the bank's customer panels. "Having real customers discuss actual experiences they have had with our company gives this program exceptional impact." The Bank of America program's purpose is summed up in its official name—"Place the Customer First Customer Panels."

WHAT TO EXPECT

Properly selected panelists will not hesitate to deliver hard-hitting feedback, both positive and negative. Here are a few examples from the bank's experiences, illustrating the range of points panelists have made:

➡ "Too many tellers are not interested in their jobs," an ex-customer complained. "I feel that they think I'm just another pair of hands with a bankbook. That feeling of not being important stays with you, even when you walk out of the branch."

➡ "We consider your account officer to be a member of our management team," the president of a contracting firm said. "An account officer must know the bank's products and our needs and make us feel that he or she is working for us."

➡ "Your collection of municipal bond coupons was too slow and too costly," said a chief financial officer. "So we dropped your service and simply started doing it ourselves."

➡ A Hollywood actor, now one of the bank's upscale customers, explained that he once left the institution, but was lured back when "two officers arranged to visit our home in the evening and talk about what was in my best interest to do with my earnings. My wife and I agreed that this advice and service were extraordinary."

DESIGNING THE PROGRAM

Chances are that your organization already uses panels of a different sort—focus groups—to involve customers in probing discussions of their wants and needs. How about letting your company's managers and executives observe these groups?

"Actually, this was our original idea," Heaps says, and we learned that it would be possible for a few of our senior people to watch focus groups through one-way glass. But we decided the scope was two-way communication. To really understand customers' needs and problems, we thought it was necessary for our people to ask questions and engage in real give-and-take with them."

Chances are that you, too, will have to create customer panels from scratch. Experience at the bank has shown that the person who runs this activity should be a manager who has a good grasp of your company's products and current customer service issues, and someone who can deal tactfully with dissatisfied customers, account officers, and senior managers.

COMPOSING A PANEL

The bank has conducted panels for mass market, upscale, small business/upscale, California corporate, and nationwide corporate customer groups (also termed market segments). Putting these panels together in a way that brings current customer service issues to life requires detailed planning.

As planning begins, the senior officer responsible for the bank's service to a segment works with Heaps to choose the criteria to be used in selecting panelists, focusing on these factors:

➡ **CUSTOMER STATUS:** Most panels include customers and ex-customers; some also include prospects. For example, a segment manager requested that one panelist be "a prospect, in a priority industry and currently with a major competitior." The overall goal, Heaps explains, "is to give our managers a realistic picture of each customer segment, including a range of experiences, viewpoints, and products used."

➡ **DEMOGRAPHICS AND PRODUCTS:** Senior officers are asked to specify the demographic factors they would like represented on a panel—e.g., age range of panelists, ratio of males to females, inclusion of minorities, selection of geographic regions and types of communities, and so on. Segment managers also indicate the types of products used by panelists.

➡ **BALANCE:** Panels that will be viewed by large numbers of employees should not tilt heavily toward either satisfied or dissatisfied customers. "A big audience will contain many people who have worked hard to please their customers, and these people can be demoralized if the panelists make only critical comments," Heaps cautions. Most of the bank's panels have included both satisfied and dissatisfied customers.

But Heaps adds that it could make sense to invite only unhappy customers if the audience is limited to a handful of managers—those who set policy and procedures for the market segment and can act to correct problems that the panel points out.

Planning the composition of a panel is a complex undertaking because so many criteria must be applied. To simplify the process, Heaps devised a one-page "panel planning worksheet" that enables senior officers to check off or write in all the factors they want represented on a panel. "This worksheet is quite valuable because it shows at a glance all the goals set for a particular panel, keeping planning on track," Heaps says.

RECRUITING PANELISTS

When a panel's desired composition has been spelled out, the next step is to find six people who fit the desired criteria, are dynamic and articulate, and are willing to participate.

You will probably have no trouble identifying dissatisfied mass market customers, since they write complaint letters to the president or branch manager, or satisfied customers, who can easily be found simply by asking managers for their names. But developing a list of unhappy corporate clients is more difficult, since account officers are not eager to advertise the fact that they have such customers. Heaps learns about dissatisfied corporate clients by calling section heads who supervise account officers; only then does he speak with the account officer.

When you have identified a customer who fits the desired criteria, the next step is a phone call to determine how candid, articulate, and forceful the person is. "This step is essential, because panels conducted before a large audience are a kind of theater," Heaps explains. "Panelist who are not dynamic will put the audience to sleep."

▷ **Screen Carefully** ⇒ To learn how a prospective panelist will come across, you have to call the person yourself. If you're looking for unhappy customers, never delegate this chore to an account officer, who may not fully appreciate the goals set for a panel and naturally will tend to select more or less satisfied customers.

"These calls must be handled with grace and sensitivity," Heaps points out. "You can't give people the impression that you are inviting them to appear on a panel, because you haven't decided that yet." Explain that you are talking with a number of potential panelists to learn more about their experiences as customers and to determine whether they might be interested in participating. When you have a clear idea of who is interested and what they could contribute, call each of them back to extend a formal invitation or explain that the person won't be needed on the panel.

BRIEFING PANELISTS

Once chosen, panelists must be briefed to ensure they understand the purpose and the format of the panel. Heaps sends a letter explaining what the panels are and encouraging panelists to "please be candid and straightforward in your remarks" and not pull punches.

He also asks panelist to be prepared with brief opening remarks covering:

- Who they are
- Where they're from
- Their background
- Description of their relationship with Bank of America or other banks
- General comments they'd like to make

The level of detail is strictly up to them—there is no need to reveal information they consider confidential.

Finally, he encloses two pages of sample questions that panelists might be asked. For corporate clients, they include:

- ★ What does our bank offer that keeps you as a customer?
- ★ Who do you think are the bank's toughest competitors?
- ★ If you were running Bank of America, what would you do to better serve customers like yourself?

CHOOSING A MODERATOR

Picking the wrong person to moderate is a sure way to destroy a panel's effectiveness. Your first choice probably will be the senior manager responsible for the market segment being discussed. But moderators should have the communication skills needed to ensure that important points are brought out clearly and that the discussion moves forward at a lively pace.

At Bank of America, some moderators are line executives in charge of the segment under discussion; others are drawn from elsewhere in the organization. One of the more successful panels was moderated by Ron Rhody, the senior vice president for Corporate Communications, who has never worked as a banker but possesses outstanding communication skills and extensive experience as a television and video moderator.

BRIEFING THE AUDIENCE

Now that you have your panelists and moderator chosen, the next step is to brief your audience. Like the panelists, the audience should be briefed in advance. Heaps briefs invited managers on paper, sending them a one-paragraph description of each panelist noting the nature of the panelist's business, the length of the panelist's relationship with the bank, and products the panelist uses.

Managers also get a copy of the sample questions, which serve as "pump primers" to start them thinking of questions they want to ask. "If there's silence when the moderator throws the meeting open to questions, it's deadly," Heaps says. "Pump priming helps, and I always ask one or two managers to be prepared to ask the first question."

POST-PANEL LUNCHEONS

Following each discussion, the panelists lunch with key senior managers responsible for the market segment and each panelist's account officer or branch manager. The luncheon is a way of thanking the panelists for their time and effort, and each receives an inexpensive but tasteful gift as an additional "thank-you."

At lunch, the senior managers can ask additional questions about issues that weren't fully explored during the panel.

The senior manager responsible for the market segment heads the small action team that meets immediately following the luncheon. Other team members are managers with the authority to make changes in policies and procedures affecting the segments.

An officer who took detailed notes during the discussions lists on a flip chart the main issues panelists raised, and members of the team are assigned to investigate or remedy each problem. For example, after panelists said that account officer turnover sometimes was a problem, proposed solutions included procedures ensuring that account officers would fully brief their successors on each customer's history and needs, then check back with customers to make sure the "handoff" went well. Designation of backup account officers was also proposed.

Audience feedback is worth noting. It would be a mistake to ignore the valuable contributions that audience reaction can make to follow-up efforts. The bank captures this reaction with an audience survey, produced on a "crash" basis to be on the segment manager's desk by the end of the day the panel meeting takes place. As they leave the auditorium, members of the audience turn in their surveys.

TERADYNE INC., ZEHNTEL SYSTEMS

Surveys are effective tools for gathering customer comments. Teradyne used a two-phased survey system to get to the heart of customer expectations.

It's one thing to be willing to make quality improvements, and quite another to know where to begin making those improvements. Sure, you can trust your gut instincts, but you will probably get better results if you turn to two sources of information that are at your immediate disposal: the people who work for your company, and the people who do business with your company.

When Zehntel Inc. (Walnut Creek, GA) launched its quality improvement program in 1980, the manufacturer of electronic testing equipment took about four years to reach its initial goals. But by late 1984, the company was asking itself, "Where do we go from here?"

"We knew that we could still improve, but the question was 'What needs to be improved?' " explains David Anderson, CPIM, systems manufacturing manager for the company, which is now known as Teradyne Inc., Zehntel Systems.

Around this same time, the electronics industry was in a slump, and the market had become extremely competitive. In the face of that competition, Zehntel knew that it had to continue the improvements it had begun in 1980 and "slingshot" past the competition to assume a leadership position.

Their first strategy, implemented in mid-1985, involved surveying company employees to find out what quality problems they perceived—both internally (in terms of problems they had with other departments and functions) and externally (problems they felt that customers had with the company).

Zehntel conducted in-depth interviews with the 50 employees in the organization who had the most contact with customers. These employees represented Sales, Manufacturing, Engineering, and Administration. "Each was asked what Zehntel was not doing well from a customer's point of view," explains Anderson. Employees answered a series of specific questions and also had the opportunity to add their own comments.

▭ **Survey Reveals Goals** ⇒ The survey took six weeks, and from it the company developed three goals:

GOAL # 1. Improve performance at every level of the organization so that any contact customers have with the company will reflect an attitude of pride in workmanship.

GOAL # 2. Ship every piece of electronic test equipment with zero defects in workmanship. Pay special attention to anything short of perfection.

GOAL # 3. Complete installation of the equipment at customer sites within one hour. Ship all appropriate parts and documents with the equipment and make sure that all accompanying electronics and software are in perfect working condition; the customer should be able to begin testing boards immediately after equipment installation.

In deciding what it needed to do to achieve these goals, Zehntel looked at a number of different options and opportunities for improvement. In some cases, subjective observations on the part of employees turned out to be inaccurate.

For example, many employees in Final Assembly complained that the quality of the parts coming from the subassembly department was below acceptable levels. But an analysis of this perceived problem indicated that quality was at the 99.8 percent level. "This study put that problem to rest," notes Anderson.

▭ **Ideas for Success** ⇒ However, other suggestions for improvement were implemented. For example:

► **Emergency Shipments.** A program was set up to ensure same-day shipments of spare parts to customers in emergency situations. The company met this goal the first year with two exceptions (one as a result of overseas paperwork complications, the other because the part ordered was incorrect).

► **International Shipments.** A program was also set up to ship all international shipments complete. Prior to this, such shipments were usually shipped partially (in two or more shipments). The company met this goal the first year with only one exception.

► **Pride of Workmanship.** Another program was created to have assembly employees sign off on their work before sending it to the next assembly stage. In this way, the company could trace any quality problems to specific employees. "In effect, this process called for each assembler to be his or her own inspector, and created a pride of workmanship that wasn't possible under the old procedure," says Anderson.

► **Employee/Customer Contact.** Another program allowed employees to visit customer locations to see how their products were used. These on-site visits let employees see firsthand how important product quality was to the individual customers.

► **Improved Support.** Another program was created to ensure that customers received their equipment instructions (manuals and magnetic tape) in prepackaged form for easier reference.

CUSTOMERS COME ON BOARD

Two years later, as a result of implementing the programs dictated by the first employee survey, the company had again improved its quality to the point that there seemed to be nowhere else to go.

Realizing that there are always opportunities for improvement, however, management decided to conduct another survey. This time, it included employees *and* customers. The process for surveying employees remained the same; but to survey customers, the company called 50 of them on the phone and asked them questions related to product and service quality.

One significant difference between the first and second surveys, Anderson found, was that while the first survey tended to focus on manufacturing issues, the second tended to focus on service issues. There seemed to be two reasons for this:

1 Most of the manufacturing issues (hardware quality, packaging, and so on) were addressed following the first survey.

2 Customers tend to rate suppliers' service issues (field repair, applications support, training, and documentation) higher than manufacturing issues.

The company also compared the results of the employee portion of the survey to the results of the customer portion of the survey. One interesting observation was that while employees ranked certain issues high in terms of importance and perceived customer satisfaction, customers ranked those same issues lower in terms of importance, and in some cases lower in terms of satisfaction.

Based on the second survey, Zehntel launched some additional improvement efforts. For example:

➡ Some customers complained that installations were not completely satisfactory. For instance, there might be screws or a supplementary cable missing, or doors might be dented.

More effort was placed on perfect installations, and the company was able to move from an 80 percent perfect installation rate to a 95 percent perfect installation rate. In addition, company representatives now call customers after installations to make sure that everything went perfectly and no problems were encountered.

➡ Other customers recommendations turned out to be opportunities for Marketing. For instance, many customers stated that they would like additional software updates. Others asked for additional documentation features such as indexes. Still others suggested new products.

Marketing has taken all of these requests under consideration and is now better able to understand and meet customer needs over the long term.

Focus on continuous improvement—Zehntel's survey process has been so successful that the company now plans to conduct one every two years. The next survey is expected to bear even more fruit and ensure that the company continues to meet customers' product and service quality requirements.

PITNEY BOWES BUSINESS SYSTEMS

" I f you work to meet your customers' expectations, you will almost always exceed your own," says this vice president of Quality. And his company uses a four-pronged approach to finding out what those expectations are.

"Once you meet customer expectations, you don't have to keep changing things internally to try to meet your own expectations," says Gerry G. Lenk, vice president of Quality for Pitney Bowes Business Systems (Stamford, CT). "You can do the right things the first time based on what customers tell you they need and want."

While many companies report that they listen to customers, not all of them take it beyond that point. "You not only need to find out their requirements, but you must drive those requirements all the way down through the design cycle into specifications on every part that goes into your products," Lenk emphasizes.

FOSTERING FEEDBACK

Pitney Bowes uses a variety of methods to remain constantly updated on what customers are interested in. These include:

1 **Focus Groups.** These groups are coordinated by interdisciplinary teams of employees representing Engineering, Marketing, Sales, and other departments. On occasion, line employees and outside consultants will take part. Members go through intensive product training in order to gain a full understanding of the products when they facilitate the focus groups, and also receive training in group process so that they can lead the meetings effectively.

When do these groups swing into action? When the company perceives a need to get customer feedback, it schedules a number of focus groups around the country to discuss the topic under consideration. "We don't just have one or two groups," notes Lenk. "We want to obtain reliable readings, and we don't want geography to sway our results."

How many people are involved? The number—both in terms of membership in individual groups as well as the total number of groups around the country—varies depending on what the company is trying to learn. "For example, if we are designing a new product and have three or four possibilities for human engineering issues—and want to find out which ones customers like—we will estab-lish as many groups as we feel we need to get reliable information." The company arrives at that number by using statistical analysis to ensure that they will achieve between an 80 and 90 percent confidence factor.

Who are they? To get participants for the groups, the company asks its approximately 100 district sales offices to invite customers *and* noncustomers (prospects) to join in. "We find that most people we ask are usually very willing to participate, because they appreciate the fact that we are interested enough in their needs to ask them what they want," says Lenk.

Focus group teams prepare for the meetings so that they know exactly what issues they want to address and how they will keep the meetings focused on these issues. "Unless we hold to our agendas, we can end up talking about all kinds of different things, and that defeats our purpose for getting specific information on certain products or ideas," says Lenk.

Possible questions for focus groups include:

➠ What are your current needs?

➠ What will your future needs be?

➠ What are the differences between your wants and your needs?

Team members may also ask participants about their level of awareness of the company's product line, how satisfied they are with the products, and what new trends in customers' businesses relate to the product lines manufactured by Pitney Bowes.

As an example of a current topic the company is addressing in focus groups is its postage-by-phone system, which allows users to reset their postage meters by phone. "We are asking customers and prospects how we can make this system more responsive to their needs," says Lenk.

In this and all other focus group meetings, team members transfer information back to the participants to make sure that it is accurate. "We are also considering starting a newsletter to send to former focus group participants to let them know what has transpired as a result of their information and how their input has helped us meet their needs better.''

2 Sales Department Feedback. In addition to getting information directly from customers and prospects in focus groups, Pitney Bowes also has a mailing advisory council composed of salespeople from around the country who meet with the company's marketing and engineering people to further communicate customer needs that they have heard while on calls.

3 Customer Surveys. Every six months, the company sends out formal customer satisfaction surveys. ''In June, for example, we sent out 11,000 questionnaires and asked customers how satisfied they were with our products and services,'' says Lenk. The questionnaires asked, among other things:

➡ How satisfied are you with the experience you have had with our salespeople?

➡ How satisfied are you with our ability to deliver products on time?

➡ What do you think of our product features?

➡ How reliable are our products?

➡ What is your degree of satisfaction with the service experience you have had from our organization?

➡ Does our value match our price?

➡ What do you think of our billing system?

➡ What do you think of Pitney Bowes as a company overall?

➡ As a company, how responsive are we to your needs?

4 Telemarketing. Pitney Bowes' telemarketing department also conducts research with customers and prospects on what their interests, needs, and wants are. ''This group also educates them about the services and products we have,'' adds Lenk.

AREAS OF OPPORTUNITY

Through its constant contact with customers and prospects, Pitney Bowes has found new areas of opportunity for improving the quality of its service and products. For example, as a result of information obtained through focus groups and customer surveys, it was found that there were some misunderstandings about the company's billing system. ''We realized that it needed to be defined more clearly, so we changed the format of our meter rental invoice,'' explains Lenk.

Another example is the creation of Access, a computerized information dispatch system linking the company with customers around the nation. The system was developed after surveying customers about service a few years ago. ''A customer who has a problem can now call an 800 number for service,'' reports Lenk. ''A dispatcher will gather all of the necessary information and dispatch it to the appropriate service person in the field. The system ensures that we meet our service response time and that we send the person who is most capable of performing the necessary service.''

And what does the future hold for Pitney Bowes as far as customer-driven quality improvements are concerned? ''While we are always interested in customer input, we are going to concentrate additional effort on getting input from prospects. This allows us to meet the needs of even more people,'' says Lenk.

ARBOR, INC.

Researching both external—and internal—customers is critical to your quality assurance effort. This company advises using a "customer quality window" to help get a handle on these customers' needs.

Statistical process control (SPC) has become a well-known tool in the quality assurance field, and Taguchi methods may be right on the cutting edge, but *customer research* could be the quality wave of the future.

"It's often overlooked, and very, very important," maintains David Saunders, director of Consulting and Training for Arbor, Inc. (Baltimore, MD). "By using customer research, you'll be able to pick quality improvement projects based on what the *customer* wants. In the past, most people involved in quality improvement projects would sit in a closed room and *they* would decide what the customer wanted and, by extension, what to work on."

Saunders points out that in his lectures to the Japanese in the 1950s, Dr. W. Edwards Deming himself emphasized how crucial it was to conduct "vigorous" customer research. "We usually just think of SPC in connection with Dr. Deming, but customer research was an integral part of his work," Saunders notes.

EVERYBODY HAS A CUSTOMER

An increased emphasis on customer research does not apply simply to external customers, but also to internal customers. Saunders' company explains it this way:

Every person, in every department, and at every level, has a customer. The customer is anyone to whom an individual provides service, information, support, or product. The customer may be another employee or department (internal) or outside the company (external).

So now that you know who the customer is, how do you go about conducting customer research? Saunders is quick to point out that "customer research" does not consist of sending out paper-and-pencil surveys to a hundred people in the hopes of getting a 10 percent response. In fact, he discourages employing this method for the following reasons:

● The questions usually aren't clear enough.

● The questions aren't tested.

● The sampling is not scientific.

● Conclusions drawn from the 10 percent who respond can be totally misleading about the 90 percent who don't respond.

Instead, Saunders advocates interviewing customers either in person or over the telephone. This method is based on the prevailing Japanese "hands-on" approach to customer research. The idea behind it is to stay tuned in to what your customers' specific thoughts, feelings, and impressions are concerning your product so that you can anticipate, identify, and resolve problems before they become serious—or before minor problems produce serious consequences, such as being dropped in favor of a supplier who does a better job of meeting customers' specific needs.

With that type of motivation in mind, how many customers should you interview? "More data is always better than less data," says Saunders. As a practical matter, however, he recommends holding 20 interviews.

"With SPC, you don't calculate upper and lower control limits until you have 20 data points, as a general rule of thumb. If you can get 20 interviews total, that's great." However, if you can't get twenty, get ten, he recommends, or five or even three. Even from a few interviews, recurring problems and specific areas of concern can become very clear.

Okay, then, exactly how do you conduct the customer research you need to focus quality improvement efforts? Saunders suggests that you follow this outline:

STEP I:
PLAN YOUR STUDY

A. Identify your customers. Although companies generally think of their customers as one large group, they really aren't, explains Saunders. Like a political candidate's constituency, they fall into different categories—each with its own unique concerns. That's why Saunders recommends beginning by doing a segmentation study; that is, dividing your customers into meaningful segments.

To illustrate how important this can be, Saunders refers to the experience of some SPC instructors who came to a workshop he taught on doing customer research. "They realized that their customers consisted of hourly workers, supervisors, and top management. So they served three segments who were very different from one another and who had very different needs."

Doing this segmentation made these instructors realize that they needed to design different training modules for each customer segment. The training modules for hourly workers were very different from the ones that would work for supervisors, and the modules for executives also needed to be tailored exclusively to that group.

Saunders cites another instance in which a team of designers learned that their engineers could be divided into three different customer groups:

► **"Heads in the clouds."** This group was difficult to satisfy, the designers determined, because they were not very concerned with engineering principles. They just said, "Here's this idea; do the drafting and build it for me." This group tended to come from academia.

► **"Feet on the ground."** From the suppliers' perspective, these were the preferred customers. They understood engineering principles, worked closely with the designers, and were helpful to the supplier. This segment tended to come from industry.

► **"Micromanagers."** These were engineers who would look over the designers' shoulders and drive them crazy. This segment tended to come from either of the other two categories, but negative experiences had resulted in their becoming micromanagers.

"This team of designers had certain improvements in mind, but they realized that one of the major improvements would make one segment happy and make the other two segments mad," says Saunders. "Consequently, they had to rethink their strategy. So just by doing the segmentation—before they even asked a question—they realized that the solution they had to a particular problem was not going to increase customer satisfaction."

B. Pinpoint what you want to know. This involves brainstorming, according to Saunders. Ask yourself the following questions about each group of customers:

► What do I want to know?

► What do I care about?

► Where is there a problem?

STEP II: COLLECT YOUR DATA

"An interview is basically a conversation with a purpose," states Saunders. "It's something that we all do. For example, when we go out to buy a car, we may interview our neighbors, friends, or relatives. We ask how they like a particular car or if they had trouble with it. Then, when we go to the car dealer, we interview the salesperson (who also interviews us). So we all know how to ask questions, probe, and gather information. We just don't think about doing it in structured way."

Before you or your staff actually go out or get on the phone to conduct interviews, however, you'll need to develop an interview guide that that lists the questions you want to ask. That way, if five people go out to separate locations, they will at least be gathering the same type of information.

To this end, Arbor has developed a model called the Customer Window^{SM} (see Figure 9). It provides a good place to start in developing your interview questions. Saunders illustrates the usefulness of this model, which involves the Department of Defense (the customer) and a defense contractor (the supplier). In response to the questions inherent in the Customer Window^{SM}, the customer pinpointed the following information:

★ **What we want and don't get:** "We want access to the right people in your organization, and a better understanding on your part of the way our organization operates."

★ **What we want and do get:** "Once we identify the right people, you are responsive and we get enthusiastic support from you. Also, we can see that you're an organization that responds to change, and we like the quality of resources available through you."

★ **What we don't want but get anyway:** "We get multiple and conflicting points of contact from you. Also, you give us good ideas, but you don't back them up. Sometimes you give us canned pitches for new products, and we don't like that."

★ **What we don't want and don't get:** The customer had no comment.

Saunders also stresses the importance of carefully designing the sequence of your questions. "You need to start with broad, open-ended questions at the beginning, then move on to the more specific questions, and get to the threatening questions at the end. Don't ask your threatening questions at the start," he warns. That will turn people off and thwart any meaningful communication right from the outset. Threatening questions include asking people their salary, about political issues within their company, or about something that made them angry.

Saunders offers a few pointers to follow while actually conducting the interview:

✍ **Take notes.** You may want to take very brief notes during the interview, then flesh them out afterwards. The reason for this approach is that you don't want your note-taking to interfere with your ability to take in what is being said.

✍ **Listen actively.** Listening is not a passive activity. To get the most out of an interview, listen carefully to what your customer is saying, ask probing questions, and paraphrase him or her to make sure you fully understand what was said.

STEP III:
CHECK YOUR RESULTS

Instead of jumping right in to take action upon completing your interviews, spend some time thinking about the results, urges Saunders. "Apply other methods to your findings, such as cause-and-effect analysis. Also brainstorm to make sure you're on the right track, and discuss the results with other people in your department."

STEP IV:
A QUALITY IMPROVEMENT PLAN

On the basis of your findings, determine what quality improvement area is the most important for you to focus on, then develop and implement a plan of action to deal with it. The Customer Window℠ provides a direction for quality circles, for instance, or can help focus the efforts of a quality improvement team.

LONG-TERM PROSPERITY

Granted, getting in tune and staying in tune with your customers is going to take time and resources; at the very least, you will have to train your staff in how to conduct effective interviews. But if you make the effort, what results can you expect from conducting customer research? Saunders says to expect that:

● Your customers will be happy.

● Your company will thrive.

● You'll achieve better internal coordination.

● Your organization's employees will be happy.

● You'll have less work.

In today's world, being right on target when it comes to meeting customers' needs has become increasingly more crucial. That means that the role you play in your organization is even more vital to its success. So as Saunders puts it, "Study your customer and prosper!"

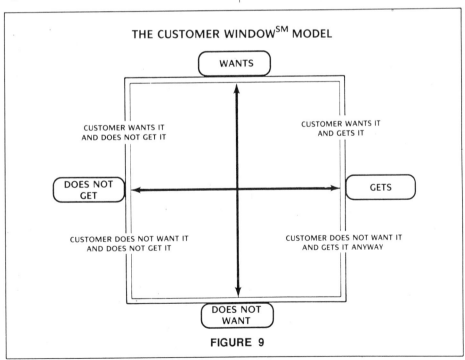

THE CUSTOMER WINDOW℠ MODEL

WANTS

CUSTOMER WANTS IT AND DOES NOT GET IT

CUSTOMER WANTS IT AND GETS IT

DOES NOT GET

GETS

CUSTOMER DOES NOT WANT IT AND DOES NOT GET IT

CUSTOMER DOES NOT WANT IT AND GETS IT ANYWAY

DOES NOT WANT

FIGURE 9

115

ASSURING VENDOR/SUPPLIER QUALITY

Assuring the quality of incoming materials is a logical—and necessary—way to assure the quality of outgoing products. Get vendors/suppliers on your quality team by working closely with them. Also, determine which ones you should be relying on, and which are less than quality conscious.

CIBA-GEIGY

Wouldn't it be great if you could be so certain of your vendors' quality that you could forgo incoming inspection? CIBA-GEIGY has a multidepartmental approach to vendor quality that allows it to do just that.

At CIBA-GEIGY's Suffern, NY, pharmaceuticals manufacturing plant, a vendor certification program is having significant impact on productivity and cost efficiency in at least three major areas: Warehousing, Purchasing, and Quality Control.

"We are in the final stages of a year-long process of working out a vendor certification program with a major supplier of a chemical we use in high quantity. They are now our primary supplier of this chemical, of which we use many tons a month," explains Bob Tice, assistant director of Quality Control. "The program is enabling us to rely on their test results to make sure the incoming raw material conforms to our quality standards. The program has already enabled us to eliminate some of our testing stages, facilitated a good deal of our materials handling, and resulted in favorable contract terms."

CERTIFICATION BEGINS WITH EVALUATION

Vendor certification—that is, agreeing to give one company the majority of your business for a particular supply and trusting that its test procedures are as stringent as your own—requires first of all a very complete evaluation of that vendor.

One of the first things that CIBA-GEIGY did in evaluating the particular company with which it is establishing the vendor certification program was to check its own records of the quality of the supplier's products. "We found they had an excellent track record with us in terms of the integrity of their products," says Tice.

Next, CIBA-GEIGY held several meetings with executives of the vendor company. These meetings were designed to fully acquaint the vendor with the criteria CIBA-GEIGY has established for its vendor certification program. These criteria include evaluation of the vendor's laboratory facilities and manufacturing process. The meetings also covered contract and materials handling issues, such as warehousing and cost-efficient lot sizes.

Once preliminary agreement had been reached on the contract issues discussed, a team from CIBA-GEIGY visited the vendor's facilities and inspected its laboratory. The team included quality control, purchasing, and warehousing executives.

"They looked at the qualifications of the people performing the laboratory tests, their training, their equipment, and their information systems," explains Tice. "They evaluated the accuracy of their data and their laboratory procedures. They also looked at equipment calibration, standard solution logs, and retention practices (whether samples of material produced were retained for the length of time required by industry standards).

"This company had the type of records and controls we required in order to certify a vendor. Both their laboratory and manufacturing procedures were at very high levels."

OUT GOES INCOMING INSPECTION

Once a supplier has been evaluated, you can move forward with certification of those who do appear able to meet your standards. When you do, you'll probably see immediate benefits, especially in the area of incoming inspection.

"Up to this time, we had always done our own extensive testing of incoming raw materials," explains Tice. "We can now rely more heavily on suppliers' Certificates of Analysis (COA) for incoming raw materials. This means that they test samples of the particular batch of material they will be shipping to us. They then send a quantity of that sample to us and we repeat the test in our own laboratories.

"What we have been able to eliminate so far is an additional test we previously did once the regular truckload shipment arrived at our site. We no longer test their truckload deliveries of this particular chemical, and we intend to eliminate testing of the samples as well, when the program is finalized."

EVERYBODY STANDS TO GAIN

The quality department isn't the only function that can expect to see real benefits from a vendor certification program. However, Tice says, you must be willing to put something in if you expect to get anything out.

◻ **Program Requirements** ⇒ "A good certification program requires close coordination of departments, such as Quality Control, Purchasing, and Warehousing," he explains. "It also requires the cooperation of Manufacturing, which ultimately benefits by having more immediate access to materials.

"In terms of favorable contract negotiations and labor, the program offers substantial productivity benefits. Simplification and facilitation of QC testing procedures, for instance, have ramifications for Warehousing, such as reduced labor and improved inventory levels. And more favorable contract terms directly affect a company's bottom line, which is Purchasing's direct contribution.

"Such a program does take a good deal of time to establish, however. And a company must evaluate the vendor it chooses for the program very carefully, making sure their quality standards are compatible with the company's," Tice concludes.

GENERAL ELECTRIC COMPANY

GE's Appliance Division shares its "Three C's" of supplier quality. Put them to work, and you may see a dramatic improvement in the goods you receive from vendors.

If you're having problems with supplier quality, you know how difficult it is to get them under control. But if you had a plan of attack for improving supplier quality, you'd probably be a lot better off than companies that are just floundering their way through. Here's a three-pronged attack you may be able to adopt or adapt for your own supplier quality needs.

As manager of Purchased Material Quality for the Appliance Division of General Electric Company (Louisville, KY), Ron Lazas is keenly interested in what it takes to develop cooperative, mutually beneficial relationships with suppliers—relations that lead to constantly improving quality. Over the years, Lazas has come to believe that the key to success with supplier quality lies in a three-pronged philosophy: commitment, communications, and control.

Here's how it breaks down:

1 **COMMITMENT.** There are two components to this commitment. The first, called the strategic component, encompasses approximately 20 percent of commitment.

Strategic Commitment—This must come from supplier top management, filtering down through the organization and ultimately moving out to the customer—in this case, General Electric. This component addresses meeting customer expectations, setting goals based on customer needs, communicating these goals to employees, and monitoring results.

Functional Commitment—This encompasses approximately 80 percent of the commitment. This is the "bottom up" commitment, which starts with the last person in the supplier's organization who touches or processes the product before it goes to the customer.

▭ **Required Element** ⇒ "If this lower level commitment is not there, the whole effort will fail," emphasizes Lazas. The challenge for supplier management, he says, is to nurture this bottom 80 percent.

Lazas adds that there are three other important things to remember about commitment:

1. *Commitment requires that everyone in the supplier organization be committed to the next user.* That is, each employee's customer is the next employee in line. "As such, the goal is to work toward the expectations of the next user, until the product or service ultimately reaches the final customer," says Lazas.

2. *Commitment should be measurable.* Lazas advises against trying to measure each employee's actions on a daily basis. "Instead, look at long-term measures, such as customer complaints, product returns, and field service calls."

3. *Commitment takes time to build.* It is not an instantaneous change; it may take years, in fact.

2 **COMMUNICATION.** As Lazas sees it, there are three elements to communication. First, it must be two-way—supplier to customer and vice versa. And Lazas emphasizes the importance of *equality* in this two-way communication. What does this mean?

"The customer is not always right," he answers. "We, as the customer, must realize that the experts are our suppliers. Just because we design parts that we think will work well in our applications doesn't mean that we understand the implications of these designs for our suppliers." Therefore, it's important to get suppliers involved up front and to learn from them so that the part designs are as cost-effective as possible.

Lazas' next point is that communication must be structured. There must be a starting point and an ending point. For example, GE's Appliance Division has a 15-step structured program for qualifying suppliers called "Quality: A Call for the Best." Both GE and its customers know where each is in the program and what is expected of the other at each step.

Finally, Lazas says, communication must be timely. It does no good to wait for disaster to strike before beginning to communicate. It must be continuous and be focused on discovering problems early to prevent them from having significant impact.

3 **CONTROL.** Once commitment and communication are in place, suppliers can then set up the controls necessary to guarantee that their processes are meeting customer expectations. While this may sound like a job for SPC to you, Lazas has found that control requires more than SPC alone.

"You may be able to control your processes with or without SPC," he notes. The key to control is not the statistics: Control must be proactive and continuous. The idea is for suppliers to take customer specs, be aware of limitations in their own processes, and then control those processes so that variability is minimized. "When suppliers do this, they will have the results that will give them the kind of control they need," Lazas emphasizes.

THE THREE C'S IN ACTION

Contrary to what many quality professionals may believe, Lazas has found that success in supplier quality comes from concentrating primary efforts on the suppliers' employees, with secondary efforts focusing on supplier management. He recommends that you shine the spotlight on supplier employees in several ways:

❏ **Visiting With Suppliers' Employees** ⇒ When customers visit suppliers to assess their capabilities, they usually spend most of their time with top management, being told how committed the suppliers are to quality and cooperation. Next, they are whisked through the plants for brief tours, and may end up the day in a dinner meeting with the supplier's top management.

"There is little, if any, time to talk to the 80 percent of the people who really make things happen—the employees," says Lazas. So when he and other GE representatives visit suppliers, they insist on taking the time to talk to employees. They want to know what employees think about their jobs, the products they make, their customers, and the role of commitment in their jobs.

"We want to find out if the employees are really committed to producing what we want, or whether they are only '8 to 5' people who come to work and go home," he explains.

How do suppliers' managements react to GE's request to speak with employees? One might think that they would be reluctant to let customers talk to line employees. To the contrary, however, Lazas has found that most suppliers' managements are happy to have GE representatives talk to their people. Why is this so?

"Supplier managements try very hard to communicate to their employees that their primary responsibility is to meet customer demands," replies Lazas. "However, it is often difficult to get this message across to employees."

When employees have the opportunity to talk directly with the customer, however, the message takes on new meaning—and has much more impact. "Actually, we have found very few '8 to 5' employees during our visits to suppliers," reports Lazas. "Almost all of the employees we meet want to do a good job and are very receptive to what we have to say."

Incidentally, there are also opportunities for reciprocal visits. Suppliers of critical components are often invited to send their employees to GE's Appliance Division plants to meet with GE hourly workers and see firsthand how their products are used. "Every quarter we bring in employees from six or seven different suppliers for these visits," says Lazas.

❏ **Training Suppliers in Quality Skills** ⇒ To date, the Appliance Division has trained over 500 suppliers in SPC and other quality improvement methods. The key focus of the training is on process control and problem-solving techniques.

"Engineers and managers can make good guesses at what problems are occurring on the line, but the ones who really know are the employees," says Lazas. "When you give employees the tools they need to control their own processes, they begin to feel in control of their jobs."

❏ **Awards—Credit Where It's Due** ⇒ It is not uncommon for customers to bestow awards on suppliers who consistently meet high standards of quality, delivery, and service. GE Appliances, however, takes a slightly different approach to these awards.

Rather than provide awards to supplier management, the company recognizes the supplier's *employees*. "We ask that the employees responsible for producing our parts be assembled, and we make a 30-minute presentation to them," says Lazas. "We find that we get very enthusiastic receptions from them, and the award ceremonies motivate them to do even better jobs."

And how have suppliers responded to this increased focus on the quality of the parts they supply to GE? "Two or three years ago, our best suppliers still came from the Far East," notes Lazas. "Today, our domestic suppliers are as good as—and in some cases better than—Far East suppliers in controlling their processes."

That's good news for GE—good news that takes tangible form on the company's 99.2 percent lot acceptance rate for *all* material the division receives. This translates into fewer line rejects and the opportunity to take fuller advantage of automated production.

In addition, service calls have been cut significantly in the last nine years. Many of those calls were related to defective parts received from suppliers, so improved supplier quality has contributed substantially to the reduction in this area.

The improved quality has also allowed the division to implement a "Satisfaction Guaranteed" program, which gives customers the opportunity to return any GE appliance (except air conditioners, which have seasonal use) within 60 days for any reason—no questions asked—for a full refund. "If we had the quality levels that we did eight or nine years ago, there is no way we could make a program like this work," concludes Lazas.

FLORIDA POWER & LIGHT

A s you know, it takes quality resources to provide a quality product or service. Here, Florida Power & Light explains the workings of its Vendor Quality Improvement Teams and Quality Vendor Process.

Every company has its own reasons for putting a renewed emphasis on improving quality. But no matter what the individual reasons are, almost every firm finds that it can't really make headway unless it focuses at least part of its improvement effort on the area of vendor quality.

Challenges during the 1970s caused Florida Power & Light (FPL) (Miami) to take a new look at the way it did business: Fuel costs were rising, inflation was out of control, there was a need for large capital expenditures, and customers were demanding higher levels of service. In addition, by the time the early 1980s rolled around, FPL realized that the deregulation taking place in the telephone and airline industries would likely not stop there; utilities might be targeted for deregulation, and there would undoubtedly be competition for electric service.

For these and other reasons, FPL launched a multipronged customer service improvement effort, a large part of which involved improving quality. The effort, called the Quality Improvement Program, covers a number of elements, including vendor quality improvement. Approximately 60 percent of the company's $2 billion revenues are spent for materials and services from vendors, so this area was ripe for improvement.

A NEW APPROACH

FPL issued its new procurement policy in late 1985, explains Carlton Hopkins, project general manager for Vendor Quality Improvement. That policy reads, in part: "[FPL will] seek, develop, and maintain a long-term business relationship with vendors who, by virtue of their management philosophy and practice, ensure that a quality product or service is provided."

With the new policy in place, the next step was the creation of a Vendor Quality Improvement Program (VQIP), which was launched in 1987. A Vendor Quality Improvement Team was created to analyze the company's procurement processes, and to develop strategies to improve these processes.

"This team was composed of representatives from a number of functions and divisions in FPL—nuclear power plants, fossil power plants, transmission/distribution, engineering, and staff groups," says Hopkins. The team proposed a number of specific action plans, for which individual teams were created to develop and pilot eight specific improvement projects.

"Some of the Vendor Quality Improvement Team members became members of the eight project teams, but the majority of the project teams were composed of all new members from the appropriate disciplines," he notes.

No matter the topic, all of the teams followed this format when tackling their projects:

1. Define the problem with data.

2. Define the current situation.

3. Perform analysis using data to determine root causes.

4. Determine countermeasures.

5. Implement countermeasures.

6. Monitor results.

7. Standardize improved process.

▭ **How VQI Teams Work** ⇨ To better understand how the teams work (and, perhaps, to spark some ideas about where you can make improvements yourself), let's take a closer look at each of the eight teams and some of the topics they looked into:

➠ **Performance Specifications for Materials and Services.** This team was created to develop a process that clearly defines and communicates FPL requirements to vendors by refining specifications and defining specific acceptance and performance criteria. The team also worked toward encouraging vendor input at the early stages of the specification process and developing as much product standardization as was practical.

➠ **Life Cycle Cost.** This team was created to develop a methodology to identify and quantify costs as they relate to the total life cycle of the products

FPL purchases from vendors (such as cost of operation, maintenance, and failures). It then applied this information to the bid process to assure overall lowest cost purchases as opposed to lowest price.

➡ **Vendor Performance Measurement and Feedback.** This team was created to develop a system to measure vendor performance in the areas of quality, cost, delivery, safety, and responsiveness to problems. "The team also created a process to identify specific areas for improvement and provide feedback to vendors to ensure continuous improvement," says Hopkins.

➡ **Vendor and FPL Education.** This team was created to coordinate the communication of FPL's new procurement policy to employees and vendors, to review information produced by the other project teams and match them with the needs of vendors and FPL employees, and to develop educational materials to fill these needs. "This has involved orientation sessions for vendors as well as internal seminars on the VQIP," Hopkins explains.

➡ **Bid Evaluation.** This team was created to improve the company's bid evaluation process by optimizing the elements of quality, cost, delivery, and safety.

➡ **Vendor Audits.** This team was created to develop vendor self-evaluation guidelines, including vendor management's ability to understand and support quality improvement efforts. "In other words, instead of going over a checklist of items that vendors should have in place, we have the vendors review their own programs to determine where there are loopholes that need improvement," says Hopkins.

➡ **Vendor Payment.** This team was created to improve the timeliness of payments to vendors from FPL.

QUALITY VENDOR PROCESS

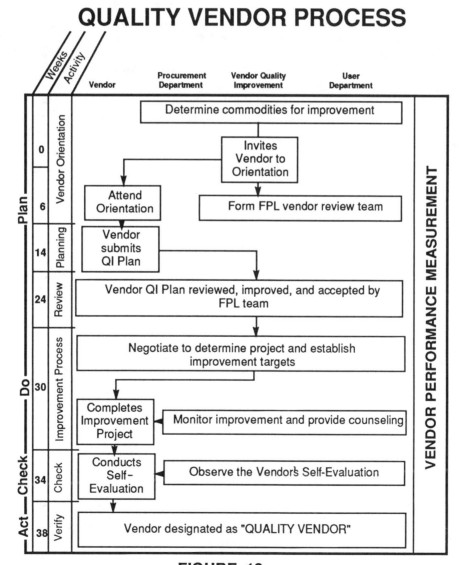

FIGURE 10

THE "VENDOR QUALITY PROCESS"

Florida Power is in the process of moving its vendors of key or critical parts through a three-phase improvement effort. The first level is "quality vendor," the second is "certified vendor," and the third is "excellent vendor."

"We have implemented the first level, are in the process of developing the second level, and are now developing criteria for the third level," reports Hopkins.

Thus, this eighth team was given the task of developing the first-level "quality vendor" process, which provides vendors with the opportunity to showcase their quality improvement efforts and therefore position themselves to participate in long-term business relationships with FPL.

"We look for vendors who are producing good products already and who are committed to quality improvement," says Hopkins. "We then ask them to attend an orientation session, where we give them an overview of quality improvement at FPL and what role they play in this process."

FPL then asks the vendors to describe in written detail what quality improvement activities they currently have in place, and indicate areas in which they would like to improve. Vendors work on these areas and report back to FPL with data on how they solved the problems or made the improvements *and* how their quality improvement programs were instrumental in these solutions or improvements. Finally, FPL asks to be invited to programs where the vendors critique their own projects and quality improvement programs. (A diagram of the process a vendor must go through to achieve "quality vendor" status is contained in Figure 10.)

The next level—"certified vendor"—will involve measuring vendor process capability. "We will look at specific characteristics and variables of products and ask vendors to use statistical process control to improve the processes which give rise to the characteristics and variables," explains Hopkins. Then, FPL and the vendors will derive measures of process capabilities to help vendors better control variation.

While Florida Power & Light's vendor quality effort is still relatively new, its Vendor Quality Improvement Teams are already producing encouraging results. "For example, our distribution transformer losses have already been reduced to zero," says Hopkins. And if the teams stay on the same track, the Vendor Quality Improvement Program is sure to be successful in the future as well.

AT&T

There's one school of thought that says it's better to work with a few dependable suppliers than to spread your business out between many different, less reliable vendors. AT&T describes its techniques for forging cooperative relationships with quality-minded vendors.

All too often, the supplier quality function within a company can be described as haphazard at best. Of course, it's much better to have a clear plan for supplier quality in place. That way, problem prevention can be practiced, and you can ensure that you would be getting the best possible quality from your vendors.

Today, AT&T is in the process of reducing its supplier base and actively involving the remaining suppliers in quality improvement and partnering activities, says Stephen E. Ford, senior consultant for AT&T (Allentown, PA).

These activities are the responsibility of commodity teams composed of representatives from Quality Assurance, Purchasing, and Engineering. These teams receive assistance from a number of quality assurance functions, and utilize a four-phase process to select the suppliers with which they will work most closely:

- **Phase I:** Identify potential suppliers.
- **Phase II:** Assess supplier capabilities.
- **Phase III:** Identify "approved suppliers."
- **Phase IV:** Identify "preferred suppliers."

"Our goal, again, is to do more business with fewer suppliers," says Ford.

THREE STEPS TO VENDOR QUALITY

The teams use a three-step approach when working with suppliers:

1 Vendor Quality Assessment. The goal of this step is to identify the right suppliers. Some tools the teams use to achieve this goal include:

- ► Vendor capability surveys.
- ► Vendor qualification programs.
- ► Engineering reviews (for specific technologies and products).
- ► Vendor quality evaluations. These evaluations, called "Quality System Audits," involve reviewing suppliers' quality systems and comparing them with AT&T's standard program to see if the suppliers meet the company's minimum requirements.

- ► Product approval. There are two types of product approval. One (which covers parts for which AT&T has internal specifications) is for coded specifications; the other (which covers suppliers' commercial parts and products) is for noncoded specifications. AT&T conducts lab tests to see if the parts and products meet its technical applications.

- ► Requalifications. "If products fail, if there are field problems, or if vendors make changes, we conduct requalification activities," reports Ford.

2 Vendor Quality Information. This involves getting the right information from suppliers so that the teams can make intelligent decisions about future business opportunities and potential rewards for the best suppliers. The teams rely on "quality activity reports" from suppliers in gathering their information.

"We have a data system where we input the various quality information from vendors into a computer base," says Ford. "The idea is to see if their products conform to our needs." The teams then rate suppliers in a formal rating system.

AT&T is also moving into a program in which suppliers will monitor ongoing reliability for the company, allowing AT&T to get predictions on failures (such as mean time between failures) earlier than before.

3 Vendor Quality Improvement. Once suppliers are selected, the teams work closely with them to help improve their quality levels. They engage in design reviews and specification reviews with the suppliers so that the suppliers can review the company's quality needs.

"We then get into the verification routine, where we 'baseline' their systems and track the changes that they make," he continues. By monitoring these changes, the company doesn't get surprised down the road with changes in supplier raw materials or manufacturing processes that might affect fit, form, or function of the parts they purchase from the suppliers.

''We also have structured vendor feedback meetings where we share quality concerns, engineering concerns, product information, purchasing information, and forecasting information,'' says Ford. The teams tell suppliers everything they need so that they can work with AT&T in a cooperative effort.

EVERYBODY LENDS A HAND

Assisting the commodity teams in working with suppliers are a number of people performing different quality assurance functions.

⊃ **Quality representatives:**

- ✔ conduct on-site quality program implementations
- ✔ handle process control reviews
- ✔ resolve customer complaints
- ✔ recommend cost reductions
- ✔ examine reports on production samples

⊃ **Field quality managers** (assigned to geographical areas):

- ✔ identify top suppliers in terms of quality
- ✔ collect and analyze quality data
- ✔ select suppliers for progression plans
- ✔ hold quality improvement conferences
- ✔ participate in quality systems audits

⊃ **Product consultants** (Ford's position):

- ✔ are assigned as the product quality contacts
- ✔ author quality programs specs and quality plans to manage the individual products through their life cycles
- ✔ track and promote uniform implementation of the programs on a worldwide basis (to ensure consistent treatment of all suppliers)
- ✔ provide training on product reviews and auditing techniques
- ✔ chair the quality program evaluations and quality system audits that provide suppliers with information on how they rank compared to AT&T's criteria.

One other tool AT&T uses to manage the supplier quality function is ''Quality Program Specifications,'' a set of customized product and process quality specifications designed to ensure that the company's quality needs are met continuously at the lowest possible costs. They are contractual documents covering:

- ⟾ activities and functions that are AT&T's responsibility
- ⟾ activities and functions that are the supplier's responsibility
- ⟾ quality expectations and requirements
- ⟾ sampling techniques
- ⟾ process control techniques
- ⟾ life and reliability tests to be performed
- ⟾ reporting guidelines and requirements

Is the plan effective? Numbers tell the story, says Ford. ''We currently have over 750 of these documents in place with our suppliers.''

STATISTICAL PROCESS CONTROL

Statistical Process Control (SPC) is a potent tool for zeroing in on the root cause of defects. And it can be used easily by everyone from workers on the line to vendors. But you need to see that SPC is implemented properly for maximum benefit, as these top companies have done.

CORNING GLASS WORKS

G iving employees full ownership of SPC is one big key to Corning's success with its statistical quality control effort. Learn how to get workers up and running with SPC.

As a quality professional, you know that achieving quality is virtually hopeless if production operators don't take the issue seriously. And one good way to ensure that they take quality seriously is to give them the bulk of responsibility for meeting quality standards.

"It's not a *program*," you emphasize to employees. "It's a *process*. Programs have beginning and ending points. This is forever!"

The employees smile at one another and nod in feigned approval and agreement. They have heard it all before. One of them leans over to a co-worker and whispers, "Sure, it's forever. It's forever until they get tired of it and start a new 'permanent' program. Or until the person who came up with it leaves, and we're back where we started again."

Such conversations—and attitudes—are unfortunately all too commonplace in U.S. workplaces. These workplaces are littered with the vestiges of "permanent" processes that management instituted over the years only to let them falter, slide, fail, and eventually die.

One place you won't encounter this type of environment, however, is at Corning Glass Works (Corning, NY), especially when it comes to quality improvement. Two cases in point are the company's statistical process control (SPC) and operator manufacturing control (OMC) efforts.

"In most companies, SPC programs have limited lifespans," observes Daniel H. Pearl, manager of Quality Systems—Ceramic Products. "The people who install the programs eventually walk away and things degrade to the way they were before. They were 'their' programs, and when 'they' left, no one else felt any ownership for them."

At Corning, management believes that operators should own their SPC processes because the operators, better than anyone else, know what is going on. "They know all of the things that they need to keep their processes running and all of the things that don't work," Pearl says.

In an effort to transfer responsibility for quality

to operators, Corning launched two separate—but simultaneous and synergized—programs. One was a traditional SPC program designed to give operators the tools for determining when the process was not in statistical control as well as the responsibility for taking the necessary corrective action. The other was an operator manufacturing control program designed to turn actual control of processes over to the operators and have them become their own inspectors.

STARTING OUT WITH SPC

The SPC effort was launched at one of the company's ceramic capacitor plants with a multitude of complex processes. A project team consisting of Pearl (as project manager), an experienced plant process engineer, a statistician, two technicians, and a data clerk began the effort by involving operators from the very beginning.

The first step was to create a "contract" with the operators to eventually transfer SPC ownership to them. "We made sure that the requirements of the contract were very clear and were understood fully by the operators, their supervisors, and their department heads," says Pearl.

▷ **Key Points** ⇒ The contract covered four key points:

1 It defined what "ownership" of the process entailed.

2 It outlined requirements for transferring ownership from the project team to the operators.

3 It detailed what constituted an operational system, training requirements, auditing, and certification of the operators.

4 It outlined what would be provided in terms of posttransfer support and provided for an external audit on a periodic basis to assure continuity.

The project team started with one department, implemented the strategy, and then moved to the next department. "We wanted to take it in small bites," explains Pearl.

But just how did the team go about meeting the

stipulations of the contract? There were a number of steps:

◻ **Determined Process Capability** ⇨ The first step was to determine the existing level of process capability. The team had a preactivity meeting with the operators to explain what would be required and how it would be accomplished. "We then solicited their input in terms of problems they were experiencing," says Pearl.

One of the problems raised by the operators in the first department dealt with the silver paste used on the ends of the capacitor chips. This paste allowed the capacitors to be impregnated with the electrode material. "It is a very critical step, because once you have a hollow chip, you need a medium to allow the electrode material to be impregnated," he explains.

Problems noted by the operators included:

✎ They often had to add solvent to the paste before it would work properly.

✎ The paste would often not work on one machine, but might work on another.

✎ The paste would not work regardless of what they did.

✎ The team asked the engineering department in the plant to address the problems reported by the operators. Concerning the silver paste, for example, Engineering made some interesting discoveries.

When they asked the supervisors how they handled the paste, some reported that they put the cans in a paint shaker for an hour. Others reported that they placed their cans in a shaker for half and hour and then put them on a series of rollers overnight to get the air bubbles out. Still others reported different preparation procedures.

It turned out that the shaft length of the stirrers on the silvering machines, that were used to keep the paste uniform, were not to print, so the cans were not getting the appropriate agitation. Stirrer speeds also varied. That is, a setting on one machine did not always produce the same rpm as the same setting on another machine.

As these and other problems were being solved, the team scheduled weekly status meetings with the operators to let them know what the engineers were finding and to get more feedback, ideas, and problems from the operators.

◻ **Provided Training** ⇨ Next, the team began to provide actual SPC training to the operators. The course was specifically geared to the operators, using real-life examples from their manufacturing processes.

◻ **Developed a Formal SPC Strategy** ⇨ The team then developed a formal SPC strategy, including the objective of running the process on the nominal with a series of corrective action techniques. "This differed from the previous approach, which involved taking action only when the process was actually outside of the control limits," says Pearl.

◻ **Piloted the New System** ⇨ The team reviewed the system with the operators and piloted it on one machine to get the bugs out.

The next step was to modify the system as needed and then implement it throughout the department. "We monitored it for four weeks, following up as needed and working with the operators to help solve their problems and reinforce their efforts" Pearl notes.

The team documented the process control system, since documentation is a very important part of Corning's overall philosophy of process management.

◻ **Transferred Responsibility** ⇨ Responsibility for the system was transferred to the operators. The team, in making the transfer, explained, "You now have the system for monitoring the process and taking the necessary corrective action. You have been a part of its development and now have the responsibility for maintaining it."

Finally, the team reinforced and recognized operator behavior on a regular basis, using informal techniques such as plant walk-throughs to ask operators how they were doing.

THE KEY TO SUCCESS

With SPC, the posttransfer monitoring of operator behavior is essential to success, Pearl has found. For instance, after solving the problems related to the silver paste, the operators ran into new problems with the paste not adhering properly to the parts.

Investigation turned up the fact that the supplier of the silver had made a change in its process but had failed to tell anyone at the plant. Engineering studied the problem and came up with a short-term corrective action strategy to address it until the supplier could change the process back.

Sometime later, Pearl was visiting operators on the floor to see how things were going in general. He happened to notice that the operators were using a corrective action strategy for the silver paste that was different from the one that had been approved.

In questioning the operators and studying their alternative process, Pearl discovered that they had, indeed, come up with a better strategy than the one that had been formally authorized—but that they had not bothered to inform anyone of it. "They just started using it on their own," he says.

Pearl took this opportunity to remind operators that—since it really was *their* process—they had the authority and responsibility to put through the formal process change documentation themselves. "If you have a better way, don't keep it a secret," he told them.

On the basis of this episode, then, Pearl recommends that after you implement such a system with operators, you should be sure to follow up for a period of time. This will ensure that everyone understands his or her role, and allows you to monitor both performance and attitudes toward the new responsibilities operators have taken on.

ON TO OMC

With SPC efforts well in hand, the Operator Manufacturing Control (OMC) initiative was led by a team composed of a senior quality assurance engineer, the supervisor of training and documentation, and the appropriate department head. OMC was divided into two specific parts:

Part I: Operator Inspection

A. The team started with a strategy session on what the concept of OMC was, namely, turning control of the process over to operators and having them become their own quality inspectors.

B. The team then arranged for every shift to have an operator spokesperson, and also identified QA trainers to train the operators in self-inspection techniques.

C. Prior to the training taking place, the test equipment in the workplace was enhanced, repaired, and/or upgraded as needed so that it would operate under control, as defined by specs.

D. Next, the team developed the training program, which included both on-the-job and classroom training elements, covering charts, standard operating procedures, inspection procedures, and so on.

E. Following the training, the operators took written tests to determine whether or not they were competent to become their own inspectors. The minimum passing grade on the test was 80 percent.

The team looked at all questions that were missed to determine whether the incorrect answers were the result of the questions being poorly worded or indicated an actual lack of understanding on the operators' part. The team then reviewed the test with the operators to make sure they were fully and properly informed.

F. The team formally certified the operators who passed the tests, posting their names on a plaque in the production area.

Part II: Process Management

A. Next, operators took on project portfolios—ongoing projects that they would have to work on as a team.

B. The first task here was to audit the manufacturing process and study the process documentation to make sure that it was up-to-date and accurate.

C. The operator teams discussed ways to improve quality and reduce variability, using some of the SPC techniques they had already learned.

The supervisors in the plant played a key role in the success of these two efforts. They went through the same training as the operators and were then charged with the responsibility of reinforcing operator behavior and reminding them of the importance of following the new procedures. If they saw operators not doing what they were supposed to be doing, they were trained to discuss the problem and reinforce the corrected behavior.

A TWIN ATTACK

The twin attack of SPC and OMC has resulted in a number of benefits for Corning Glass Works. For instance:

➡ The operators now come forward with their own ideas on how to make further improvements, because they know that management is willing to listen and take action where appropriate.

➡ One-and-a-half years after the training, SPC was still being successfully run by the operators. "We walked away, and the process kept going," says Pearl. Currently, there are over 700 control charts in the plant.

➠ There have been reductions in long-term standard deviation. Reductions were in the neighborhood of 15 percent in the first six months of implementation and they are still trending downward.

➠ Stabilization of the processes has also meant reduction in waste, resulting in significant dollar savings.

➠ There was a 20 percent increase in out-the-door yields in the first 18 months. "And only half of the process steps in the plant had been put under statistical control at that time," notes Pearl.

➠ Operator teams have begun to confront those among them who are content to simply "get by." In the past, that type of performance was either tolerated or ignored.

➠ The process is now being controlled to its capability, rather than to engineering specs (where the original control limits were established). As a result, quality outputs are now higher than ever before.

OHIO PRINTING COMPANY

If you work in a competitive industry (and actually, who doesn't these days?), you need all the help available to put out a quality product and maintain your edge. OPC realized that SPC was just such a tool. Here's how the company launched its SPC effort and gave production and quality a big boost.

If you work in a competitive industry, then you know that every little edge you can gain on others in your field translates into more dollars for your company. Of course, one of the best ways to gain an edge is by providing customers with better quality products or services than they can find elsewhere. And one of the best ways to do *that* is through the use of SPC.

Members of the commercial printing industry face a number of problems peculiar to their operations, says Jerry Cozart, technical director for the Ohio Printing Co. (OPC) (Dayton, OH). These include:

1 The printing industry itself is very competitive, and profits traditionally are not as high as they are in other industries.

2 Printing is also a risky business. "The work may have to run through 10 different stages, and if any one of those stages has a problem, then the whole job may have to be scrapped," says Cozart.

3 Traditionally, it has been very difficult to standardize anything. Unlike specialty printers who can become very efficient and cost-effective by handling only one line of work (such as newspapers or business forms), commercial printers must handle a variety of different projects (posters, labels, advertising brochures, annual reports, and so on), and thus must deal with a great deal of variability.

4 In recent years, the trend has been toward more and more full-color printing, so in order to remain competitive, commercial printers must provide this service. However, full-color printing involves even greater degrees of variability and difficulty.

As a result of these challenges, OPC found itself practicing "crisis management" most of the time. Every color job, for example, was "like walking through a minefield," according to the company president, Bill Franklin. "Everyone knew something would go wrong; the only question was when."

Even the experienced press operators weren't comfortable with the new equipment. Also, sales-people remained constantly nervous, wondering when the problems would occur and how they would explain them to their waiting customers. Because of the lack of control, spoilage and rerun costs soared while profits suffered.

"Even when we invested in a lot of new equipment designed to help us begin to standardize, we still found a lot of the same spoilage and rerun problems existing," adds Franklin.

◻ RESOLVED: A New Direction ⇨ OPC realized that some changes needed to be made. So, the company resolved to:

GOAL #1: Implement adequate controls to stabilize operations. This would help to:

- ⇢ reduce spoilage and reruns (internal "failures") and
- ⇢ eliminate poor-quality final work that ultimately is rejected by the customer (external "failures").

GOAL #2: Blend the newest available technology with the skilled judgment and experience of the company's craftspeople to ensure consistent, problem-free work.

GOAL #3: Place the focus for quality on individual employees performing the jobs, not on inspectors.

The experienced quality professional will quickly realize that one possible solution for achieving these three goals is statistical process control. "One of quality expert W. Edwards Deming's points is that if you give employees responsibility for making a quality product, they will come up with a way to do it," says Franklin. "Then it's management's responsibility to change the process to make it possible for workers to put their ideas into motion."

SPC IMPLEMENTATION

Having recognized that, the company began SPC implementation. In this case, the implementation was a matter of:

⊃ Reducing variables. The first step that OPC took was to stabilize the production processes so that it could measure what it was doing. This involved reducing the number of variables, which required standardization. At the time, the technology that allowed standardization had become available. For example, the company now uses one kind of film instead of five, and one plate instead of three.

⊃ Developing standardized procedures. At the same time that variables were being reduced, the company developed standardized procedures so that everyone could perform the same job in the same way. It also created printed checklists for each stage of production so employees could sign off on the work they had performed, thus ensuring consistent quality.

⊃ Encouraging employee input. A short time before implementing these changes, the company had built on an addition to its facility and had sought the input of both suppliers and employees for work-station configuration and layout design.

"The company had previously operated in a rather traditional top-down manner," says Cozart. "However, when people realized how effective employee participation was, they realized that it would be beneficial to obtain it for this process, too. SPC and employee involvement, in other words, came along together at the right time."

So, management called together the company's 80 employees, gave them an introduction to SPC and what was being planned, and asked for their assistance. "We knew that they would be uncomfortable doing things in a new way, but we also told them that we would listen to them, because they held the key to the success of SPC," says Franklin.

⊃ Instituting formal SPC training. The company contracted with two local professors with SPC training experience to develop a training program specifically for OPC. The first training group consisted of 23 employees who were taught to:

- define chronic and sporadic problems
- set priorities for problem-solving projects based on cost-savings impact
- make corrections immediately, or seek help in taking corrective action
- place emphasis on prevention rather than inspection

- forget the concept of "private turf": share information with co-workers who handled jobs before and after their operation
- apply various SPC techniques to printing applications

⊃ Creating SPC project teams. During training, the 23 employees broke up into four project teams, with employees from different departments on the same team. One team, for instance, is composed of four pressmen, a pre-press technician, and an estimator.

At first, many of the employees were concerned about their abilities to handle the math involved in SPC and to use it in practical applications. To address this concern:

- The professors reassured them that if they could look at their paychecks each week and calculate whether or not they were paid the right amount, they had enough math ability to perform SPC calculations.

- They also made sure that at least one employee on each team was comfortable and experienced with a calculator.

⊃ Identifying problems to solve. The company had always kept excellent records on the cost of each of its jobs. "We used this data to determine where our most serious problems were," notes Cozart. "Our intent was to take the most serious problems and work on them one by one."

Management selected four problems and allowed each team to choose the one on which it wanted to work. The teams began working on the problems while they were still receiving the training, then continued with them after the training was complete. The problem-solving process the teams used involved:

- defining the causes of the problem
- collecting data on a limited test basis
- beginning to analyze results
- continuing to monitor the process as new procedures were implemented

Each month, the teams report their findings and progress to management, which then decides whether to keep testing the procedures or introduce them plantwide.

⊃ Monitoring progress. Teams also develop "models of excellence" for each step of each process. The definition "excellence" is determined by customer demands, and then each employee is told what needs to be done to reach those goals.

⊃ Providing recognition. To remind employees how much management appreciates their efforts, Cozart produces a regular "Good News Letter" that reports on team successes and names each team member.

THE TEAMS IN ACTION

Here are some examples of the projects tackled by the teams:

EXAMPLE #1: Stock Control. One team focused on the problem of stock control. "On a number of jobs, we found that we couldn't account for some sheets," notes Cozart. "For example, we might estimate needing 5,000 sheets for a particular job, end up not having enough, and then have to go back to the stockroom for more."

After studying the problem, the team came up with a plan involving the creation of a staging area as well as a better system for organizing stock.

EXAMPLE #2: Color Variation. In studying the problem of production reruns, one of the teams found that color variation was the single most common and expensive cause of reruns. During a test period, for example, the team found that five reruns for color variations cost more than $14,000 (34 percent of the total rerun cost).

Research into the problem led the team to conclude that poor workmanship was a significant cause, and they took steps to improve that. They also recommended a new press make-ready procedure on one of the presses. Projected savings are $7,500 per year.

EXAMPLE #3: A third team tackled the problem of uneven ink drying times. While some jobs dried within the time expected, others took much longer. Still others, *never* dried and had to be scrapped. At first, many of the employees suggested that changes in humidity and temperature in the pressroom were causing the problem. To test out this hypothesis, they plotted temperatures, humidity levels, and drying times, but found no correlation.

Next, they noticed that the batches of slow-drying jobs all came from one stock. After standardizing the stock and still not completely solving the problem, they began to monitor ink and fountain solution characteristics, and found that this was the real cause. That is, most of the variations in drying time were caused by fluctuations in these properties. The team then developed a procedure to monitor these properties on a regular basis and keep them within specified limits.

Those measures eliminated the problem instantaneously. Spoilage rates dropped from 20 percent to one percent. As a result, inventory was reduced, jobs could be done faster, and the company was able to reduce its price for such jobs while at the same time increasing its market share and improving its profits. In fact, the savings on this project alone over the course of one year paid for the cost of the SPC training program.

"This project also clearly illustrated that employees are willing, and in some cases eager, to follow new procedures when those procedures have been designed—not by managers—but by respected colleagues," says Cozart.

MORE THAN DOLLARS

While there have been hard dollar savings, as we just learned, there have also been other benefits that OPC can point to as a result of its SPC team approach:

#1. Gaps between departments have begun to close. Employees now communicate with one another and help co-workers solve problems. Employees have also begun to realize that management is listening to their ideas, and mutual trust has begun to flourish.

#2. Supervisors have become better communicators and better listeners. Instead of functioning as department problem solvers and overseers, supervisors work with employees to solve problems. They now function more as facilitators, tapping the skill and knowledge of the craftspeople. "Supervisors today are concerned about building a climate that allows employee input, reduces employee fear, and encourages quality," says Franklin.

#3. Individually, employees have become analytical about their jobs and the work they do. "They feel very involved in the management of their jobs," adds Cozart.

#4. The company's sales force has a great deal more confidence in the quality and timeliness of the jobs they bring in from customers.

Now there isn't nearly as much chance of jobs "blowing up in their faces."

 # 5. OPC is now considered one of the best printers in the region. "We have regained some customers that were lost in the past, and we now enjoy an excellent reputation," Cozart asserts.

And like any successful operation, OPC has no intention of resting on that reputation. It has plans to eventually train all of its employees in SPC. In fact, a second group of employees has already been trained and added to the existing SPC project teams.

In addition:

- *One of management's specific goals is to improve communication even more.* "We communicate a great deal, but we can do more of it and we can do it even better," Cozart maintains. "Fortunately, everyone is sincere about improving. In other words, it's a question of improving our skills, not our desire; the desire is there."

- *OPC has also started to research and compile the quality requirements of individual customers.* "Quality for one is not necessarily quality for another," Cozart explains. "This is a very subjective industry, and it is our job to translate subjective requirements into objective specifications so that we do a better job for our customers."

- *Finally, the company has plans to begin working with its suppliers of paper, ink, and photographic supplies to improve their quality.* Eventually, they plan to limit their business to only the ones that show the most improvement. "We used to just shop around for the best price," Cozart concludes, "but now we look for the best quality and service."

ROBERTSHAW CONTROLS COMPANY

Here are seven false assumptions that can jeoparize your SPC efforts. Breaking through these dangerous misconceptions can help you implement this valuable quality control tool successfully.

Assumptions are a fact of life when it comes to making decisions. Unfortunately, they can lead you down paths to disaster if they turn out to be wrong. And you never know you've made the wrong choice until *after* it's been made and it's too late. And if what you've been making assumptions about is how to implement SPC in your company, you might as well prepare yourself for some quality problems.

When the New Stanton Division of Robertshaw Controls Co. (Youngwood, PA) decided it was time to improve quality by doing things right the first time and getting employees involved in quality, they realized that it was time for statistical process control. However, they wanted to make sure they implemented it properly.

Many organizations feel they can cut some corners to expedite the process. That is, they make some assumptions, most of which turn out to be false. Fred Cox, director of Quality Assurance for the division, discusses some of these assumptions, why they are false, what the appropriate alternatives are, and how to implement them.

FALSE ASSUMPTION # 1: "WE DON'T NEED TOP MANAGEMENT SUPPORT"

Why is this assumption false? "Top management support is absolutely crucial to the successful implementation of SPC," emphasizes Cox. "One of W. Edwards Deming's key points is that 85 percent of a company's quality problems rest with management."

In addition, such support is crucial because it will determine the commitment that lower levels of management and line employees have. "When top management is involved, they will be out on the floors, studying charts, and talking with people about the progress of the effort," he explains. "When employees see this kind of concern, they will become concerned, too."

What can you do? Quite simply, members of management must learn about SPC, its benefits, and their roles in making it work. Cox accomplished this by showing Deming's videotaped program for SPC

implementation several times a week during lunch-time sessions, but you may be able to think of other effective ways that suit your own needs.

FALSE ASSUMPTION # 2: "WE DON'T NEED A PILOT PROGRAM"

Why is this assumption false? While it may be relatively easy to gain top management support—and even line employees' support—for SPC, it is traditionally difficult to gain first-line supervisory support for it. Supervisors often counter attempts to put such a process in place with, "We've been doing things the same way for years: Why change?"

Trying to implement SPC plantwide does not allow you to focus your energies on getting it running successfully in any one area, particularly if that area has a reluctant supervisor undermining your efforts. This is a two-edged sword: If supervisors see that positive results are not forthcoming, fewer and fewer of them will support SPC, and they will sit back to wait for it to fade away.

What can you do? The answer is to adopt a pilot program that focuses your efforts on one particular area. "We chose a screw machine area of the plant for out pilot program because we felt we could get good results there," relates Cox. "Employees and supervisors received 10 to 12 hours of basic SPC training, including charting experience based on their actual work.

"During this test period, we found that some of our machines were not capable of producing parts consistently; they were unable to hold their tolerances." Once the problem was remedied, results were immediate and dramatic: Scrap and and rework dropped an impressive 47 percent right away and another 13 percent later on. And when these initial results were made known, supervisors became convinced of the value of SPC.

FALSE ASSUMPTION # 3: "WE DON'T NEED VENDOR INVOLVEMENT"

Why is this assumption false? During the division's test program, it became evident that a second problem (in addition to the problem of certain machines being unable to hold tolerances) was present: inconsistent raw materials from vendors. "Many of these materials were not good enough to allow us to make parts consistently," Cox reports.

What can you do? To address the problem, management invited all of its vendors to visit the facility to discuss SPC and to launch an 18-month vendor improvement program. "Only one vendor—a small one—did not agree to the request for improvement," recalls Cox.

Once the program was under way, the division tightened acceptable quality levels for the vendors every six months. "We also began a vendor rating system that is different from most," he says. "We didn't feel that it was fair to grade vendors only on the number of lots received versus the number of lots accepted, because some vendors may send only one or two lots per year to us."

Instead, the division came up with a point system that involves assigning points for:

- lot acceptance percentages

- response time (how quickly vendors respond to problems)

- delivery (on-time versus early or late)

- cost (compared to other vendors supplying similar or comparable parts)

Vendors receive monthly, quarterly, and year-to-date reports. "If we find that a vendor is not meeting our standards, we will begin looking for an alternative source," says Cox. Most vendors, however, have shown excellent improvement."

FALSE ASSUMPTION #4: "WE DON'T NEED CONTINUOUS TRAINING"

Why is this assumption false? "Initially, we had a goal of training everyone in SPC within two years," says Cox. "However, as we got more involved with the training, we realized that we needed even more. Eventually, we saw that in order to guarantee continuous quality improvement, we needed continuous training."

What can you do? The division trained one of its quality engineers to become a full-time training coordinator and invested in training tapes. "One of the series of tapes covers individual machines that we use," Cox explains. The tapes show how to set the machines up properly for running without tolerances.

"We require operators to check out the 7- to 14-minute-long tapes about the machines that they use, view the tapes, and then take tests on them. They must achieve 100 percent on the tests. If they don't, they keep reviewing the tapes until they are able to make 100 percent on the tests."

Having passed the test, employees are expected to know what they're doing when setting up machines. "And if the setups are correct, then it is just a matter of watching the process and making sure that it remains in control limits," says Cox. "If setups are incorrect, there will be problems all the way through."

To offer an even stronger safeguard against improper setups, a specialized setup person or the machine operator will set the machine up based on a 10- to 15-point checkoff sheet covering critical points defined by Quality Assurance, Engineering, Production, and/or the customer.

When the setup specialist or operator feels the machine is properly set up based on a sample that is run, he or she will call the production supervisor to recheck the sample. If the supervisor agrees, then and only then will a quality inspector be called in to verify the setup.

From that point on, operators are trained to make notes on their charts if and when points go out of control. "By making notes, we are later able to determine why points have gone out of control and what is needed to bring them back in control," says Cox.

FALSE ASSUMPTION #5: "WE DON'T NEED TO MONITOR PROGRESS"

Why is this assumption false? What gets measured gets attention. In other words, unless employees, supervisors, and managers know that someone is keeping track of how they are performing, it is very easy for them to dismiss, ignore, or forget about the effort.

What can you do? At the New Stanton Division, production supervisors set limits, based on capability studies, and hold employees responsible for keeping these up-to-date. Quality engineers then randomly select charts on a daily basis, review them, and make sure operators are doing their work correctly. Operators have the authority to shut down their equipment if the machines begin producing parts that are beyond control limits.

With this authority comes responsibility: Employees are expected to inspect their work periodically throughout their shift. "We start with five samples every 30 minutes," says Cox. "Once we are confident that the process is running in control and using no more than 75 percent of the tolerance ban, we reduce the sample frequency to five samples every hour. In cases where the process runs in control and uses 50 percent or less of the tolerance ban, we take five samples every two hours.

Precontrol or X Bar R charts are kept on dimensions such as diameter and length on screw machine parts. On punch press, plastic, and die-cast parts, one or two dimensions are controlled with the knowledge that, if they go out of control, something else has gone out, too.

During the shift to SPC, Cox found that, with precontrol and X Bar R charts, "go/no go" gaging was no longer appropriate. "As a result, we purchased as much electronic gaging as we could, as well as laser measurement systems, optical coordinate measuring machines, and computerized coordinate measuring machines," he says. In addition, the division created the appropriate computer data gathering systems (handled on PCs), which customers often require to accompany their orders.

FALSE ASSUMPTION #6: "WE DON'T NEED TO EXERCISE CAUTION"

Why is this assumption false? "Once you see improvement in one area, there may be a tendency to push SPC quickly into other areas," says Cox. "You can't do it! You must implement it slowly, because you need to train employees properly before they can work with it. Without this training, SPC just becomes a lot of paperwork that no one pays attention to."

What can you do? In implementing SPC in other areas of the plant (which has over 200 screw machines, 65 punch presses, and complete machining, die casting, and plating departments), management looked for areas that had the highest scrap rates. "We chose another screw machine area first, and then moved it into the punch press department," says Cox.

"Again, resist the temptation to do it all at once," he reiterates. "We find that if we get a little piece of the pie now, we can go back for more later. Doing it a little bit at a time makes sure the training takes hold."

FALSE ASSUMPTION #7: "WE DON'T NEED TO SET GOALS"

Why is this assumption false? Goal-setting is crucial to SPC success. Without setting goals for which employees, supervisors, and managers can strive, continuous improvement becomes difficult. People soon become satisfied with the status quo, and that's a death knell for SPC, which, by its very nature, involves continual improvement.

What can you do? "There's a tendency to let things slide once you start getting some results," says Cox. "Don't do this. The key to success is continuing to push for improvement—forever.

"We set goals and milestone charts for each department and work toward these slowly," reports Cox. "We don't make the goals either too easy or too hard. However, we do revise them upward each year."

Cox stresses that such goals should be negotiated with employees and supervisors, rather than forced on them. With negotiation, you get cooperation. With force, you get resentment and resistance.

THE PLUS SIDE OF NOT ASSUMING

Because his division doesn't make assumptions—false or otherwise—about SPC implementation, Cox is able to report that scrap and rework have been cut dramatically, as has the need for inspectors.

"We used to do batch inspections," he explains. "If we ended up with 5,000 rejected parts, they would sit in a corner somewhere awaiting disposition. In the meantime, we would have to run an additional 5,000 parts to meet our schedule. Now, we don't have to run 10,000 parts to get 5,000 good parts. As a result, our productivity has also improved."

Finally, when customers visit the facility, they see SPC in operation and develop a feeling of confidence in the division's ability to meet requirements in terms of quality, cost, and service. "And this gives us the edge over our competitors," Cox concludes.

GENERAL ELECTRIC COMPANY

Can SPC being used outside your company help you to assure quality? Yes, if it's used by your suppliers. GE's Aircraft Engine Group offers its advice for teaching vendors the ins and outs of SPC.

Most companies that use and benefit from statistical process control would like to see their suppliers adopt SPC as well. In fact, some even require it of their vendors. But suppliers may not know where to find proper training or simply can't afford it. That's where your company can play a valuable role.

"The aircraft engine business has changed drastically over the past five to seven years," reports Paul Robinson, manager of Quality Training for General Electric Company's Aircraft Engine Group (Cincinnati, OH). What form have those changes taken? For example:

■ The Group began to experience many of the pressures of a "world economy" in terms of quality demands and customer expectations.

■ The U.S. Department of Defense, once representing only 20 percent of the division's business, now represents closer to 60 percent. And because the Defense Department has been under pressure from Congress, it has been forced to change the way it does business with suppliers, learning to use competition to its advantage and demanding even higher levels of quality.

■ Commercial airline customers, reacting to the pressures of deregulation and fuel costs, require much more of engine manufacturers in improved acquisition and operating costs in order to meet their competition.

■ The work force, in terms of skilled craftspeople, is aging. "The craftsmen on whom we've learned to depend to 'read between the lines' of what we really want on the production line are retiring," notes Robinson. "Their replacements are younger and less skilled, so we have to spend a lot more time debugging our processes and depending on the quality of the design of our processes, rather than on the knowledge of the employees."

■ Demand for the Group's engines is growing, requiring it to become even more efficient in order to meet the demand. "We must get the very best out of our processes," says Robinson.

What does the Aircraft Engine Group see as the logical approach to addressing these challenges? *Statistical Process Control,* says Robinson.

"We realized that we had the opportunity to change before we were forced to change," he says. "We also realized that it would make no sense not to take the opportunity to begin implementing SPC in the mid-1980s."

So in late 1984, the Group scheduled a symposium for its own managers as well as for the CEOs and quality managers of its 200 largest suppliers. "We explained why we were adopting SPC as a way of life and asked our suppliers' cooperation in implementing it in their companies, too."

The Group went on to explain that, eventually, having SPC in place would become a condition of doing business with suppliers. And unlike some companies who make such pronouncements and then leave suppliers to their own devices, the Aircraft Engines Group promised to provide the necessary SPC training to its suppliers free of charge.

If any supplier was still reluctant to sign on after all that, there was an additional incentive: Each supplier has a "bank account" of 100 points related to quality. Fifteen of those points are tied to the implementation of SPC.

Suppliers were told that they did not have to implement SPC initially, but that without it, the best they could do would be an 85 percent rating. And since 60 percent is the minimum "passing grade" to remain a Group supplier, the vendors quickly realized the importance of getting SPC up and running.

Finally, the Group explained that the suppliers should not implement SPC just because it was being promoted by the Group, but because it was a way to maximize their own profits and help them meet their other customers' expectations.

ALL ABOARD FOR TRAINING

Initially, training took place at the Group's two plant locations (Cincinnati and Lynn, MA), but now that the bulk of the training has been completed with over 85 percent of the dollar volume of the

Group's suppliers trained to date, training now takes place only in Cincinnati.

Each class is limited to approximately 20 participants. The Group asks that suppliers, when they feel they are ready to receive the training, send two representatives. One of these should be the person who will be responsible for going back and training the rest of the employees. The second representative should be the person designated to be the supplier's SPC project manager—the person who will be responsible for the overall implementation of SPC in the plant. Suppliers are responsible for paying their representatives' travel and living expenses during the week-long training, but there are no charges for the course itself or the materials used during the training.

The program is based heavily on videotapes, which were produced by General Electric's Technical Education Group in Bridgeport, CT. The sessions focus on three key areas:

1 BASIC TRAINING. Since SPC is new to many suppliers, they learn the fundamentals of the techniques and the skills they will need in order to be able to perform a process capability study *and* monitor the process following the study.

2 "TRAIN THE TRAINER." Since the idea is to have the participants return to their respective organizations and begin to conduct training with key managers, staff, and line employees GE also presents modules that help train vendors' SPC resource people.

"We spend some time coaching them on using videotapes themselves so that they can train their own people," says Robinson. During these practice sessions, the participants learn how to generate discussion among their employees, and also receive coaching and critiques on how well they performed during their practice training sessions.

Although the Aircraft Engine Group does not require that its suppliers use its methods of training to educate their employees about SPC, it does make its videotape packages available on long-term loan and offers the textbooks, workbooks, and other printed material at cost to those who are interested in using the Group's approach to training.

3 CORPORATE CULTURE. The Aircraft Engine Group also exposes participants to some of the research it has conducted for its own benefit on how to bring about general change in the corporate culture. "This allows the participants to spearhead attempts to get their people interested in implementing SPC," explains Robinson.

The Group then asks the participants to develop implementation plans so that when they return to their companies the following Monday, they can sit down with their CEOs and report what they learned, what their companies need to do, and how they should go about doing it.

Once the training is over, it certainly isn't forgotten. The Group ensures this by following up with suppliers approximately two months after their representatives have received instruction. This function is carried out by purchasing representatives, who say to suppliers, "When you left here a couple of months ago, you had a pretty good implementation plan under your arm. When is it convenient for us to stop by and see how you're coming with it?"

Robinson notes that such an effort requires excellent cooperation between the quality department and Purchasing. In his case, the cooperation was not difficult to obtain since most of the Group's purchasing people have been trained in SPC themselves and realize its benefits.

KEEPING THE PRESSURE ON

At least partly as a result of its cooperative venture with suppliers and its training efforts, the Group has found itself able to meet its ever-increasing profit targets. "Our business has been growing by leaps and bounds because our customers prefer our products to those of our competitors," says Robinson.

In addition, the organization has been able to cut costs and meet its schedules, two things that definitely add to customer appreciation. "When you have quality problems, you can never fully get on top of your schedule," he adds.

What does the future hold? "We plan to keep the pressure on. When we started this effort, we realized that it would take between five and seven years to make fundamental changes in our corporate culture, so we will continue our efforts in this direction," Robinson concludes.

DESIGNED EXPERIMENTS/TAGUCHI METHODS

Companies have found that they can eliminate flaws that impair quality by using these tools to study designs and processes. And the good news is that implementing designed experiments and Taguchi Methods is not as complicated or difficult as it might seem.

UNITED TECHNOLOGIES AUTOMOTIVE

Y*ou* know that designed experiments enable you to test designs and processes to improve quality. But how do you convey this idea to managers and other nonstatisticians?

People don't buy into things they don't understand. So how can you sell the idea of something as complex as design of experiments? Alfonso Enriquez, QC engineer at United Technologies Automotive (El Paso, TX), has an effective solution: "Initiate training classes for all levels of the organization. Then, keep the training simple; don't try to overwhelm them with too much technical jargon."

You want to cover the basics about design of experiments: what they are, why they're effective, how they're used. And you'll want to make them understandable as well as overcome resistance to them. As you try to spread the word about design of experiments, you'll be asked numerous questions. Let's look at some of the most common questions—and some of the answers you can offer in reply:

❏ **What are designed experiments?**

Experiments are usually conducted in order to prove theories—or to separate fact from fiction. Almost all of us do some experimenting, like when we try different gasolines in order to eliminate an automobile engine's knock. Inexperienced and untrained experimenters, however, tend to make their changes in a disorganized fashion. The net result is a series of inefficient tests.

Design of experiments was developed to increase the efficiency of testing, and to reduce the risk of drawing the wrong conclusions. In industry, managers are prone to refuse to allow testing when it appears that the experimenters are getting little information at a great cost.

Many experimental designs require the use of complex analyses such as the Analysis of Variance (ANOVA). Although the theory behind ANOVA is complex, it is still a valuable tool that can be used by nonstatisticians. ANOVA is particularly useful where computer programs are available to do the calculations. By using ANOVA, the statisticians are freed from tiresome number-crunching; they are able to spend more time on teaching potential users and interpreting test results.

❏ **Why run designed experiments?**

Designed experiments are much more efficient than random, disorganized testing; they help you get more for your testing dollar. "In addition," says Enriquez, "designed experiments help you to":

1 **Verify tolerances.** Tolerances can be set subjectively; the designer can think up a good number and put it on the print. In some cases, the resulting tolerances can be too tight. When this happens, high scrap rates often follow—even though the user might accept less difficult limits. In other cases, the tolerances can be too loose, and the plant will put out a sloppy product that doesn't meet the competition. With designed experiments, it is possible to determine which variables are critical to a product design and which are less important. Then, more effort can be put into the critical variables and less time wasted on the unimportant ones.

2 **Confirm or reject old recipes.** "Old recipes" involve chemical formulations that have been used for years, but which can be improved. In some cases, designed experiments enable you to come up with a better product at a reduced cost.

3 **Reduce variability.** Variability is a major source of scrap and rejects. By running designed experiments, you may be able to identify which parameters or materials contribute to variability. Once you know what to control, you can reduce variability and improve the quality of your product.

4 **Increase capability.** Capability often identifies whether you can meet the quality of the competition. Designed experiments can help you identify your capability as well as your ability to meet the requirements. They can also help you identify which variables must be controlled if you want to improve that capability.

❏ **Where can you use designed experiments?**

Designed experiments have been used to determine cause-and-effect relationships. Examples range from studying the factors that help you lose weight efficiently to the factors that contribute to a good weld. A few of the experiments that Enriquez completed for United Technologies Automotive include:

► Determining the variables having the most effect

on the pull-test results of crimped wires

► Determining the variables having the most effect on the pull-test strength of a soldered pair of wires

► Determining the variables having the most effect on the bond produced by an electrode welding machine

► Determining the variables having the most effect on the bond produced by an ultrasonic welder

► Determining the variables having the most effect on a molded part's flashing

► Determining proper terminal, process sequence, and voltage for a water immersion test

What kind of training is involved?

"In order to get the most benefits from our testing, we initiated a training program in the design of experiments," says Enriquez. "We didn't stop at training quality engineers and statisticians; we trained a variety of personnel at different levels of the organization."

But you must take into consideration the backgrounds of the students when planning classwork. For example, the backgrounds and education of managers with limited exposure to math are different from the backgrounds and education of engineers who use math all the time.

The training classes were designed to minimize time and cost. Time is always in short supply among managers and executives; costs have an obvious influence on the bottom line. Acknowledging these constraints, United Technologies changed the classes to have less theory and more practical material. It also included extensive hands-on personalized training. That's because when classes stress theory, the material is soon forgotton unless the students have a chance to apply what they learn.

There's no denying that the design of experiments is a complex subject. "To get more people interested," says Enriquez, "we made extensive use of response graphs and other graphics. There is an old Chinese proverb that says, 'one picture is worth more than a thousand words.' This observation also applies to charts and graphs."

Early classes at United Technologies Automotive were for QA managers and engineers. The material covered included:

● Demonstrations showing that the Taguchi methods had a theoretical basis

● Examples showing the savings that could be obtained by using designed experiments such as orthogonal arrays

● An emphasis on the use of linear graphs to explain relationships and interactions among variables

● An explanation of the signal-to-noise ratio, showing how a portion of the variation was explained by the experiment and a portion was not

● Discussions about the loss to society caused by poor quality

Although the original training program was designed to provide one week of introductory work and one week of advanced work, Enriquez adjusted the schedule to have less class work and more applications training out in the plant. As a consequence, the class work was reduced to a one-day seminar and a two-day advanced seminar.

"This reduced classroom time," explains Enriquez. "It was supplemented by practical applications: We ran an actual experiment in each plant for the people who attended the one-day theory class."

Once the training program proved successful, it was expanded to cover other areas of the plant. "We have trained people from the maintenance, manufacturing, equipment engineering, and industrial engineering departments," explains Enriquez. "By bringing other departments into the program, we are able to make additional converts to the design of experiments process. Once employees know the tool is available—and are able to use it—they can come up with a variety of places where it can be applied in their work areas."

How can I make design of experiments understandable?

One of the best ways is to stress the percent contribution each factor makes to variability. Managers are seldom interested in statistics like the "F" value of a variable. They are interested in how each one influences the total variability. In most cases, the factor with the highest contribution to the total variability is the one you will have to watch.

Charts can help you present data in an easy-to-understand manner. Figures 11, 12, and 13, for instance, show how three variables influence a solder joint. The joint, in this case, was subjected to a pull-test; the higher the value, the better.

For the levels tested, temperature had only a slight

effect; the slope of the line connecting the two points is very flat (Figure 11). The immersion time had a slightly larger influence; the slope of the line is a little less flat (Figure 12). The quality of the solder, however, was the dominant variable; the slope of the line is much steeper (Figure 13). When using charts for this type of comparison, be sure to use the same scale for all three. Otherwise, you will give at least one variable an unfair advantage over the others.

Another point you may want to consider is the use of data transformations. They sometimes make simple experiments look complex. It is possible, for example, to transform all the data to logarithm—but are they needed?

In his work at United Technologies Automotive, Enriquez found transformations unnecessary. "We analyzed the experimental data with and without transformations and found that transformations did not improve the results. In addition, the elimination of transformations helped our managers and engineering personnel to understand what was going on. Transformations would have added nothing but confusion."

◻ **How can I overcome resistance to using design of experiments?**

"When a person takes a design of experiments seminar, it is very likely that the idea of finding the optimal conditions will be in his or her mind," notes Enriquez. "He or she often considers optimal conditions as the only purpose of the study. Therefore, people confronted with particular problems are often afraid of failing to achieve better results," he points out.

"The world is divided into two kinds of people according to their attitude about risk: the ones that love it and the ones that hate it. In a manufacturing environment, you are more likely to find people hating risk; they have been taught to follow procedures and manuals. When you ask them to openly attempt an experiment, a good number of them will give all kinds of arguments to avoid taking the risk. At times, they even generate false data to avoid having to make a change.

"An alternative approach is to consider each experiment a success. This makes sense because we always learn something from it. As an example, if the variables we study turn out to be less important than we thought, we have learned that our previous assumptions were wrong.

"Sometimes, we think we can get a better response from a process. If the experiments show that the optimal settings are in fact the normal conditions, we have learned a little more," Enriquez concludes.

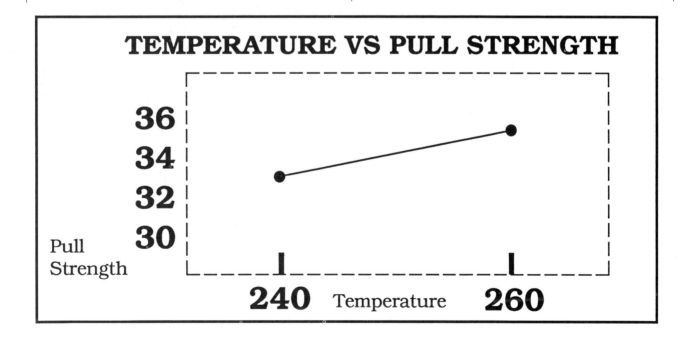

FIGURE 11

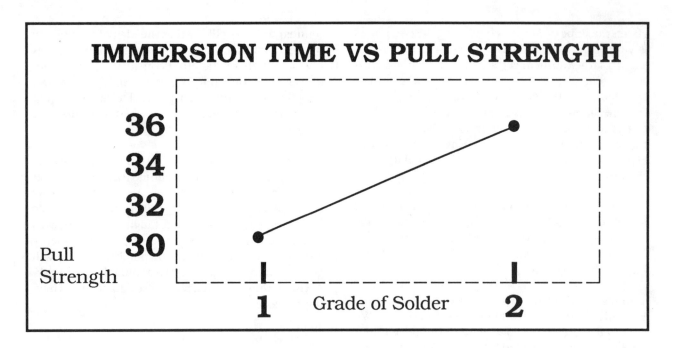

FIGURE 12

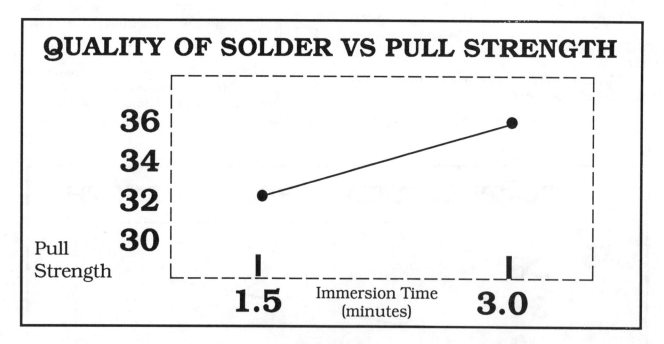

FIGURE 13

ITT

ITT uses Taguchi methods to pinpoint and solve production quality problems. In one case, the company realizes seven-figure savings annually.

When Timothy Reed was with an ITT division that manufactured fiber optic cables for the telecommunications industry, his organization was experiencing some yield problems with its product. Cables were composed of a number of "primary tubes," each of which contained one to twelve fibers cushioned by a gel. The problem had to do with optical attenuation—the ability of the fibers to carry their signals under severe changes in temperature.

To begin to address the problem, Reed, who currently is a senior manufacturing engineer at ITT's Electro-Optical Products Division (Roanoke, VA), attended two weeks of Taguchi training and one week of statistical training at the company's quality training facilities in Michigan.

Upon his return, the division organized a task force of representatives from Quality Control, Engineering, R&D, and operators and their supervisors. This group met for several days of brainstorming on the optical attenuation issue. They came up with a number of possible factors for the problem, and then narrowed them down to the most important ones. These were separated into two groups:

1 Controllable factors. These are factors that could be controlled in the manufacturing process.

2 Uncontrollable ("Noise") factors. These are factors (such as factory temperature and humidity) that could not be controlled in the manufacturing process but *could* be controlled in an experimental or laboratory setting.

Next, the team set up a series of experiments using these factors against each other. "We tried to determine which set of *controllable* factors made the process most 'robust' against the noise factors," explains Reed. In other words, the idea was to experiment with the various controllable factors to determine which combination of controllable factors' levels could best resist the impact of the uncontrollable factors. This technique is considered the Taguchi design's most powerful analysis.

To conduct the experiments, the group set the various controllable factors they had chosen at two or three "separable" or "statistically distinct" levels.

For instance, extrusion temperatures were set at 400 degrees and 600 degrees for experimentation.

The group studied the changes in attenuation under the various sets of conditions and eventually found the optimum set of controllable factors. What they discovered was that gel viscosity was the root of most of the problems. The cables in which the silicone oil-based gel was contained were used in all types of environments, from Arizona deserts to the Arctic Circle. In very hot environments, the gel would often ooze out of the cables and drip onto the ground and/or separate into its primary components—silica filler and silicone oil. In very cold environments, the gel would harden, causing the fibers to buckle and kink. Both situations led to attenuation problems.

"We needed a gel that would combine all of the best characteristics and give us the lowest optical attenuation at room temperature, but would be the most immune to temperature changes in the field," says Reed. In short, the gel viscosity had to be much more uniform and consistent at room temperatures and also perform well at extremes.

GROUP ACTION

Since the division manufactured its own gel (because it was unavailable for purchase from any qualified suppliers), the group identified the most important characteristic that would be required of the gel. These included:

► Nominal room temperature viscosity

► Drip prevention (so that gel would not ooze out of cables and drip on the ground)

► Oil separation prevention (so that gel would not degrade back into its original components of silica filler and silicone oil)

► Immunity to temperature changes in the field

The group got together again to brainstorm the factors that might be involved in these problems and came up with 16 major factors. Among them were:

● The ratio of filler to oil

- The temperatures of the oils when they were mixed

- Mixing ratios of high- and low-viscosity oils

- Speed of the mix

- Time of the mix

- The type of stabilizer that was added

As a result of its findings, the group was able to adjust the processing parameters so that:

■ The nominal room temperature viscosity became immune to mixing time, which allowed the operators to mix for a long enough period of time to get the gel homogenous.

■ Drip was eliminated completely.

■ Oil separation was reduced substantially below specification.

■ The gel became more immune to temperature changes.

In addition, by controlling the gel mixing process more carefully, waste was reduced from 50 percent to zero. "The silicone oil was very expensive—approximately $1,000 per barrel," explains Reed. "Once the gel was mixed, it could not be reworked if it had the wrong quality characteristics. In addition to the cost of the wasted gel itself, the substance was considered a controlled waste, so it could not simply be dumped; we had to pay people to haul it away."

THE POWER OF TAGUCHI

Exactly what did the use of Taguchi methods mean to Reed's organization? Without the power of those techniques (which allowed the division to set the statistically distinct levels for the controllable factors and test them against "noise" factors), Reed calculates that it would have taken about 65,000 experiments to arrive at the correct combination of factors.

"Using Taguchi methods," he notes, "we were able to accomplish the same results with 16 experiments." And as a result of the improved quality and reliability of the cables, the division was able to save approximately $2,000,000 annually—as calculated using Taguchi's loss function.

FORD MOTOR COMPANY

How can you solve quality problems before they happen instead of after? Ford's Casting Division uses five steps to implement design of experiments and has had excellent results.

Statistical Process Control (SPC) is an effective way to control process variables, but it analyzes a problem *after* it has happened. For example, if a part is defective, you can figure out why and by how much the item strayed from the target variables.

The problem is that target variables are often determined by past personal experiences of process engineers and other experts. This method has never ensured that the nominals or target levels are optimal—only that they "seem to work." And since most processes involve many variables, it's difficult to determine the separate contributions that each variable makes to the final results. More important, you don't know what contributions they make *in combination with each other.*

There is a solution to this dilemma: Design optimal procedures *before* you begin production. By conducting *design of experiments,* which involves choosing key variables and testing them under different conditions, you can find the best overall target level for each variable. Ford Motor Company's Casting Division (Dearborn, MI) has had excellent results using this approach. Tom P. Enright, the division's quality control manager, explains the five steps involved:

STEP ONE: CONDUCT A BRAINSTORMING SESSION

At this diagnostic stage, all of the employees involved in the process (including process engineers, product engineers, quality control personnel, and machine operators) meet to discuss which factors might have an influence on the process. These might include temperatures, ingredient quantities, timing, or other factors. The division often uses an Ishikawa or "fishbone" diagram to help outline ideas at this stage.

■ **The first phase,** getting as many people as possible involved, is very important, Enright believes. "People are limited by their own shortcomings," he explains. "If, for example, a process engineer thinks that she knows the cause of the problem, she will want to try her own solutions. However, the machine operator may have

an equally valuable idea as to the cause, so it's important to get his input, too."

■ **The second phase** of the brainstorming session involves narrowing down the list of possible variables to those that the group most strongly believes have the most influence. With the design of experiments approach being discussed here, it's possible to have up to seven variables.

"The beauty of being able to experiment with so many variables at one time is that everyone in the group ends up being happy," notes Enright. "In other words, the chances are that at least one or two of the variables that each person thinks are important will be listed among the seven, and as long as *their* key concerns are going to be addressed, they don't really care what the other variables are."

This, of course, is a vast improvement over the old, "one at a time" approach used in traditional manufacturing settings, where the variables tested are controlled by an inner circle of engineers or superintendents who insist on testing out only their own personal theories. With design of experiments, everyone's theories can be tested at the same time.

■ **The third phase** of brainstorming involves initially determining two separate and distinct level settings for each variable to be tested. This, also, is a key element of design of experiments. If you choose a number of different levels and a number of different variables, then you would have to perform hundred of experiments in order to test all of the different levels of all of the variables. By choosing only two levels, you can minimize the number of experiments.

This last point may concern you. After all, aren't you risking error by choosing only two levels of variables? Not really, says Enright. For instance, if "pouring temperature of a certain metal is one of the variables you wish to test, you could choose half a dozen different levels (2000 °F, 2100 °F, 2200 °F, 2300 °F, 2400 °F, and 2500 °F) or you could choose two separate and distinct levels initially (say, 2000°F and 2500°F). If the results of the experiment indicated that pouring temperature was indeed an important variable, and that results were better at 2000°F than at 2500°F, then additional experiments could further narrow the temperature down to the ideal. For instance, experiments could be run at 1900°F and 2100°F to determine which level was best. In this way, you need only run a limited number of experiments."

STEP TWO:
SELECT THE DESIGN OR LAYOUT

The method used to select the design or layout of the experiments usually involves *orthogonal arrays*—rows of experiment "runs" to be performed and columns of the variables to be tested, each column having a combination of different levels at which the variables will be tested.

The number of orthogonal arrays that can be developed is limited only by the number of variables to be tested and the number of levels at which they are to be tested. Even with only seven variables at two levels, the complete orthogonal array is extremely large (27 = 128). This means that in order to experiment with each variable at each level *in combination with all of the other variables at each of their two levels,* it would take 128 experiments.

One of Dr. Genichi Taguchi's greatest contributions to the classical design of experiments is the creation of some easy-to-use, simple examples of orthogonal arrays that capture the most significant combination of levels for the variable to be tested. Using a two-level, seven-variable example, for instance, the ideal orthogonal array to use would be the "L8," which looks like this:

COLUMN NO.	1	2	3	4	5	6	7
1	1	1	1	1	1	1	1
2	1	1	1	2	2	2	2
3	1	2	2	1	1	2	2
4	1	2	2	2	2	1	1
5	2	1	2	1	2	1	2
6	2	1	2	2	1	2	1
7	2	2	1	1	2	2	1
8	2	2	1	2	1	1	2

The L8 provides the level settings for each of the eight runs (eight rows) involving the seven variables (seven columns). The "1" or "2" signifies the level setting at which each experiment will be conducted.

For instance, using the example of pouring temperature variable we discussed earlier, Level One would be 2000°F, and Level Two would be 2500°F.

Taguchi found that the setting combinations in the L8 help the experimenter to narrow down the key variables and the most appropriate settings for those variables, and to do so through an experiment that has a *balanced design.* That means that each of the variables gets tested at each setting an equal number of times.

"What Taguchi has done, in other words, is give us a 'family' of typical arrays that can be used over and over again, rather than forcing people to go through all of the possible combinations," says Enright. "Using this method, you can test all seven variables at two level settings with only eight experiments, rather than having to conduct 128 separate experiments."

STEP THREE:
CONDUCT THE EXPERIMENTS

Experiments should be conducted very carefully and under controlled conditions. "The validity of the resulting data is a function of the adherence to the design," stresses Enright. "Shortcuts don't work; all experiments must be run at the levels stipulated."

STEP FOUR:
SUMMARIZE THE DATA

This involves mathematical computations to determine what changes have taken place in the processes as a result of testing the variables at the different levels.

STEP FIVE:
DETERMINE THE BEST COMBINATION

Once the best "run" and the key variables and levels are determined, additional runs can be performed to get down to more specifics. Again, for example, if 2000°F is found to be better than 2500°F for the pouring temperature variable, then additional runs can be made at 1900°F and 2100°F.

Finally, a confirmation run can be made using all of the levels believed to be ideal for the variables being tested. "Another reason for performing the confirmation run is to be sure that the levels of the various combinations of variables don't accidentally cancel each other out," says Enright.

"For example, using the L8 Orthogonal Array, let's say that the best combination turns out to be Variable

1 at Level 2, Variable 2 at Level 2, and Variable 3 at Level 2. A check of the L8 indicates that this specific combination was not run as part of the eight experiments. It is important to make this run to be sure that none of the variable settings cause problems or cancel the effects of each other out, " Enright explains.

For instance, if an experiment involved testing pouring temperatures and the moisture content of sand being used for casting, two Level 2 settings (high pouring temperature and high moisture content) would cause problems. "High pouring temperature and high sand moisture content produce instant scrap," says Enright. If the confirmation run *does* indicate such problems, then the experiments must be set up again in order to get around the problem.

"It's been our experience that this rarely, if ever, happens," Enright says, however. "In fact, in all of the experiments we've run, we've never yet had this problem occur."

A CASE IN POINT

One of the many opportunities the Casting Division has had to utilize the design of experiments concept involved the pistons for the 3.8-liter (3.8L) engine at the Division's Essex Aluminum Plant in 1986.

"Continual process improvements had resulted in substantial improvements in quality, both in-house and in customer plants," says Enright. One of the problems that the plant has had was that of "shrink" on the piston domes. While the problem had decreased significantly over the years as a result of plant personnel conducting "one at at time" experiments, the problem still existed. By 1986, it had leveled off to a scrap rate of 0.6 percent, but the Division still felt there was room for improvement.

Team members met to brainstorm the problem, and developed an Ishikawa diagram covering all of the possible variables involved. (See Figure 14.) They then narrowed that list down to what they felt were the most important seven variables:

FACTOR	PROCESS PARAMETER	TO BE STUDIED
A	MOLD TEMPERATURE	2
B	DOWNSPRUE RISER	2
C	METAL TEMPERATURE	2
D	MOLD CASTING APPLICATION	2
E	RISER DESIGN	2
F	MOLD DESIGN	2
G	MACHINE CYCLE	2

3.8L PISTON

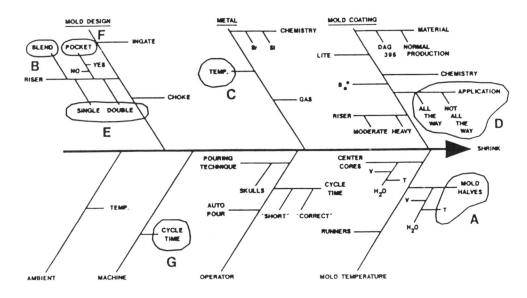

FIGURE 14

The team chose the L8 Orthogonal Array with which to conduct its experiments and then selected the levels at which each variable would be tested. (See Figure 15.)

Five hundred piston castings were run for each of the eight experimental production runs and were then evaluated for shrink defect and overall percentage defective. Mathmatical calculations determined that the three key variables and their appropriate settings were downsprue riser (Level 1), mold coating application (Level 1), and mold design (Level 2). (See Figure 16.)

The confirmation run indicated that these were indeed the key variables and settings. And as a result of using the new levels in the process, scrap was reduced significantly further—down to less than 0.2 percent.

"These improvements have been holding steady over time," adds Enright. "In fact, if and when any problems do occur, we know exactly why by looking at the control charts. It's then a simple matter of bringing the process back under control."

What final advice does he have for other quality professionals using—or about to use—these methods? "Choosing the variables to be tested and the levels at which to test them are the most important steps of the whole effort," Enright emphasizes. "In fact, it's about 90 percent of it. If you choose the wrong variables to test in the first place, then you'll end up with the wrong answers—it's that simple."

FIGURE 15

3.8L PISTON SHRINK STUDY
EXPERIMENTAL LAYOUT

RUN	A	B	C	D	E	F	G
1	1	1	1	1	1	1	1
2	1	1	1	2	2	2	2
3	1	2	2	1	1	2	2
4	1	2	2	2	2	1	1
5	2	1	2	1	2	1	2
6	2	1	2	2	1	2	1
7	2	2	1	1	2	2	1
8	2	2	1	2	1	1	2

		OPERATING	
FACTOR	PROCESS PARAMETER	LEVEL 1	LEVEL 2
A	MOLD TEMPERATURE	375-425° F	500-550° F
B	DOWNSPRUE RISER	STANDARD	REDUCED SIZE
C	METAL TEMPERATURE	1220-1260° F	1180-1215° F
D	MOLD COATING APPLICATION	ALL THE WAY	PARTIAL
E	RISER DESIGN	SINGLE	DOUBLE
F	MOLD DESIGN	POCKET	NO POCKET
G	MACHINE CYCLE	CORRECT	"SHORT CIRCUIT"

FIGURE 16

3.8L PISTON SHRINK STUDY
RESPONSE TABLE

	RESPONSE		PARAMETER LEVEL	
PROCESS PARAMETER	LEVEL 1	LEVEL 2	LEVEL 1	LEVEL 2
MOLD TEMPERATURE	0.5%	0.5%	375-425° F	500-550° F
DOWNSPRUE RISER	0.0%	0.9%	STANDARD	REDUCED SIZE
METAL TEMPERATURE	0.4%	0.5%	1220-1260° F	1180-1215° F
MOLD COATING APPLICATION	0.1%	0.8%	ALL THE WAY	PARTIAL
RISER DESIGN	0.5%	0.3%	SINGLE	DOUBLE
MOLD DESIGN	0.8%	0.1%	POCKET	NO POCKET
MACHINE CYCLE	0.3%	0.5%	CORRECT	"SHORT CIRCUIT"

EATON CORPORATION

What's the best application for Taguchi Methods? Eaton Corporation demonstrates that the greatest benefits can be realized in parameter design.

"In the United States, Taguchi Methods are being used most commonly to improve existing manufacturing processes," says Diane Byrne, a specialist in Eaton Corporation's Quality Institute (Southfield, MI). "In Japan, Taguchi Methods are predominately used during product design."

But where can Taguchi Methods best be applied during product and process design? Consider the following three steps:

1 System Design. This step requires the talents and skills of scientists and engineers. Designers may be innovative in their selection of design concept and various components.

2 Parameter Design. This is the step where designed experiments are conducted to optimize the proposed system. In parameter design, the best nominal values for design factors are determined so that a product exhibits a high level of performance with the least sensitivity to "noise" (uncontrolled factors). The goal is not just to design a system that works, but one that will be cost-effective as well.

3 Tolerance Design. If variation is not sufficiently reduced through parameter design, then tolerance design may be needed. Here, tolerances are tightened around specific design parameters.

However, the emphasis should be on using Taguchi Methods during the parameter design step and finding the best nominal values for all of the parameters. Then you can work on tightening tolerances during the tolerance design step to improve quality even further, if necessary. "You want to do tolerance design last," says Byrne, "because at the parameter design step, quality can be improved without spending additional money."

PARAMETER DESIGN STRATEGY

The strategy behind design of experiments in performance design is to obtain the best performance and the greatest resistance to noise factors at the least possible cost.

Here's a brief explanation: During production there are certain factors that are controllable and other factors that are not controllable. Using parameter design, it is possible to design a product so that it is minimally affected by noise factors (such as heat, cold, and humidity) during the production process. When products and processes are minimally affected by noise factors, they are referred to as being "robust." By designing products with the possible effects of noise factors in mind and conducting experiments to determine the combination of controllable factors that will best minimize the effects of noise factors, it is possible to make the products and processes "robust."

Of course, you must consider preparing the people who will be making use of design of experiments for parameter design. Fortunately, this isn't much of a problem, believes Byrne. "One of Dr. Taguchi's greatest contributions has been making design of experiments a common engineering tool," she says. "Engineers can now learn it quickly because it is simple. It's not a statistically or mathematically rigorous process anymore."

Training engineers to use parameter design techniques involves the following steps:

► First, it is important to explain the concept— the theory, how it is applied, how easy it is, and how powerful it is.

► Next, participants should have a project on which they want to work, so that they can actually use the concept during training.

"We ask engineers to come as a team and to have a project goal identified so that they can gain hands-on experience with the methods," says Byrne. And once engineers find out how simple the methods are to use and what they can accomplish with them, they readily embrace them, she has found.

► To ensure follow-through back at the plant, however, Byrne recommends having at least one individual trained thoroughly in Taguchi Methods. If the engineers return to their plants without resource people who can help them with the techniques, they may drift away from the techniques eventually.

"We have found that engineers at plants with

resource people use Taguchi Methods daily—almost routinely,'' Byrne relates. ''However, those at plants without resource people usually give up.''

THE REWARD: REDUCED COSTS

While your focus will most likely be on the engineers when it comes to parameter design and Taguchi Methods, don't overlook the gains that can be made elsewhere. Byrne reports on a situation where a production foreman at a plant without a large engineering staff used the methods with his operators.

The work group ran a wave soldering process and were experiencing a lot of solder defects on PC boards. The group looked at its controllable factors and noise factors and then conducted a series of experiments that led to a dramatic reduction in the number of defects.

''The estimated annual savings on reduced scrap and rework alone were $20,000,'' says Byrne. ''However, when we took the long-term effects into consideration, it turned out to be about $94,000 per year in savings.''

With cost-cutting like that at your fingertips, you might consider using Taguchi Methods for parameter design in your own operations.

SHELLER-GLOBE CORPORATION

How does a major supplier to the automotive industry remain competitive? It manufactures top-quality products by using Taguchi Methods.

"Being a part of the very competitive auto industry, our survival is based on quality improvement programs," says Paul F. Barth, director of Statistical Methods for Sheller-Globe Corp. (Detroit, MI), a major supplier to the auto industry. "Since 1983, following a trip to Japan, our executives' primary goal has been quality improvement. We started out with SPC and we've come a long way since then."

One of the many advances the company has made since 1983 is the implementation of Taguchi Methods. "We have found that they expedite the implementation of quality improvement methods for us," he says.

THE METHODS MAKE A DIFFERENCE

Like anything else, success with Taguchi Methods depends on where and how you use them. For example:

► **During the production phase,** the goal of Taguchi Methods is to reduce process variation for the controllable factors providing uniform products with very low scrap. In this area, Taguchi Methods can help you:

- determine the sources of variation and then control them as a result of the response you get from the experiments

- explain the common-cause variations on certain processes that have been plaguing you for years

- increase your process capability on the shop floor, which helps reduce the number of nonconforming parts

The key to success during this phase, according to Barth, lies in having cross-function teams that plan and implement the methods. Teams are composed of representatives from various departments that have a vested interest in solving the problems. The most critical tasks that the teams must master are:

➡ Choosing the most important projects on which to use Taguchi Methods (preferably by using Pareto charts to isolate the high-cost problems).

➡ Selecting the proper variables and levels to be tested. "If the teams don't come up with the right variables that contribute to the variation, they won't get the answers that will totally solve their problems," emphasizes Barth.

➡ Running a validation experiment after getting their results to make sure that the results are indeed predictable.

► **During the design phase,** the goal is to provide designs that prevent scrap from being generated in the production phase by optimizing the design parameters and levels. This results in products being manufactured with very little piece-to-piece variation and that are robust against their functional environments as well. In other words, the goal during the design phase is to remove the *effects* of the causes, rather than to control the causal factors or reduce the variation of the causes.

This brief review should be of some help if you aren't getting the most out of Taguchi Methods. Take a look at your current methods to ensure that you're applying them appropriately in either the design or production stage. The Methods work best when you draw on the appropriate strengths for each given phase.

ECHIP, INC.

If you're just getting your feet wet in Taguchi Methods or other design-of-experiments techniques, you may not be ready for Robust Product Design. Then again, it never hurts to look to what may be the future of quality assurance.

Statistical process control (SPC) is widely used to identify quality problems on products that don't meet specifications. In fact, SPC is becoming something of a standard in North American industry. But one expert maintains that SPC mainly "counts dead bodies. It provides little information on how to design the product and process to be on target in the first place in order to prevent problems," says Dr. Thomas A. Donnelly of ECHIP, Inc. (Hockessin, DE).

So how can you make products right on the first try? One way is through the use of experimental design. An experimental design is a set of experiments in which many variables are simultaneously controlled at specified levels. These sets of experiments maximize the information that can be obtained while minimizing the amount of data that needs to be collected. Depending on the type of experimental design that is run, one can:

➪ identify the few significant variables in a large group being studied

➪ detect interactions between variables

➪ generate response surfaces (pictures of the process) relating the measured characteristics to the controlled variables

The more descriptive or predictive you want your knowledge about the product to be, the more experiments you will need to conduct. For example, the vise that seals bags of potato chips requires the proper combination of temperature, duration, and pressure on the plastic. To test the bond strength, you can use a machine that pulls the seals apart and measures the force per unit area required to do this.

An experimental design consisting of 15 unique combinations of control variables can be analyzed to produce response surfaces relating the bond strength to the applied temperature, duration, and pressure. Figure 17 illustrates one such surface with the pressure set at a constant value.

The response surface is interpreted just like a topological contour map. The example in Figure 17 shows the top of a ridge running from the upper left to the lower right of the map. There are several things to note. Some regions of the contour are less steep than the others, like the top of a ridge. Picking any contour line (for instance, the H = 77.4), it can be seen that there are many combinations of temperature and duration (for the stated pressure) that yield such a bond strength. At low temperatures the bond strength increases as the duration increases ("going up the hill") while at high temperatures the opposite is true ("going down the hill"). Such a strong interaction between the temperature and the duration is quite obvious in response surface experimentation but is easily missed in classical "one variable at a time" experimentation.

BEYOND TAGUCHI

Many engineers in North America, particularly those in the automotive industry, have first run into experimental design in the the methods of Dr. Genichi Taguchi. As good as these "textbook" methods are, Donnelly says there are better designs and strategies. The newer methods take advantage of the improvements in statistical methodology and computer technology of the last two decades.

For example, using Taguchi L8 (eight trials, three variables at two levels) or L9 (nine trials, three variables at three levels) experimental designs for the potato chip bag sealing problem discussed above would result in identifying the important variables and detecting the interactions, but it would not have the predictive capability of the illustrated response surface design.

When it comes to designing products to be robust or insensitive to "noise" factors—an idea that is certainly among Taguchi's greatest contributions—the new strategies are significantly more efficient than those proposed by Taguchi himself. A robustly designed product will be minimally affected by noise factors, such as temperature, humidity, vibration, tool wear, and component deterioration.

The weakness in Taguchi's approach is that you collect noise information everywhere that you collect response data or signal information. What's the problem with that? "It requires taking lots of information about noise in the regions where the signal just isn't that interesting," explains Donnelly.

In other words, there are regions in the experiments (for example, test runs of certain combinations of variables) that indicate very poor yield. No matter how consistent the parts might come out or how resistant to the environment they might be, you would never run the process there.

"Therefore, collecting noise information in these places—where you will never run your process—doesn't make much sense," says Donnelly.

The real problem becomes evident when you consider the number of experiments you have to run in order to test for noise using Taguchi methods. For example, if you decide to run 27 experiments (combinations of control variables) and you also want to test for noise, you will also be required to run noise experiments (combinations of noise variables) at each of the 27 control experiments. Let's say this requires 18 separate noise trials at each location: You will be forced to run 486 experiments to determine the effect of noise on the process.

THE EASIER WAY

For quality professionals looking for an easier method of design of experiments, Donnelly suggests Robust Product Design (RPD). RPD is similar to the approach of Taguchi in that you study both the control variables and noise variables. The difference is that with RPD, you only collect noise information where the signals are interesting, which substantially reduces the number of trials required.

Using the example cited above with RPD, you might run 27 experiments with the control variables, and then examine the response surface that the data support. By studying this picture, you can decide where it is best to run your process.

For example, you might not want to run your process in a "valley," because the signal information is poor there. Similarly, you might not want to run it on a steep "peak," because if there is much variation ("falloff") during the production process, it will have a dramatic effect on the response. The best place to run the process is usually on a "plateau"

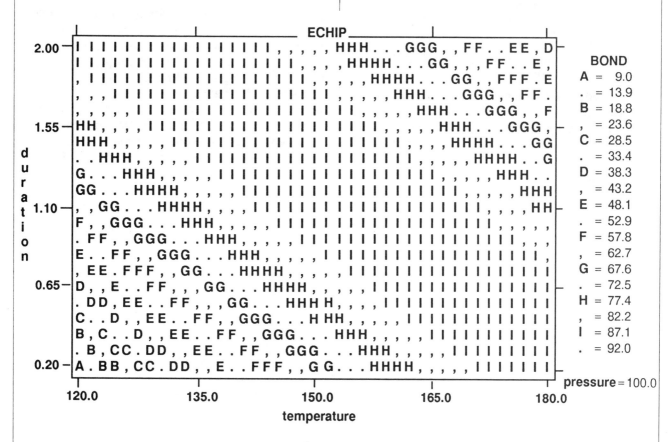

FIGURE 17

(preferably high in this case), where the results are good and where the variation won't have a major effect on the response.

Once you have determined the point (or even several points) where you want to run your process because these signals are interesting to you, then you can run your 18 noise trials. The total number of experiments is then 45 (27 + 18), a far cry from the 486 otherwise required. Of course, by not running the 441 extra trials that were run in the Taguchi approach, you can't conclude anything about the noise where the signals were uninteresting—but, on the other hand, that's no loss.

RPD IN ACTION

For a better understanding of RPD, consider this example: Let's say you have already designed and run experiments that have given you a response surface characterizing the output of a circuit for an electronic component that is to be installed under the hood of an automobile. After identifying the interesting locations or desirable sets of conditions to which you wish to build parts, you want to study the noise factors. For instance:

• One type of environmental noise will be the temperature ranges under which the component will have to operate (-40 °C to 150 °C).

• One type of process noise will be the tolerance of the resistors being used. For example, the design may call for a 100-ohm resistor. If Manufacturing uses resistors with one percent variation (relatively expensive), the resistors will vary from approximately 99 ohms to 101 ohms. If, on the other hand, Manufacturing uses resistors with 10 percent variation (relatively less expensive), the resistors will vary from 90 ohms to 110 ohms.

The goal, of course, is to identify conditions where the response signal is acceptable and at the same time minimally sensitive to variation caused by the noise factors. A second experimental design is constructed and the corresponding data are collected and analyzed.

These new surfaces are studied and conclusions are drawn about the trade-offs between robustness and cost. In terms of the process noise, for example, this may require using more expensive components, such as one percent resistors instead of 10 percent resistors. Or one may find that the effect of the environmental noise factor (temperature) swamps the process noise factor (resistor tolerance), and that 10 percent resistors are no less effective than the one percent resistors but are less expensive.

FOOD FOR THOUGHT

If you've only recently gotten a handle on the concept of Taguchi methods, you may not be quite ready for an approach that refines them even more. But there's certainly no harm in keeping up with the latest developments in the quality assurance field—and there's always the chance that you can apply some or all of the concepts of Robust Product Design to your own operations. Only by learning about new ideas can you sift through them and choose the ones that will work best for you.

QUALITY AND OTHER DEPARTMENTS

United, you stand; divided, you fall. That statement accurately sums up the relationship between QA and the other departments at your company. When each department marches to its own drummer, achieving your goals may be difficult—even impossible. Working co-operatively is a must if you want to keep quality on track.

INTERNATIONAL SWITCHBOARD CORPORATION

The quality department is often regarded as the "bad guys" by other departments. By following this company's strategy, you can promote teamwork with other areas at your firm and break down the barriers to harmonious—and quality-effective—relations.

Is the quality department looked on as the enemy by the production department—as well as others—at your company? "It's an all-too-common problem," acknowledges Leon Fassy, quality assurance manager for International Switchboard Corporation (Sugar Land, TX). "The truth is that we and they have much in common and the best way to accomplish mutual goals is to work in harmony with each other."

Fassy speaks from his own experience, since he had to change QA's negative image when he took over that department at ISC. How he did that provides valuable instruction for other quality professionals who find themselves in the same boat.

ALL FOR ONE AND ONE FOR ALL

What advice does Fassy have for those who want to create a more harmonious relationship between QA and other departments? He recommends taking the following steps:

❏ **Meet with other departments.** Get together with the heads of Production and Engineering and set up a meeting of engineers, designers, and material control and production workers. At this gathering, explain the function of Quality Assurance as it applies to other departments: to assure that the product is designed and engineered correctly, and that it is then manufactured in accord with the specifications.

❏ **Initiate a participatory problem-solving program.** While a worker's goal should always be to reach the zero defects level, it usually isn't realistic to expect perfection at all times. Therefore, you need to have a problem-solving mechanism in place, one that allows everyone to participate. As soon as a problem is recognized, it should become *everyone's* (QA, Engineering, Design, Material Control, and Production) task to work together, determine why the problem exists, and come up with a solution.

❏ **KEEP IN MIND** ⇒ When pinpointing the cause of the problem, you may discover that an individual employee was at fault. At many companies, this would be *the signal* for the adversarial relationship to go into full swing. "But if you do determine that it is human error, the emphasis—at least initially—should be on preventing the problem in the future, not on discipline," says Fassy. "You can always take disciplinary action later on if you've determined that the employee cannot—or will not—do the job as it needs to be done."

PEOPLE POINTERS

What other steps can you take to promote a good work atmosphere between your department and others?

★ *Look for good interpersonal skills when hiring QA people.* If the people on the quality staff are good communicators to begin with, chances are that fewer misunderstandings will arise and lead to full-blown conflict.

★ *Arrange to have people from other departments spend at least some time working in Quality Assurance.* For instance, at ISC, all new engineers spend their first four to six weeks in QA, performing final inspections and testing. This allows them to see, firsthand, the practical effects of design and engineering on quality assurance, and gives them an understanding of the role QA plays within the company.

★ *Ask your staff to encourage production workers to come to them with quality-related questions instead of taking them to their supervisors.* This is not done to circumvent supervisory authority, however. "While we're all part of the same team, it's important to realize that sometimes employees, especially new employees, may not want to ask their immediate supervisors too many questions," he points out. This also lays the groundwork for a helpful relationship between QA and the employees who come to them with questions.

COOPERATION IS CRUCIAL

No matter how you approach it, it's crucial that the quality department maintain a sound work relationship with every other function within the company. To do otherwise makes the workplace a less than enjoyable place to come to each day, and jeopardizes your company's chances of providing a quality product or service to your customers.

FEDERAL EXPRESS

FedEx's plan to involve its maintenance department in QA has kept its planes flying high and its customers satisfied. You can assure both interdepartmental cooperation and quality by taking a similar route.

Traditional quality control efforts have tended to rely on the "CCCE Formula"—Critique, Confrontation, Conflict, and Enforcement. At Federal Express (Memphis), this formula was in effect for a number of years. Contributors (FedEx's term for nonmanagement employees in the line haul organization) in the quality assurance department were also responsible for assuring quality in the maintenance department. The contributors would critique the work performed by the people in Maintenance, and confront them with the errors or oversights they found. This often led to conflict as the two sides questioned each other's standards. But the end result was usually the same: The quality staff would enforce its decisions.

While quality and reliability levels in the company were the highest in the industry, the approach still left something to be desired in terms of departmental cooperation and—more important—diminished opportunities for improving quality and reliability even further.

"We have always operated under the principle that Federal Aviation Administration (FAA) requirements are the very *minimum* with which we must comply," says Bob Kurtz, managing director of Quality Assurance. "We are constantly looking for ways to do more than is simply required by law."

A NEW APPROACH

The CCCE approach began to fall by the wayside when Jim Riedmeyer, a senior vice president in Line Haul Operations, introduced an approach he had found to be successful at another company during the 1950s. It had been Riedmeyer's experience that in traditional environments, maintenance people were usually not interested in meeting specs. Rather, they were primarily interested in seeing whether they could get their work past the QC inspectors.

When Riedmeyer saw the faulty logic with this approach, he proposed that the maintenance people take responsibility for their own quality, and the QC inspectors be responsible for auditing the work and helping Maintenance solve problems. This proposal met with success; the two groups dropped their adversarial relationship and began to cooperate, and quality improved dramatically.

"Under Riedmeyer's approach, the QA Department would no longer be the 'bad guy,' " explains Kurtz. "QA's job would simply be to tell Maintenance how it was doing." As a result, FedEx launched an effort to make Maintenance responsible for its own quality and to have QA provide feedback.

BRINGING CHANGES ON BOARD

To implement the new approach successfully, FedEx made a number of changes. First, it completely reorganized the QA department so that it is now made up of:

➡ **The quality control function,** which includes—

✔ **Aircraft Maintenance Quality Control.** This group develops QC practices for aircraft maintenance, has primary responsibility for meeting FAA requirements, and performs aircraft maintenance audits in Memphis.

✔ **Technical Audit.** This group audits FedEx's component maintenance suppliers and its fueling suppliers on a worldwide basis.

✔ **Weight and Balance.** Since it's important to know the weight of each airplane and how it is physically balanced in order to be sure that its flying characteristics are not adversely affected, this group audits weight and balance activities by watching ramp activity to make sure freight is loaded properly.

✔ **QA Administration.** This group ensures proper aircraft weight (which can vary over time as it collects dirt or sustains repairs), conducts *ad hoc* investigations in Memphis, and grants temporary authority to designated field mechanics around the country to conduct specific inspection activities.

✔ **Nondestructive Testing.** This group performs X-rays and other nondestructive testing of aircraft structures to check for cracks and other defects. It also manages FedEx's special tool calibration program.

✔ **Group Support Equipment.** This group performs inspections and audits on FedEx's 13,000 pieces of group support equipment, including fuel trucks, loader/lifters, and cargo tugs. Inspections occur when the equipment is first purchased, immediately after overhauls, and randomly while in service to ensure constant availability.

"Loader/lifters are so unique, for example, that you can't lease or rent them," notes Kurtz. "If you have one down, then you can't get freight off an airplane; they need to be in constant working order."

➠ **Field Quality Assurance,** which includes—

★ **Project Managers.** This group performs physical condition evaluations of aircraft that FedEx is considering purchasing. It also has on-site reps at the facilities where the aircraft are being built as well as where heavy maintenance and modifications are being performed on already owned airplanes.

★ **Field Quality Control.** This group is the field counterpart of Aircraft Maintenance Quality Control, performing aircraft maintenance QC at locations outside of Memphis. In addition, they visit major airframe and power plant repair vendors that perform work on FedEx aircraft to ensure that they are following the proper procedures and policies.

➠ **Reliability,** which includes—

✎ **Data Analysis.** This group analyzes the data generated by Aircraft Operations and Maintenance and turns it into useful information for use by Engineering to assist Maintenance in improving reliability and productivity. The group also assists Maintenance in troubleshooting ongoing problems.

✎ **Maintenance Program Support.** This group ensures that the scheduled maintenance program is effective (by making sure maintenance tasks are performed at the right frequency) and productive (by making sure the tasks detect deterioration as planned or provide needed service).

➠ **Maintenance technical training,** which includes—

▶ **Airframe and Power Plant.** This group trains maintenance people, not surprisingly, in the areas of airframe and power plant maintenance.

▶ **Avionics, GSE, and Facilities.** This group trains maintenance people in the maintenance of the aircrafts' electronic components.

▶ **FAA Liaison.** This is an individual contributor who is responsible for keeping track of changes made by the FAA and maintains daily contact with FAA's Memphis office. "Anyone at FedEx who needs information on the FAA contacts this person," says Kurtz.

Aside from these changes to the structure of the QA organization itself, the company also changed the titles of the individual QA contributors from "inspectors" to "auditors" to better reflect their new roles.

At first, some of the individual contributors didn't like the new designation: They had been trained in the past to believe that "inspector" was a premier title in the technical field, and it took some retraining to help them understand the vital role that auditors could play.

Training didn't end there, however. FedEx launched new education programs for both Maintenance and QA.

One area of concentration is improved technical training for the technical staff, while another is designed to teach the QA auditors how to perform their jobs better and work in a spirit of cooperation with Maintenance.

"We don't want to be in conflict," stresses Kurtz. "We want to provide feedback in positive, nonthreatening ways to help Maintenance people do their jobs better."

KEEP 'EM FLYING

Perhaps the greatest testimonial to the fact that QA and Maintenance *are* working together successfully at Federal Express is this: In its 15-year existence, the company has *never* sustained an aircraft crash, a particularly impressive record in these days of frequent reports of crashes.

"Our record is unblemished, and we have one of the best reliability records of any fleet of DC10s and 727s in the industry," says Kurtz. "We feel this is directly attributable to the professionalism of our work force."

SHELL CHEMICAL COMPANY

In order to improve quality and increase productivity, your department may need to closely examine production procedures. Here's how QA worked with the production staff at one of Shell's facilities and found ways to boost quality *and* quantity.

With the demand for quality increasing in recent years, most companies have come to realize that value and dependability—and not necessarily price—are what influence customers. One company that fully understands this concept is Shell Chemical Company.

"We began to realize a few years ago that if we could not provide a high-quality product consistently and dependably to our customers—even if we could sell it cheaper—our customers would go elsewhere," says Tommy Weatherly, a supervisor for Operations for Shell's Deer Park Manufacturing Complex (Deer Park, TX).

Shell's customers needed to take the company's product and use it directly in their manufacturing processes—without their own verification. "If our certificate of analysis met the requirements, they would use it in their processes," Weatherly explains.

One of the ways the plant chose to improve its quality to meet customer requirements was to implement statistical process control (SPC). One of the first things they realized in trying to implement SPC, though, was how low plant reliability was overall.

"We had low reliability because we had low output at the time," explains Weatherly. In other words, when demand for business increased and output had to increase, the plant discovered that it was not prepared to meet the increased capacity and produce quality products at the same time. "We didn't have reliable equipment to get us where we needed to be," he says. So the goal was to increase production while eliminating *off-spec* production.

In investigating the problem, the plant found that approximately 30 percent of the controllers on the equipment were being adjusted manually by the operators, rather than automatically, which was the way they should be adjusted. This presented four problems:

1 It cut down on the throughput of the plant.

2 It reduced product quality.

3 It was not making the best use of the operators'

skills.

4 Energy costs alone amounted to about $100 a day more when the operators had to adjust a controller on manual.

"Because of these factors, we realized that the first step to reaching our goal was to have all of the equipment operate on automatic," says Weatherly.

Next, it was necessary to train the employees to utilize the equipment to its full capacity. "After this, we arranged to have operations and maintenance personnel get together to discuss plant reliability so that hardware could meet what the process needed or what had to be done operationally to run equipment properly," he continues.

The plant was able to eliminate about 25 percent of its repeat maintenance work simply by having the operators work with maintenance personnel and get the "right fix," regardless of operational or hardware changes. Once the right fix was implemented, the operators did not have to spend time adjusting the instruments manually.

THE PEOPLE FACTOR

"We found that the key to success was getting the right people involved," observes Weatherly. "The person who knows the equipment best is the person who operates or maintains it every day. That person knows more about the specific things in it than anyone else. The closer you get to the process, in other words, the more you know about it."

Weatherly recalls sitting in meetings where people would try to explain why certain things were going wrong and would engage in a lot of theorizing. "All we had to do was go out to the field and talk to the operators to find out what was *really* going on," he reports.

▻ **KEY POINT** ⇨ You shouldn't be afraid to give employees a lot of responsibility, freedom, and authority to make their own decisions, Weatherly maintains. "In almost all cases, people know the right things to do," he says. "So I encourage employees to go with their 'gut' feeling,' because most of the time that will be right.''

Finally, he does not ignore suggestions—good or not so good. ''They have to be addressed,'' he emphasizes. If you ignore them, that could turn employees off to offering more suggestions—some of which are certain to be good—in the future.

QUALITY PAYS

As a result of the plant's drive to increase production, production is up between 25 and 40 percent. Right in step with that, quality has been improved, and is consistent. In addition, off-spec material has essentially been eliminated.

''In the meantime, we have gone from a buyer's market to a seller's market,'' says Weatherly. ''In a seller's market, we have the opportunity to sell products without a lot of customer input or interface, but we have stuck with selling only quality products and working with customers to meet common goals. This tells me that the company is really committed to quality and customer service. Quality is paying off for us and will continue to keep us on the top.''

HEWLETT-PACKARD COMPANY

There's much to be gained by keeping the peace with other departments and avoiding "turf" wars. Here's how H-P's quality department turned Marketing into a strong ally.

For many quality departments, success is measured by the number of rejects they catch at the end of the line. For others, it is measured by their ability to implement SPC and other line-owned quality efforts.

But for other quality departments—those within "cutting edge" companies—success is measured by the service they provide to *all* other departments in the organization.

The Colorado Computer quality department at Hewlett-Packard Company's Fort Collins facility, for example, has established partnerships with a number of different departments. These partnerships are designed to promote universal quality thinking and provide the best quality assurance service possible.

QUALITY LENDS ITSELF TO MARKETING

One of the earliest partnerships took place between QA and Marketing, according to Henry J. Kohoutek, quality manager. Kohoutek feels that there are a number of opportunities for the two departments to work together toward their common objective of customer satisfaction. These opportunities include:

☐ **Customer Needs Analysis.** Kohoutek has long been enthusiastic about a definition of quality proposed by K. Monroe and S. Petroshius that appeared in the February 1973 issue of *Journal of Marketing Research* in an article titled "Buyer's Perception of Price: An Update of the Evidence." The definition seems to be a precursor of the Quality Function Deployment effort now sweeping the United States, and reads as follows:

"(Quality is) a multiattribute product characteristic which can be expressed by a generalized, overall rating which is based on multidimensional measurements that reflect rank ordering of preferences and their relative importance."

Thus, Kohoutek sees opportunities for QA to assist Marketing in issues related to "quality deployment tables translating customer language about quality characteristics into the local engineering specifications used to manage internal quality improvement programs."

☐ **Market Research.** QA can also assist Marketing in the area of market research. The statisticians in the quality department are usually very familiar with the methods conducive to good market research, such as correlation analysis, regression analysis, probability sampling, factor analysis, multiattribute modeling, and causal analysis.

☐ **Forecasting.** QA statisticians can also assist Marketing in forecasting orders from customers.

☐ **Technology Assessment.** QA can help Marketing to study and understand the technologies needed to achieve the quality levels required by customers.

☐ **Competitive Analysis.** Here, QA can provide information about the company's quality as compared with competitors' quality, and analyze the trends of important quality attributes and levels.

☐ **Supplier Performance.** Since more and more customers today are concerned about their suppliers' suppliers, QA can help Marketing make sure that the company's suppliers will meet customer expectations and requirements.

☐ **Customer Tours.** Quality representatives can also participate in plant and facility tours for customers, detailing the company's quality philosophy and practices for them.

☐ **Ad Analysis.** Since product ads often discuss quality attributes as well as warranty and support information, it makes sense for QA to assist Marketing in developing accurate, appealing ads. "The quality community should help in assuring credibility of advertising by controlling—or at least auditing—the accuracy and completeness of presented information and of the supporting processes," says Kohoutek.

☐ **Pricing Strategy.** QA can also assist in setting product prices since, as Kohoutek notes, customers balance quality and price when making purchases.

☐ **Information Quality.** QA can review user manuals to make sure that the information is technically correct, concise, and clear.

PARTNERSHIP IN ACTION

"One of the first partnership improvement attempts between QA and Marketing at the Fort Collins facility took place in 1984. There were several reasons why the attempt was made in the first place:

► Corporate quality management policies and guidelines suggested the need for QA's close contact with the customer and required information feedback about customer satisfaction and product field performance.

► There had been previous close cooperation between both departments in terms of pricing proposal preparation, service contract pricing, and field training and support.

► The changing business and market situation imposed new performance requirements on Marketing and thus opened up opportunities for QA to contribute.

The first effort at partnership involved expanding existing surveys and field data collection to include other product attributes besides quality. However, Kohoutek admits, this effort was not very successful, primarily because some of the people in Marketing felt that QA was trying to impose some unwanted external requirements on them.

The second effort involved having QA offer services as a support function to Marketing. "We began helping Marketing indirectly by helping the field sales and service people directly," explains Kohoutek. Since the field people knew specifically where they needed quality-related assistance, QA was able to target and meet these needs. QA found that it could best help the field people in the following ways:

✔ providing product quality data sheets (bulletins containing conservative, factual test condition and test result data that allowed the field personnel and their customers to make their own interpretations)

✔ making direct contact with the field personnel via training sessions, presentations, and facility tours so that they could see firsthand what QA was capable of doing for them

✔ developing and distributing documents describing and exploring internal quality assurance and improvement programs

ENSURING SUCCESS

With the success of this second effort, Kohoutek is able to provide a formula for success in building a QA/Marketing partnership. He says that:

★ It makes sense to begin your effort with field sales. "This approach not only provides indirect support to Marketing but helps create an environment of cooperation," he says. "Once Marketing sees the benefits to customers through the sales function, it will want to work more closely with you."

★ Next, try to put yourself in Marketing's shoes and understand their goals and challenges. "This is almost a necessary condition for success," Kohoutek emphasizes.

★ Make sure you don't move into Marketing's "territory" without authorization. "It is important to eliminate the fear that many departments naturally have, the fear that there will be additional levels of unwanted controls when the quality department comes in," he cautions.

★ Once Marketing people see the benefits of your input, you can teach them problem-solving strategies and expose them to other technical tools. "You can't teach the tools before they see the benefits," Kohoutek notes. "However, once you show benefits, they will want to learn the tools themselves."

According to Kohoutek, the key measure of success is the marketing department's willingness to provide funds to QA for services delivered.

LENDING A HAND

If you follow that formula for success, then chances are that—like the quality department at the Fort Collins facility—QA will be able to assist Marketing in the areas of:

✎ standards and regulations

✎ customer interface

✎ field sales training

✎ customer service support

✎ Total Quality Control process analysis and process improvements

✎ human factors information

✎ product quality information

✎ reliability engineering

✎ product audits

✎ process audits

✎ statistical consulting

✎ special product testing

✎ safety testing

✎ warranty administration
✎ federal procurement processes

FORGING AHEAD

As if that weren't enough, the QA/Marketing partnership at Hewlett-Packard also plans to forge boldly into the future. "We want to become even more involved in the area of customer satisfaction: for example, in gaining a better understanding of trends in customer needs and priorities," report Kohoutek.

"In addition, we want to work on improving the quality of Hewlett-Packard services, not just products," he says.

Of course, forward-thinking companies can create opportunities for improvement throughout the organization by seeking to build partnerships between the quality assurance department and other groups within their firms besides Marketing.

PROMOTING QUALITY IN THE SERVICE SECTOR

Quality assurance is just as important in the service sector as it is in Manufacturing. And it takes the same type of commitment, training, and tools to make it work. The following service sector companies share their successful strategies for "keeping the customer satisfied."

NATIONAL WESTMINSTER BANK USA

Having trouble finding a service quality strategy to fit your needs? Then you might be better off designing your own improvement plan, as this bank has done.

One of the biggest laments of quality professionals working in service industries is that most "prepackaged" quality improvement plans have few applications to their situation. Because such plans are more frequently aimed at the production environment, QA managers looking for ways to foster improvement may have to do what this organization did: It designed its own improvement plan.

When William T. Knowles, Chairman and CEO of National Westminster Bank USA (New York City), joined the institution as president in 1981, "Our profit position was unfortunately bleak," he stated in a 1987 speech. "There were a number of problems, including a seeming lack of direction."

Between 1981 and 1985, the bank built a team of professional people, upgraded its systems, and reached a competitive level of performance. But Knowles was not satisfied. "We caught up with the competition," he says. "Now, the challenge was to move out ahead. How could we differentiate ourselves from the many banks in our market?"

The bank chose to concentrate its efforts on quality improvement as one of the strategic elements for outdistancing its competitors. "We realized that this would make good sense both financially and culturally," says Neil Metviner, vice president at the bank and manager of the Quality Improvement Divison.

The bank formally launched its Quality Improvement Process in early 1985. Its goals were to:

➡ enhance the bank's reputation for providing superior service and products

➡ reduce processing costs

➡ improve customer relations

➡ eliminate or reduce errors

➡ improve staff training

➡ provide greater employee recognition

➡ increase profits

The bank's Quality Improvement Steering Committee (about which we'll learn more later) issued the following statement as part of its open letter to employees on the Quality Improvement Process:

"With the dedication and hard work of all, we can move NatWest USA from being a good bank, with a reputation for good products and services, to being the best bank among our peers. In the long run, we are striving to establish a superior reputation, so that when other banks look for a standard by which to measure quality, they look to NatWest USA."

And just how does NatWest itself measure quality? "Overall, it means excellence throughout the organization and adherence to the highest standards," says Knowles.

"It also mean developing an environment in which all employees are constantly aware of customer needs as well as the need to deliver superior products in a timely way. Consistent with this, I see courtesy to customers and the creation of an operating environment in which we strive to be error-free as being very much a part of quality. In everything we do, quality means performing professionally and with distinction."

From Goals to Action ⇨ That's certainly a desirable goal, but how did NatWest go about achieving it? The first step involved analyzing the quality programs of other organizations to see how they operated and to see what was offered by outside consultants.

Management found, to its delight, that there was much to be learned about quality improvement from some of the cutting-edge manufacturers around the nation. But there were few models of quality improvement in banking, and the consultants were not able to offer the bank exactly what it needed in this area. As a result, management decided to organize its own effort internally.

Before rolling the plan out to the employees, the bank made several decisions about the effort:

1. It would be driven by top management commitment and involvement.

2. It would be a long-term process, not a short-term program.

3. It would provide the resources necessary to ensure success.

4. It would be tailored specifically to the bank's environment.

5. Decisions would be made and actions would be taken with the customer in mind.

6. Employee involvement would not be based solely on voluntary employee initiatives, because the most knowledgeable employees might not take part, and because the company wanted employees to see quality improvement as part of their jobs (not something extra), among other reasons.

CREATING THE FRAMEWORK

With these "rules" established, management created a Quality Improvement Steering Committee composed of approximately 10 top executives in the bank whose responsibility it was to create the Quality Improvement Process, oversee its implementation, and monitor its progress.

The committee then created an eight-person Quality Improvement Division (headed by Metviner) to work full time on the Quality Improvement Process implementation. The Division:

✔ conducts quality training programs

✔ provides quality consulting services to anyone in the bank who needs such services

✔ coordinates the annual planning process

✔ implements the measurement and reward systems

"The group serves as quality facilitators, not quality police officers," emphasizes Metviner. "Its role is to consult, not to confront."

AWARENESS: THE FIRST STEP

Once their roles were defined, the Quality Improvement Steering Committee and the Quality Improvement Division began their efforts by developing an employee awareness campaign. The idea was to get name recognition and give the process a unique identity. The first phase was a bankwide party called "It's Just a Beginning."

Next, the bank created a mascot for the Quality Improvement Process, a cartoon character named "DIRF" (Do It Right First). DIRF is now seen on notepads, key chains, and posters throughout the bank. Employees participated in a slogan contest with the winner being "Do It Right First, It's the NatWest Way."

In addition, the March 8, 1985, issue of the bank's internal magazine was entirely devoted to the Quality Improvement Process and provided employees with a 25-point quality improvement checklist designed to be removed from the magazine and placed in a prominent place as a reminder of what they could do individually to further the cause of quality and customer service improvement.

TRAINING: THE SECOND STEP

The next step was a massive undertaking: Train all of the bank's 4,600-plus employees in quality improvement techniques. Everyone in the bank, from the chairman to entry-level employees, was required to participate in the training. Officers received two-day training sessions, while non-officers received one-day sessions. The training process, which is still in operation today to train new employees, took approximately two years to reach all of the existing employees in the bank.

▭ **Proven Training Strategies** ⇨ The Quality Improvement Division, in conducting the training, made use of some interesting strategies:

1 Classes were composed of employees from different backgrounds, departments, functions, levels, and lengths of tenure. "Often, students can learn more from other employees' war stories than from the instructor's examples," explains Metviner. An additional benefit of the heterogeneous groups was they gave employees an opportunity to learn about the problems confronting others in the bank.

2 A top bank official led wrap-up sessions to put the training in perspective and to emphasize top management's commitment to the process.

3 Resisting the temptation to take the easy way out by using "off the shelf" training materials, the Quality Improvement Division created its own tailor-made material to fit the needs of the banking environment, its employees, and its customers.

4 Training was broken up with a mix of approaches, including lectures, break-out groups, case studies, and individual exercises.

5 Employees were encouraged to speak up and discuss problems and concerns they had that prevented them from providing the best quality possible.

"This training was really the first time that many

of the employees were able to go to a class not aimed specifically at improving their jobs, but rather at making them feel like a part of the whole bank—while giving them the opportunity to address problems they were having,'' points out Metviner.

PLANS OF ATTACK

What do NatWest employees and officers do with all that training? Each of the 12 areas of the bank sets annual Quality Improvement Plans, which result in Quality Improvement Projects. These projects are designed to allow managers and employees to use a uniform approach to address weaknesses in their areas.

Quality Improvement Teams are composed of managers who identify high-priority quality improvement opportunities in their divisions. Once approved by management, these opportunities become Quality Improvement Projects incorporated into the annual Quality Improvement Plans.

Quality Action Teams, on the other hand, are composed of employees who report to the managers on the Quality Improvement Teams. The Quality Action Teams are given responsibility to analyze the details of the opportunities, develop solutions, and implement the changes necessary to make the improvements.

''The idea is to get the employees to solve their own problems and make their own improvements,'' explains Metviner. ''They know best what needs to be done, and improving what they do is their ultimate responsibility, not that of a consultant or a staff professional.''

To that end, Quality Action Team members use the skills they learned in training to make flowcharts of their job processes and then analyze and simplify the workflows to eliminate problems, errors, and other weaknesses or inefficiencies. Currently, there are about 100 Quality Action Teams in operation in the bank, according to Metviner.

◻ **Why People Work for Improvement** ⇨ There are at least three reasons why so many employees take the time to improve their jobs in order to improve quality, says Metviner. The first two are internal (or personal) rewards, while the third is an external (or system) reward:

Reason #1: During training, employees began to realize that they would have the opportunity to take responsibility for the way they performed their jobs.

Reason #2: They soon realized also that by getting rid of the problems that plagued their daily worklife, they would be able to enjoy their work more and feel more rewarded with a sense of accomplishment.

Reason #3: Last but not least, employees are rewarded by the bank for their efforts with incentive and recognition programs. For example, under the Quality Achievement Program, managers who see their employees do something outstanding can write the incidents up and send them to Metviner's department. Metviner will then give the employees $100, and make them eligible for year-end lotteries with prizes that include a one-week, all-expenses-paid vacation for two—including the vacation time from work.

IT'S NOT ONLY THE EMPLOYEES THAT REAP THE REWARDS

While employees are benefiting from both personal and system rewards, the company as a whole is also seeing a number of positive results from its quality improvement effort. For instance:

⊃ It's not uncommon to walk through the bank now and see employees at break time huddled around performance charts showing volumes, error, timeliness, rework, and so on, and discussing strategies to improve their work and meet their goals. ''They see themselves as being part of a team and can see how vital their work is in the overall scheme of things,'' says Metviner.

⊃ Communication between and among employees in different departments and divisions has improved tremendously. In fact, it is now a regular practice for employees in one area to visit employees in another area to better understand how the latter perform their jobs.

⊃ When the bank sponsored ''Teamfest '88,'' a party designed to showcase the activities of 47 of the bank's Quality Action Teams, Metviner hoped that as many as 500 employees would show up, since the party was held during a weekday evening on employees' time. However, ''over 2,000 employees showed up to see what the teams were doing!'' he reports.

There are hundreds of examples of realized improvements, all of which have allowed the bank to roll its improvements out to its customers in the form of money-back guarantees for certain services. For example: ''In 1988, as part of an ad campaign called 'Raising the Standards of Banking,' we offered money-back guarantees to customers if we didn't issue letters of credit on our TRADE-BEAM product (an automated issuance system)," reports Metviner. Other promises the bank has made include:

⟹ A $50 refund if an approval or report on an installment loan application is not provided by 5:00 p.m. the following day.

⟹ Standard checking account fees are refunded if customers are not fully satisfied with the bank's checking account product for any reason within the first 90 days.

⟹ Five-dollar gifts from the branch manager are given to customers if they are not satisfied with the way they are greeted by bank personnel at the branch.

"We have been able to count the number of claims in these areas on one hand in the last year," reports Metviner. "As a result, we are now expanding our guarantees significantly to bring on more products and services."

FORD MOTOR COMPANY

Here are five keys used by Ford Motor Company to assure service quality. Based on the teachings of Dr. W. Edwards Deming, they can work as well for service functions as they do for manufacturing.

While manufacturing operations have had many tools to improve production quality, the perception in service operations has too often been that there seem to be too few tools applicable to their needs. For the quality professional committed to improving service quality, then, the solution may simply be to adapt the production improvement tools already being used.

When Ford Motor Company began its foray into quality improvement in the early 1980s under the tutelage of Dr. W. Edwards Deming, the lion's share of the initial publicity and results centered on production quality improvement. However, there was more going on at Ford than met the eye of many observers.

"We were looking at the application of Dr. Deming's ideas not only on the product side but also on the administrative, service, and support side," reports Harry L.M. Artinian, chief statistician for Finance and Financial Services Group. "We set as a goal to improve the quality of these support systems just as we intended to improve product quality."

While the challenge and steps involved in improving service quality are different in some ways from those involved in improving product quality, there are more similarities than differences, Artinian stresses.

"In terms of implementation, there are very few differences," he states. "About the only major difference at all is that, in service quality improvement, employees can't actually *see* the processes in place. In manufacturing, of course, they can see the operations taking place and all of the processes in action."

▭ **Five Key Components** ⇒ Artinian sees five important components necessary for improving service quality:

■ **Key #1: Senior Management Involvement.** "This is one area that you can't overemphasize," stresses Artinian. One way to foster that involvement is to train top management so that they not only understand how the improvement process works but what value it has *and* what their roles should be in promoting the improvements and resulting changes. "It's important to explain their need both to sponsor individual projects and to follow up on them."

At Ford, gaining senior management involvement was not as difficult as it might be in other organizations, because senior management already understood the concept of business process. "We have Total Quality Excellence, which means that every Ford employee—from the chairman of the company to the newest hire on the line—is responsible for managing a process," explains Artinian.

One of the tools of TQE, then, is process improvement, and since senior managers used the concept themselves, they began to support its use at lower levels in the organization. "In other words, process improvement at Ford is a generic concept. That makes it very powerful because everyone at all levels sees how things work not only at his or her own level but at other levels as well."

■ **Key #2: Strong and Knowledgeable Teams.** The employees involved in cross-functional improvement teams should be familiar with the processes with which they are involved—and be willing to tackle any and all upstream stages where there are indications that improvements can be made.

"If you make a list of your most inviolate processes and procedures, you have before you a list of areas that represent the greatest potential for improvement," says Artinian. "With this understanding in mind, there are no processes or procedures at Ford that are sacrosanct. We view *every* process as an opportunity for improvement."

■ **Key #3: A Framework and Methodology.** Employees involved in process improvement teams should understand how to dissect and analyze the processes they intend to tackle. At the same time, the teams must also have a grasp of what constitutes "quality" for these processes.

As noted earlier, the only major difference between improving product quality and improving service quality is in trying to visualize the processes. "And so, it takes more time for employees on the teams to come to agreement on how the processes that they are studying actually function," says Artinian.

In the product environment, of course, there is less disagreement on what the stages and the steps of the process are. In the service area, most people know how their individual part of the process is formed, but they may not know where it goes after them, how it is used, or even if their customers—the next people in line in the process—are satisfied with the work they have passed on.

"Sometimes, work might even come back to them, and they don't know why," he says. "When you extend this lack of understanding over a number of stages, you can see how complex it is to fully understand how complete processes work. And over the years, stages have usually been added to processes for various reasons, so ultimately no one person in the organization knows how the complete process works."

That's why it's important that teams have available to them methods that allow them to:

⟾ identify and outline processes

⟾ determine what customers expect in terms of quality

⟾ locate areas in the processes where these quality requirements are not being met

■ **Key # 4: An Improvement Method.** At this point, the teams need access to any of the various tools, such as SPC, that can help them improve the processes under scrutiny.

■ **Key #5: An Emphasis on Change.** Second only in importance to gaining senior management support, according to Artinian, is getting everyone to understand that the emphasis of process improvement is a change in the way people think, act, and believe, *not* a set of tools or techniques.

"It is really a total systems view," he emphasizes. "In fact, although I spend some of my time on statistics, because it forms the cornerstone for continuous improvement, I spend the majority of it trying to show people that quality is getting them to understand internal supplier-customer relationships and taking a systems view of the organization instead of a functional view."

MAJOR REDUCTIONS, MAJOR INCREASES

As a result of focusing efforts on service process improvements, Ford has seen major reductions in cost as well as increases in quality, productivity, and employee morale. "In every case, employees become excited because they have the privilege to better understand the importance of what they do, improve their work, and take pride in it."

In 1984, for example, the company began a process improvement effort in one of its export supply organizations, which had a number of administrative functions, such as financial services and material control. One area that a team tackled was the freight audit and payment system. There was a problem with the payment of carrier invoices (the invoices that carriers sent Ford for payment of the services they rendered). In fact, 34 percent of the invoices that carriers submitted were being rejected from the system for one reason or another. Others were taking 40 to 60 days to be paid.

"These problems had an impact not only on the financial side of the business but also on the operations side," reports Artinian. "For instance, we might have a shipment that we needed to move quickly from a supplier who used a specific carrier, but the supplier would tell us that the carrier was resisting further shipments because it hadn't been paid for the previous work it had done for us."

The team studied the process and within five months had reduced the invoice rejection rate from 34 percent to under 1 percent. In addition, they cut the number of days before payment was made from 40 to 60 down to 6.

"Some people questioned the wisdom of paying faster," admits Artinian. "They noted that this would only reduce our cash flow. I explained that cash flow was only a visible cost. The invisible costs—such as demoralized employees 'fighting fires' and coping with inefficiencies, the cost of dissatisfied customers, and so on—were much greater."

▷ **The Bottom Line** ⇒ Employees feel themselves beginning to gain control over the process and understand their role in making it work most effectively. And when that happens, they take more pride in the quality of their work as well as in the quality of service provided by their organization.

NASHUA CORPORATION

When it comes to customer service, does your company provide its reps with the tools they really need to get the job done right? This world-class manufacturer shows you how to get maximum output from all your service reps.

"We realized that if we wanted to provide total customer service and quality, we would have to make similar gains in nonmanufacturing areas, such as customer service," explains Earl Dodge, mechanical design group leader in Nashua Corporation's Computer Products Division.

FOCUS ON A NEW AWARENESS

To bring the service function up to the new expectations, the company began with an employee education program. The focus was on encouraging employees to begin participating more actively in changing their tasks than on improving technical skills. "We did introduce some techniques, but the idea behind the education was primarily to get employees to think and question why they had been doing things the way they had," states Dodge.

Awareness sessions were followed by training sessions designed to teach employees problem-solving. Here's how employees at Nashua were introduced to problem-solving:

STEP 1: Dig into problems deeper than the symptoms in order to get to the root causes.

STEP 2: Come up with a number of alternatives (possible solutions).

STEP 3: Choose the best solution, and know why you're choosing it.

STEP 4: Implement it and monitor its results.

PROBLEM-SOLVING IN ACTION

These steps enabled the employees to root out problems and solve them effectively. Here are some of the problems they faced:

❏ **Ducking Difficult Orders** ⇒ It seemed that some employees processed easy orders immediately and stacked problem orders in a pile off to the side to process at a later time. One of the basic tenets of JIT philosophy is that WIP inventory be eliminated, and stacks of problem orders are, in an office setting, WIP "inventory."

⇒ *Solution:* The system was revised in such a way that employees would process all orders in the sequence in which they were received—no "problem piles." "This helped us to pinpoint specific problems and solve them at once instead of ignoring them and making the same mistakes over and over again," explains Charles Marshall, controller in the company's Office Products Division. "In other words, we began addressing problems in a timely manner and solving them to prevent recurrence."

❏ **Error Correction** ⇒ Another "glitch" that employees identified in their processes was that when they received work containing errors from fellow employees in other departments, the employees *receiving* the work were responsible for correcting the errors. This, of course, did nothing to get to the root of the problem, which was: *Why are the errors being made in the first place?*

⇒ *Solution:* To determine the answers to this question, the process was revised so that errors were returned for correction to the employees who made them in the first place. This did two things:

● It highlighted recurring problems that could be addressed. For instance, if employees were making the same errors over and over, it might be determined that more training was needed.

● It focused employee attention on their own lapses in quality. Since no one likes to see his or her own errors, employees made a special effort to be more careful in doing their work right the first time so that it wouldn't have to be returned to them for corrections.

FLOWCHARTING: A VALUABLE TOOL

Although returning errors to employees for correction was effective in bringing down errors, more had to be done. Nashua found that one of the most powerful tools that employees were able to learn about and use was flowcharting. There are two ways to create waste, says Marshall. One is by not understanding what you do. The other is by doing what you do sloppily.

❏ **Key Concept** ⇒ Flowcharting helps to uncover

both of these problems by forcing employees to look at each job as an ordered sequence of steps.

To train employees in flowcharting, instructors began with simple examples, such as the steps taken when brushing one's teeth. The purpose of choosing something so simple was to illustrate the importance of detail, detail, detail in flowcharting. "When employees first began flowcharting the process, they had the toothpaste on the toothbrush before they had even taken the cap off the toothpaste!" Dodge laughs.

By the third and fourth sessions, the instructors began helping the employees translate the theory and examples into practice, asking employees to flowchart their own work processes and to identify areas in which they could make improvements by uncovering waste.

The instructors found it extremely valuable to bring in people from outside the customer service department for these sessions. Why? To take advantage of their objectivity. "These outside people don't know all the details of what Customer Service does, so they ask simple *but basic* questions: 'What do you do next? Why? How do you get from here to there?' etc. The people who perform these tasks every day have a tendency to skip a lot of the details because they're so used to doing them without thinking about what they're doing," he explains.

What did this experience teach employees? Employees realized that:

- They were performing a lot of unnecessary activities.
- There was a great deal of duplicated effort.
- Many tasks and process steps could be combined.

Prior to teaching employees about flowcharting, order processing had occurred this way:

1 Employees would take orders over the phone and write them on forms.

2 Employees would send these forms to the credit department for credit checks.

3 The orders would then be rewritten on new forms.

4 The order would then be entered into the computer.

5 The employees would then make copies of the forms.

6 Employees would file them in a number of places.

Besides being inefficient, the process was error-prone. It was common for employees to transpose customer numbers or order numbers when copying information from one form to another. This, of course, caused problems downstream in the process, and time had to be taken to locate the errors and correct them.

In tackling the problems of inefficiency and errors in the process, employees found that they could combine forms to eliminate the need for rewriting orders after the credit check, develop multipart carbonless forms to eliminate the need for making copies, and completely eliminate the need to file in one particular file. "We found that the only purpose for this one file was to prove who did or didn't make errors," states Marshall. "We eliminated that file in three seconds!"

Management then gave the customer service employees the authority to make the credit checks themselves, eliminating the need to send all orders to the credit department.

As a result of the changes, the new process looks like this:

1 Employees take orders over the phone, write them on multipart forms, and check credit.

2 The orders are entered into the computer.

3 Only necessary duplicate copies are filed.

Errors decreased dramatically, and employees rewrote 300 fewer orders a week and eliminated 600 copies a week. "We ended up saving 20 hours a week with this new streamlined process," reports Marshall.

VESTING AUTHORITY

A vital component of success needed in Nashua's JIT program is the giving of additional authority to employees in order to allow them to take responsibility and make decisions. Naturally, the authority has to be confined within certain guidelines, and employees must be trained in how to make these decisions.

The following three examples show what can be achieved when employees are given the power to act independently and to make improvements.

EXAMPLE #1: Prior to the changes in customer service, employees had to obtain approval before they could air-freight shipments to customers in need. In investigating the issue, the department realized that one of three situations was involved when a customer requested air freight:

1. The customer had miscalculated needs and would thus be willing to pay the extra charges.

2. Nashua had made a mistake, and being willing to ship via air freight would help them look better to the customer.

3. Regardless of where the problem lay, shipping by air freight for a customer in need would help the company show its concern for its customers.

With these realizations, management authorized employees to approve air-freight shipments when appropriate and within certain guidelines. As a result, employees saved themselves time by not having to locate someone for authorization, saved time for the customers by being able to get their shipments out quicker, and looked more professional in the eyes of their customers.

EXAMPLE #2: If there were problems in receiving payment for orders, the company's credit department was usually the first to hear about them. In most cases, late payments were the result of customers' problems with the orders they received (incorrect items, incorrect counts, damaged items, etc.).

The credit department had developed an elaborate system to notify customer service personnel of such problems and make sure that they were following up on these problems to resolution. Besides being inefficient, the system was ineffective, because it turned out that only one person—not the customer service department as a whole—ultimately had responsibility for claims (invoices that customers refused to pay because of problems.)

To streamline the process, the claims specialist was trained to become a regular customer service representative, and all employees in the department were given responsibility for following up on problems. Additionally, the credit department was told that there would be no need to follow up on the customer service department's efforts in this area and that Customer Service would take full responsibility for follow-up.

EXAMPLE #3: Customer Service also took over some of the responsibilities formerly assigned to the company's product managers. Product managers were supposed to be developing and launching new products, but they were often so inundated with customer calls and letters relating to product application questions, product quality problems and complaints, and requests for bid prices that they had very little time for developing and launching new products. "As an example, one product manager came back after being gone for two days to find 60 phone messages waiting on his desk!" reports Marshall.

To address this problem, Customer Service was given the responsibility and the authority to deal with these areas. The necessary training was provided, and management promised to back up reps on their decisions, right or wrong. Support, both Dodge and Marshall emphasize, was vital to the success of this change. As long as employees knew they would be backed up, they felt comfortable with making the decisions they felt were appropriate.

The goal in Customer Service has come to be called the "one-stop program," designed to eliminate the need for transferring customers to a number of different people in the company. "Before this program, customers often didn't know with whom they needed to talk or if they had the right people at all," admits Marshall. "Now, customers can call our customer service representatives and have all of their questions answered. In essence, the representatives have evolved from being order-takers to being territory managers."

BOTTOM LINE: QUALITY PERFORMANCE ACROSS THE BOARD

By streamlining operations and eliminating many unnecessary steps, Nashua was able to increase its productivity while providing excellent service to its customers. These changes resulted in many profitable benefits for every department in the very first year.

WOOLRICH, INC.

To ensure quality service, you must gain the commitment of employees and suppliers. Here's how to get these two key factions on your service quality team.

When it comes to quality, you may be quite willing to accept the axiom that "the customer is always right." The only question is, just what is it that the customer is right about? In other words, if you don't know what consumers are looking for, any improvements you are able to make will be the result of blind luck.

Many companies have taken steps to improve quality in recent years, but a large number of them have missed the boat in one very important area: They've attempted to improve quality in a vacuum. That is, they forge ahead without knowing what to improve, how much to improve it, or why it needs improving. And why don't they have this information? They have failed to get specific input from their customers.

One company that realizes the importance of getting quality feedback directly from customers is Woolrich, Inc. (Woolrich, PA), manufacturers of rugged outdoor apparel since 1830. In the last five years, the company's customers (department stores, specialty stores, sporting goods stores, and mail-order retailers) have been promoting a "quality first" attitude among their suppliers.

"Their customers—the consumers—are demanding quality, so it is up to us to provide that," explains Richard Holcombe, vice president of Sales Service. "We've been number one in our industry for over 150 years, and we plan to stay that way."

With that commitment in mind, Woolrich set a number of goals for itself.

✍ **GOAL # 1:** Take a proactive role in quality so that it could anticipate quality problems and prevent them before they occur.

✍ **GOAL # 2:** Develop a QA effort that is:

A. Coordinated—a cooperative effort among all departments in the company. "Our drive for improved quality has been a catalyst to create other communication programs between the various departments," notes Holcombe. "In this way, if we have to report any bad news to customers, we can do it three months in advance instead of the day something is supposed to be shipped."

B. Comprehensive—covering the process all the way from the company's raw material suppliers through distribution to customers. This includes:

✓ specifications for raw materials
✓ inspection and testing of the materials when they arrive
✓ on-line QA inspections
✓ a sampling plan for finished goods

"We don't load anything into our three distribution centers without a QA sign-off," reports Holcombe.

✍ **GOAL #3:** Base the program on customer input (such as return rates, voluntary customer information, and surveys). "We survey our customers to see how they perceive our quality and how *their* customers perceive our quality," explains Holcombe.

BLUEPRINT FOR SUCCESS

As Woolrich sees it, the key to a proactive QA effort is employee commitment, says David Gay, director of Apparel Resources. The challenge is to get employees to focus on quality first, and productivity second.

"It has required some additional technical training for the quality staff, but mostly it has involved a reorientation of all of the employees to the importance of quality," says Gay.

"We emphasize the importance of producing products that they would like to purchase themselves," adds Holcombe.

The fact that employees like to know how they are doing has provided yet another opportunity for getting workers to gear themselves toward quality instead of productivity alone. "Our focus in the past was to reprimand employees who failed to produce quality products," notes Gay. "Today, we concentrate on informing everyone of how they're doing, praising employees who do good work, and letting everyone know how they can do even better."

SUPPLIERS JOIN THE PARTY

The emphasis on involvement doesn't stop with employees, however; suppliers are also brought into the fold at Woolrich. Gay says that the creation of raw material specifications has been extremely helpful in gaining supplier cooperation for quality improvement.

"For the most part, suppliers are being cooperative, but a few of them think our specs are too stringent," relates Gay. "We have to explain to them that our customers are requiring this of us, so we must require it of our suppliers."

Once you do have suppliers taking part in the QA effort, you'll have a real head start toward making quality improvements, one you wouldn't have if you restricted your efforts solely to your own plant. "If you start in your plant, you may have to begin by working with raw materials that won't perform properly until you bring your suppliers on line, regardless of how good your manufacturing quality processes are," says Gay.

NOT SO MANY UNHAPPY RETURNS

With the firm commitment of both employees and suppliers, Woolrich products are now being produced with more consistent quality, as evidenced by a steady decline in customer complaints and returns. And the company is using those complaints and returns to improve quality even more.

"Our customers have excellent information on consumer returns, so we want to get even more feedback from them on why customers are dissatisfied with our products," says Gay. "We have a report that breaks these returns down by individual reasons, and we plan to integrate this into our QA system even more in the future."

"Once we get this information back to the plants, we will be able to eliminate even more quality problems," concludes Holcombe.

CONCLUSION

You've read what these leading companies do to put their commitment to quality excellence into action. You've seen how they put pride and hard work behind their quality efforts. You've learned how they set standards, and you've witnessed how closely they work with customers to make sure their quality standards are right on target. And you've seen the different techniques they employ to meet those standards. But the best ideas in the world are effective only when they're used.

So, now it's time to take these ideas and make them work for you. Learn from these experts. By adapting their experience to your situation, you may meet or even exceed the quality standards you have set. Let these ideas help you turn problems into opportunities for improving the quality delivered to your customers.

Put emphasis on your primary resources—your employees. Since they do the actual work, they have the ultimate responsibility for quality. Emphasize the importance of doing a job right the first time, and make sure your people have the skills they need to do just that. Show them how to make quality not just an ideal, but a realization. With that kind of attitude, your employees will take personal pride in the reliability and quality of the products or services they produce.

Don't overlook the importance of dealing with only quality-minded vendors/suppliers. And take advantage of tools such as statistical process control and designed experiments to improve quality control.

Once you've taken steps like these to improve quality, get the word out. By letting your customers know about the special emphasis you put on quality, you promote your company's quality image—and that leads to increased profitability.

Using these blueprints for success can earn you the reputation of a leader in quality assurance. Put them into action today!

INDEX